THE CASE FOR CRITICAL LITERACY

# The Case for Critical Literacy

*A History of Reading in Writing Studies*

ALICE S. HORNING

UTAH STATE UNIVERSITY PRESS
*Logan*

© 2024 by University Press of Colorado

Published by Utah State University Press
An imprint of University Press of Colorado
1580 North Logan Street, Suite 660
PMB 39883
Denver, Colorado 80203-1942

All rights reserved

 The University Press of Colorado is a proud member of Association of University Presses.

The University Press of Colorado is a cooperative publishing enterprise supported, in part, by Adams State University, Colorado State University, Fort Lewis College, Metropolitan State University of Denver, University of Alaska Fairbanks, University of Colorado, University of Denver, University of Northern Colorado, University of Wyoming, Utah State University, and Western Colorado University.

ISBN: 978-1-64642-625-6 (hardcover)
ISBN: 978-1-64642-626-3 (paperback)
ISBN: 978-1-64642-627-0 (ebook)
https://doi.org/10.7330/9781646426270

Library of Congress Cataloging-in-Publication Data

Names: Horning, Alice S., author.
Title: The case for critical literacy : a history of reading in writing studies / Alice Horning.
Description: Logan : Utah State University Press, [2024] | Includes bibliographical references and index.
Identifiers: LCCN 2024002450 (print) | LCCN 2024002451 (ebook) | ISBN 9781646426256 (hardcover) | ISBN 9781646426263 (paperback) | ISBN 9781646426270 (ebook)
Subjects: LCSH: Literacy—Study and teaching—United States. | Reading (Higher education)—United States. | Language arts—United States. | English language—Rhetoric—Study and teaching (Higher)—United States.
Classification: LCC LC149 .H667 2024 (print) | LCC LC149 (ebook) | DDC 808/.0420711—dc23/eng/20240417
LC record available at https://lccn.loc.gov/2024002450
LC ebook record available at https://lccn.loc.gov/2024002451

Cover photo: © Shutterstock/Ju Jae-young

*My connection to Norbert Elliot is entirely the fault of Ed White, who introduced us years ago after saying more than once that he thought Norbert and I would work well together. Ed's judgment was perfectly correct, and the result has been years of collegial cooperation throughout which I have been the happy, lucky beneficiary of Norbert's generosity and expertise in the field of writing studies.*

*In this project, Norbert has read every chapter at least once, provided endless resources, offered different perspectives, and saved me from many errors and flaws. He has had an important influence on my thinking about how to capture the features of critical literacy in both the text and the visual representation of the model as it unfolds throughout the book. While we have not agreed on everything I've written, he's forced me to be clear about my ideas and findings. Through all of these activities, we have, amazingly, remained good friends. He has my profound respect and gratitude; this book is thus affectionately dedicated to him.*

# Contents

*List of Illustrations*  ix
*Acknowledgments*  xi
*Preface: Preview/Overview/Plan for the Book and a Model of Critical Literacy*  xiii

## Part 1: The Status of Students' Reading  3

1. Introduction  5
2. Varied Approaches to Reading: Complexities and Equity  28
3. More Reading Now than Ever: The Current Reading Landscape  57

## Part 2: The Lost History of Reading in Writing Studies  83

4. How We Got Here Part 1—Early History  85
5. How We Got Here Part 2—Writing Studies as a Distinct Discipline  109

## Part 3: Making the Case for Critical Literacy: What Writing Studies Can/Should/Must Do for Students Now  151

6. Textbooks, Digital Tools, and Reading  153
7. What to Do on Monday—Steps to Address Students' Reading Needs  180

*References*  213
*Index*  237

# Illustrations

*Figures*

0.1  The complete model of critical literacy   xv
0.2  Definition of critical literacy   4
1.0.  Criteria for evaluation of sources   18
1.1.  Information literacy source evaluation: student strategies   21
3.1.  Core definition of critical literacy   63
4.0.  Partial model of critical literacy   84
6.0.  The complete model revisited   152
7.1.  The complete model in final form   191

*Tables*

3.1.  Trend in time spent reading for personal interest, 2009–2019   76
5.1.  CCCC sessions with presentations on reading or literacy   146
5.2.  Journal articles 2019–2021 with "reading" or "literacy" in the title   147

# Acknowledgments

Book writing appears to non-authors to be solitary, and some might say lonely, work, but in fact, a book of this kind is much more like a team sport. There are lots of players on the team who have contributed to making this book a group effort. I am grateful to all of the following and anyone I have inadvertently overlooked. Errors and omissions are, naturally, mine alone.

For help with the entire book: Norbert Elliot, Marc Loustau, Ellen Carillo, Laura Aull, and two anonymous readers for Utah State University Press (USUP). I am also grateful to Rachael Levay and the staff at USUP for their help with all phases of book preparation and for putting up with a gazillion emails from me in my efforts to produce a manuscript that was easy to turn into a finished book.

For help with the introduction: Alison Head, Jinrong Li, Tricia Serviss, and Sam Wineburg.

For help with chapter 2: Peter Adams and Brett Griffiths. Particular thanks to one of the anonymous readers for USUP who provided helpful guidance, encouraging me to look closely and carefully at the complexities of two-year colleges.

For help with chapter 5: Erika Lindemann, Annette Vee, Kristen Ritchie, Cinthia Gannett, and John Brereton. Special thanks to an anonymous reader for Utah State University Press who pointed out the omission of reader-response theory and other approaches to reading in a draft of this chapter. The relevance of this work clearly warranted careful consideration and was later added in response to the feedback provided.

For help with chapter 6: at W. W. Norton and Company, Marilyn Moller, Melissa Goldthwaite, Emma Peters, and Sarah Touborg. At Macmillan, Joy

Fisher Williams and Jimmy Fleming. Also for this chapter: Dana Driscoll, John Brereton, Dan Melzer, John Bean, and Lynn Bloom.

For help with chapter 7: Joel Breakstone and Howard Tinberg.

Some folks read some or all of various chapters, some sent me additional sources or information about forthcoming work of their own or of others, and some talked to me about the relevant issues discussed here.

I am grateful for all the help I received in the preparation of this book. Thanks to the whole team.

# Preface

*Preview/Overview/Plan for the Book and a Model of Critical Literacy*

Reading can fairly be described as an important issue in higher education today. More precisely, students' novice-level critical reading abilities are an area of concern that warrants a great deal more attention than has been paid until now. This book has three specific goals, realized in its three parts. First, I offer a detailed review and analysis of students' current situation with respect to critical reading and, more broadly, with respect to critical literacy. Part 1 reviews students' novice status, how this status has come about, and why, despite a lot of reading and writing in the digital environment, they remain novices. At the end of this part, readers should have a clear sense of where students are today with respect to critical literacy. To understand fully how the current situation has developed, part 2 reaches back to the origins of writing studies as a field. The two chapters in this part focus first on what some scholars consider the starting point of the field with the offering of English A at Harvard starting in 1885, tracing the treatment of reading from then to the important conference at Dartmouth College in 1966. The second chapter in part 2 picks up with the Dartmouth meeting and explores the intermittent attention to reading from 1966 to the present. At the end of this part, readers should understand how the history of the field reveals its treatment of reading, including times when reading has been in focus and times when it has been overlooked. Part 3 offers two ways of addressing students' needs to develop much-needed expertise in critical literacy: first, through textbooks and digital tools to improve critical literacy and second, through evidence-based approaches to teaching. At the end of part 3, readers will be able to see the best ways to help students become efficient and effective critical readers, writers, speakers, and listeners through the use of textbooks, digital tools, and evidence-based strategies suitable for writing classes and in every college course.

https://doi.org/10.7330/9781646426270.c000

Along the way, I share a few snapshots of my own development as a reader, from the pesky little sister always begging to be read to by my older sister who taught me to read, to the persistent advocate I have become for critical reading on campuses, in presentations, and in publications. It's not just my longstanding love of reading that motivates me, though that is certainly part of it. It is that reading has had a profound influence on me as a scholar and teacher; I'm convinced that it can make an important difference to student success and to helping everyone understand our differences across political, social, and economic lines. I don't think critical reading can solve all our problems, but I do think it can improve our empathy in ways that might make greater collaboration possible. If I had my way, every teacher on every campus would commit to helping students become successful critical readers in every course, regardless of discipline. Through what I hope is a detailed and thoughtful look at where we are with respect to reading in writing studies and beyond, I am confident that this goal can be achieved. In the final chapter, I offer a set of evidenced-based ways to do just that.

Within these broad goals, there are limitations on what I have been able to include. My focus is chiefly on students sometimes referred to as FTIACs, as they are first-time-in-any-college traditional new high school graduates entering college immediately. However, recent research by Michigan Tech rhetorician and former chair of the Conference on College Composition and Communication (CCCC) Holly Hassel has shown that the postsecondary population now more commonly includes a wide range of students who vary by age and background (Giordano and Hassel 2019). These students are less likely to start at selective four-year institutions and more likely to at least begin at two-year, four-year, and open access colleges and universities across the country. As these students make up a much larger portion of the current undergraduate population, I consider them a key part of the student body who can benefit from more attention to reading. Where pertinent, I will include relevant research findings and appropriate classroom strategies for this now substantial portion of the student population.

A further point is needed here about the current US adult population at large. Across the entire population, the level of adult literacy is not where it could or should be. Again, recent research makes clear that many adults lack the critical literacy skills needed to function well and to participate in the current environment, with political, social, and economic information coming at everyone from many directions online and off. Research on this claim was done by the Gallup Organization for the Barbara Bush Foundation

Preface : xv

for Family Literacy (Rothwell 2020), relying on both international studies and United States Department of Education findings. The work that has been done across a sample of US adults shows that 54 percent lack literacy proficiency (3). Literacy proficiency is defined in this report as the ability to understand complex ideas and evaluate claims from printed materials on paper or on screens (6). Thus, the need for much more consistent attention to critical reading and literacy pertains not only to college students but also to the population at large.

Included in each part of this book is a series of sketches of a developing model of critical literacy. The model is intended to provide a visual representation of the key ideas presented in the text. It is only a sketch, proposed as a starting point for ongoing discussion of the urgent need to develop students' integrated abilities in reading, writing, speaking, and listening. For the purpose of "coming attractions," here is the complete model (figure 0.1). The

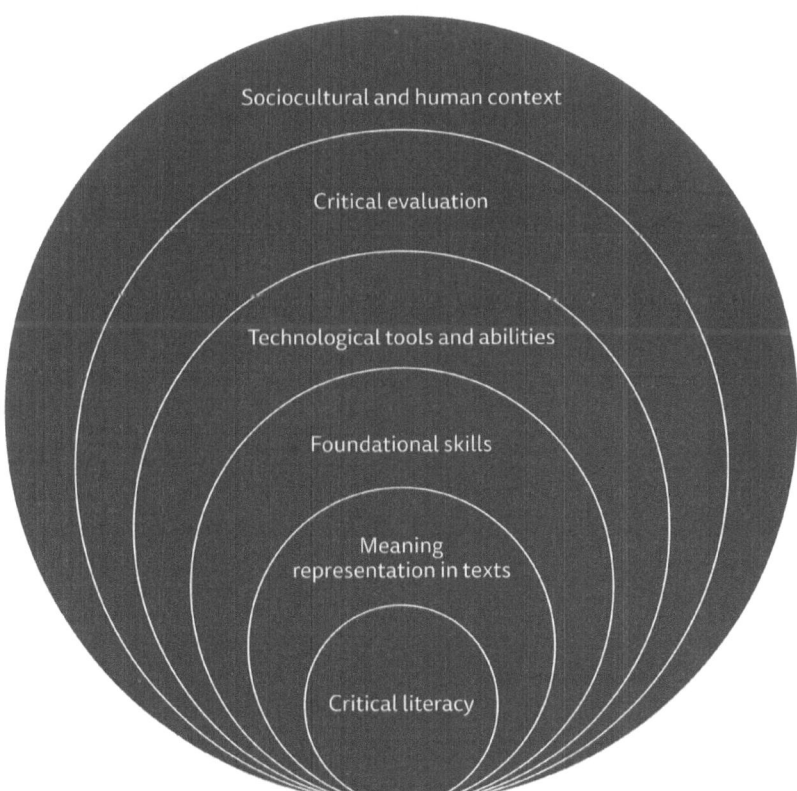

FIGURE 0.1. The complete model of critical literacy

rationale and explanation of the parts of the model will unfold over the course of the book. Readers should understand that critical literacy entails a highly complex set of skills and abilities, pared here to their absolute essence as currently understood.

Following is a brief summary of the chapters, providing an overview of the entire book. Each chapter reflects the interplay between a commonplace observation about students' critical reading/literacy and the realities of teaching and learning in the field. The commonplaces are meant here to capture often stated concepts about students' reading that will be explored in the text.

## Part 1: *The Status of Students' Reading*

### CHAPTER 1: INTRODUCTION

Commonplace: They don't read, won't read, can't read.

The book opens with a review of where students are now with respect to reading, making clear the scope of the problem. Large-scale testing (ACT, SAT, PISA, NAEP), careful analyses of students' use of sources (the Citation Project), and studies of online reading (Stanford History Education studies) all show students' current reading status as measured both by standardized testing and by direct observation of students' writing and their performance on un-timed exercises that show their actual abilities.

### CHAPTER 2: VARIED APPROACHES TO READING: COMPLEXITIES AND EQUITY

Commonplace: It's someone else's fault.

For a long time, faculty in education at every level have blamed students' weaknesses on the earlier work teachers did or failed to do. College teachers blame high schools, high schools blame middle schools, middle schools blame elementary schools. Even in the best school districts, high school students in particular don't get enough—or any—reading instruction. The Common Core State Standards set requirements designed to address these complaints, but it will take a long time for them to make a difference. And many poorly funded schools—schools under emergency managers, schools with outdated textbooks and lack of access to the internet, schools struggling with remote learning in the current/recent pandemic—do not have the resources to do substantive work on reading for all students. This chapter also looks at the status of students who are the first in their families to attend college, for whom academia could fairly be described as a foreign country. In this connection, the chapter touches on the history and status of reading instruction in two-year and open access institutions, where recent and significant change has occurred, making strategies like corequisite courses in reading or integrated reading and writing as well as stretch models more widespread and important.

### CHAPTER 3: MORE READING NOW THAN EVER: THE CURRENT READING LANDSCAPE

> Commonplace: Students are reading a lot because of social media.

This commonplace points to the fact that plenty of young people spend hours and hours on their phones or tablets reading postings and even longer texts. True that. However, in the current environment of misinformation and disinformation, what they are reading and how they are reading it shows clearly that many are unable to sort truth from fiction. Fake news is everywhere. Students need much stronger skills to be able to evaluate texts of all kinds, online and offline. A thorough definition of critical literacy, focused initially on reading alone, is developed in this chapter to set up the review of the history of reading in writing studies. This definition is the core of a full model, as sketched and proposed later in the book.

## Part 2: The Lost History of Reading in Writing Studies

### CHAPTER 4: HOW WE GOT HERE PART 1—EARLY HISTORY

> Commonplace: Not even Harvard students can write.

Writing studies was launched when Harvard University began offering English A in 1885. That course was invented in response to entering students having failed a writing exam based on lists of readings (of the famous or infamous "uniform lists") they were supposed to have done prior to admission. It was clear to Harvard faculty that students could not write well enough to do the work expected of them and so would need specific instruction in writing. A number of scholars have addressed this part of the history of the field, but not with an eye toward the reading piece. This chapter examines the early history of the field, from the launch of Harvard's English A to the Dartmouth Conference in 1966.

## CHAPTER 5: HOW WE GOT HERE PART 2—WRITING STUDIES AS A DISTINCT DISCIPLINE

> Commonplace: Writing studies is a separate field from literature, so never mind about reading.

Part of how we got here has to do with a big split in English studies overall. Composition used to go hand in hand with literature. Freshman composition, for example, when I took it as a student in the late 1960s, was a composition and literature course. We read extensively, analyzed and discussed texts and literary criticism, and wrote about all the reading we did. This chapter traces what happened when writing studies emerged as a separate field and sometimes as a separate academic department. The 1966 Dartmouth Conference is sometimes thought to be the starting point of writing studies as a distinct discipline. This chapter traces the last fifty years in the history of the field from a holistic perspective, to show how reading came to be so neglected. While reading was getting some attention by scholars using reader-response theory, critical literacy studies, and other approaches, that work did not address the kinds of critical skills students need now. The resulting version of the model of critical literacy reveals the current limited role of reading in the field.

## *Part 3: Making the Case for Critical Literacy: What Writing Studies Can/Should/Must Do for Students Now*

### CHAPTER 6: TEXTBOOKS, DIGITAL TOOLS, AND READING

> Commonplace: There are plenty of textbooks to help students with reading.

If only this commonplace were true. Yes, there have always been textbooks that tried to address students' reading needs and certainly, in recent times, compilations of readings—both fiction and nonfiction—have served as the basis of writing courses. Early textbooks, such as *The Practical Elements of Rhetoric* (Genung 1886), paid scant attention to reading and then as now included some readings to serve as models or springboards for writing. But in fact, none of them really help students with the nuts and bolts of reading or with critical analysis of materials of all kinds, online and off. How are students supposed to learn about deep fakes (altered images); about careful bias and disinformation, so abundant on the internet; or about the difference between and the value of published sources as opposed to the first item in a Google search? A few recent books, like Ellen C. Carillo's *MLA Guide to Digital*

*Literacy* (2022), move in this direction, but there are few of these and they are not as widely used as they might be. Textbooks old and new as well as new tools for reading are reviewed in this chapter.

## CHAPTER 7: WHAT TO DO ON MONDAY—STEPS TO ADDRESS STUDENTS' READING NEEDS

> Commonplace: Teachers say, I don't have the preparation to teach reading; teaching writing is hard enough without doing anything else or anything more. I don't have the time to teach reading when I am supposed to be teaching writing (and add any discipline), and I should not have to teach these basic skills when I am a teacher of XXX (fill in the discipline, including writing).

Research (Carillo 2015) shows that few college faculty have any sort of preparation to teach reading; this claim is true of writing teachers and the rest of the faculty as well. So, step one needs to be to prepare college faculty to work on reading in every class. Help can come from faculty development, possibly through centers for teaching excellence, and from the few of us who have expertise in reading pedagogy (Sullivan, Tinberg, Carillo, myself). Graduate programs in writing studies can connect with colleagues in education and psychology for additional resources. A key source is the library; librarians who are members of the Association of College and Research Libraries are doing their own work on these matters, and every librarian has skills and strategies to help faculty address students' reading needs more effectively.

This chapter also discusses what faculty really need to know: the basic psycholinguistics of reading. While there is much research in this area, the essential features of the reading process and a few key references offer a basic starting point for the "Monday morning" material in chapter 7. Psychologists, education scholars, cognitive scientists, and others have been studying reading for years. The essential processes involved are fairly well understood. Appropriate faculty preparation should include some knowledge of the reading process along with its psycholinguistic features. Faculty can do a much better job of helping students become effective critical readers. Their preparation might come, for pre-service faculty, from coursework either as part of their disciplinary graduate program or a psychology department or as an education course; for practicing faculty, in-service workshops can provide the relevant background and tools for the classroom. With this backdrop, the complete version of the model of critical literacy is presented and discussed. This book won't be the last word because the reading landscape will continue to change, but I hope it represents the nature of critical literacy as discussed here and provides a basis for much more, and more consistent, attention by writing studies teachers and scholars to helping students become effective and efficient critical readers, writers, listeners, and speakers of all kinds of texts in writing studies and beyond.

Concrete, evidence-based Monday morning solutions are presented here to address learning goals or outcomes in every class. Little time and energy are required to help students improve their reading. An assortment of specific approaches can help faculty achieve their own course goals. Showing students how textbook material is structured, addressing vocabulary development, and drawing on the apparatus (depending on quality) provided with textbooks are all good starting points. More relevant given the current information environment is the use of note-taking tools like PowerNotes, Perusall, and Hypothes.is and other techniques such as lateral reading, bias charts, and algorithm awareness to address the internet's widespread resources. These tools offer practical starting points to work on effective and efficient critical literacy.

### *Some Notes on Terminology*

As an author, I have confronted a few challenges in preparing the text of this book having to do with terminology and capitalization, among other issues. While the University Press of Colorado and Utah State University Press generally ask authors to follow the *Chicago Manual of Style*, using its author-date format for citations and references, they differ on some points. I have followed their preference to capitalize the term Black and also the abbreviation BIPOC for Black, Indigenous, and people of color but not to capitalize white or brown.

With respect to the terms used to refer to groups of students judged (often by test results) as not ready for college-level work, I have tried to avoid various terms like *remedial* or *developmental* that suggest a deficiency of some kind. I hope the terms I have chosen, such as *novice, advanced beginner, competent, proficient,* and *expert,* are less fraught and convey the path readers should be on. These terms draw on research by philosopher Hubert L. Dreyfus and engineer Stuart E. Dreyfus (1986), who have studied the development of expertise.

Finally, following guidance from author Amanda Oliver (2022) in her book about the current status of public libraries and their patrons, I acknowledge that while I have tried to use appropriate terms and capitals in the entire book, some readers may take exception to those words. As Oliver says: "It is never my intention to purposefully harm anyone with my words, but I have been a ... human long enough to understand that harm inevitably happens in writing, especially in nonfiction. No part of this book is intended to demonize, shame, or otherwise disparage specific persons, organizations, or institutions" (iv). I hope I can also make this claim, so well said by Oliver.

THE CASE FOR CRITICAL LITERACY

PART 1

# The Status of Students' Reading

The first three chapters of this book provide an overview of where contemporary postsecondary students are with respect to critical reading. This status report derives from a number of different kinds of sources, including standardized tests with all their flaws and weaknesses, careful studies of students' actual work, and other sources. Further insight comes from different approaches arising from efforts like the Common Core State Standards (CCSS) for reading, as well as special programs for students who are novices at college-level reading and writing. A number of different factors and forces play an important role in the development and current status of students' critical literacy, such as their experiences (or lack of) in earlier schooling and the responsibility for literacy teaching as shared by K–12 schools and teachers. Issues of funding, fake news, and, of course, the impact of technology all come into play, as do the different roles played in the postsecondary realm by two-year colleges and open access institutions (abbreviated throughout the book as TYCOAs), as well as more selective four-year schools.

    The specific goal of this first part of the book is to present a full picture of where undergraduates currently stand with respect to their reading, writing, speaking, and listening abilities, based on evidence of various kinds. Although these chapters look at recent historical developments such as the

CCSS, readers will leave part 1 with a full picture of students' critical literacy status. The end of part 1 offers a proposed definition of critical literacy as a starting point for the discussion (figure 1.0), reflecting the limited view of reading taken initially by writing studies as a field at its beginnings and pointing toward a fuller view that might now be possible. This definition is the core of a full model of critical literacy, proposed later in the book.

FIGURE 0.2. Definition of critical literacy

# 1
# Introduction

Over the past few years, I have been invited to speak on a handful of campuses, talking to faculty about student reading problems and how to address them in writing classes and across the disciplines. I often start my talks by recounting typical presentation experiences. On campuses across the country, I report that I ask faculty (regardless of discipline) what is the greatest problem they face in the classroom, and inside of five minutes, we are talking about reading. Even when I am not the so-called reading specialist, brought in to help with reading, the conversation moves almost immediately to what I call the "don't, won't, can't problem." At conferences, my audience typically starts nodding as soon as I mention these exchanges: the reading problem is the proverbial elephant in the room. Everyone knows it is there; it is much too big to ignore. However, no one seems to know what to do about it, despite the fact that there are straightforward, evidence-based strategies that can be used in every classroom. Moreover, faculty adopting these approaches will be able to achieve their own teaching goals more effectively, a positive outcome everywhere.

Plenty of evidence indicates that faculty members are not alone in their experience with students' reading troubles. Whether the evidence comes from large-scale standardized testing or close, careful examination of students' writing or anything in between, and whether it comes from students' work

https://doi.org/10.7330/9781646426270.c001

with online digital, visual, or audio material or traditional printed texts, the results or findings are fairly consistent. Between 50 percent and 80 percent of students cannot do the kind of careful critical reading essential to success in college and beyond. The evidence shows clearly that students do not read the kinds of extended nonfiction prose expected in college-level work, and they won't do this kind of reading unless it is required of them. Most important, though, the data show that they really *can't* read the way most faculty expect. That is, students can't get the main ideas and details of an extended argument or synthesize differing points of view on a topic, and they specifically don't know how to evaluate any kind of text for authority, accuracy, currency, relevance, appropriateness, and bias. They are especially weak in their ability to evaluate bias.

Far too often, these claims appear to be just a pejorative view of students' abilities or lack of them. Students are seen as deficient, in need of remediation, according to this view of the data. Moreover, an entire line of argument leads to basic writing, developmental reading, and other kinds of skills-based, often non-credit, courses required of students before they are admitted to college or are able to move on to credit-bearing work. This argument was classically presented and clearly refuted by Mina P. Shaughnessy in *Errors and Expectations* (1977) in the open-admissions days at the City University of New York and by Mike Rose in *Lives on the Boundary* (1989). Both of these and many other books and articles in the forty-plus years since demonstrate students' underlying abilities; their troubles arise from poor preparation, socioeconomic factors, systemic racism, and related issues. Furthermore, academia can fairly be described as a foreign country for many students. They, like other travelers, do not read, write, or speak the language; have no interest in permanent residence; expect to spend little time for any reason; and intend to leave quickly. Teachers need to take all of these factors into careful account.

It is increasingly clear, furthermore, that remedial courses do not actually help students succeed or improve degree completion rates. This claim is based on a comprehensive study of remedial coursework by the United States Department of Education in 2016 (Chen 2016). Although Xianglei Chen's study was done prior to the pandemic, it also covered a number of years, so there is reason to think that little has changed despite the challenges of remote instruction and other issues. According to a careful analysis building on Chen's work by Maria Elena Oliveri, Robert J. Mislevy, and Norbert Elliot (2020, 348–349), Subgroups enrolled in a higher percentage of remedial courses had lower percentages of graduating students. For instance, Black and Hispanic students participated in a higher percentage of remedial courses (78 percent and 75 percent, respectively) in 2-year institutions and had the lowest graduation rates (24 percent and 34 percent, respectively). Comparatively, in both 2- and 4-year institutions, white and Asian students participated in fewer remedial courses and had higher graduation rates. It appears that remediation is not having the desired effect on graduation rates.

It should be clear that remediation is not the solution, but it is especially important to note two further points. First, remedial courses don't help students complete a degree, as these authors point out. But in addition, the reading problem is more widespread than any of these numbers suggest. The findings about students' reading discussed below show that half or more of all students—regardless of race, ethnicity, socioeconomic status, high school preparation, or any other factor—simply don't read as well as they could or should. This outcome appears in both large-scale standardized tests and in detailed studies of students' own writing, in their work reading traditional alphabetic texts, and in their abilities in the digital realm with online materials of various kinds. Given the findings, critical literacy warrants much more attention in every college classroom than it is presently receiving.

Many of the reports and publications mentioned thus far generally address students' reading problems somewhat indirectly, as in degree completion rates. When the focus is directly on students' actual reading, as I have been arguing over the many years since I published "The Connection of Writing to Reading: A Gloss on the Gospel of Mina Shaughnessy" (Horning 1978), the data deliver the same message repeatedly. I pointed out there, and in dozens of publications and talks since, the relevance of reading to the teaching of writing. I have been motivated by the message in the data and by a lifelong love of reading, as far back as my older sister teaching me to read around age four, well before I started school. She taught me to read so I would stop pestering her to read to me and is herself a voracious, speedy, and expert reader. While I did not study reading directly through coursework, I went to graduate school in Michigan in the heyday of the work of Kenneth and Yetta Goodman at Wayne State University and of much intense focus on the psycholinguistics of reading, leading to my doctoral research project on textual redundancy and its impact on reading comprehension. For virtually my entire career, not counting recent detours into literacy history (Horning 2018, 2021a), I have been raising my voice about the need for writing studies and all other faculty in higher education to pay much more attention to critical reading. A few years ago, I caught the attention of the chair of the Conference on College Composition and Communication (CCCC) (Asao Inoue), who established a task force, which I co-chaired, to create a formal position statement on reading for the organization (CCCC 2021). Otherwise, I do not think my message has been widely acknowledged and integrated in ways that impact students and faculty. This book is just the latest attempt to shine a bright light on the need for much more attention to critical reading in college writing classrooms and across every campus.

In thinking and writing about students' current reading status, as detailed below, while I don't blame technology for the decline in students' reading abilities, lots of other people do. The reading problem has little to do with whether a text is alphabetic or visual or whether it appears on a paper page or a screen; the psycholinguistic processing needed is the same in all cases, as is the need for critical evaluation and sustained attention. A lot of data show that students clearly lack the skills needed for effective, efficient, critical reading and evaluation of texts of all kinds. Before exploring the origins of this situation, a review of the evidence for students' current status with respect to reading is in order, with the important caveat that all the standardized tests have strengths and weaknesses, as do naturalistic studies discussed later. The rationale for this look at standardized tests is that they are in widespread use, frequently cited, and commonly thought of (albeit not necessarily correctly) as valid measures of student ability. The larger point is that no matter what kind of assessment is used, warts and all, they show that students do not read as well as they could and should.

### *Large-Scale Testing: ACT, SAT, NAEP, PISA*

#### ACT

It seems best to start the survey of recent large-scale standardized test data with the findings of the ACT from 2020, the latest year for which results are available. In 2020, 1.67 million students took the ACT, which includes a separate test of students' reading ability (ACT 2020). That number, according to ACT, represents 49 percent of the high school graduating class that year; while many students taking the ACT choose to do so for college admission requirements, some take the test because their state uses it for assessment purposes, so it is at least in part a self-selected sample. The exam itself is a timed, paper-and-pencil, multiple choice test. In the reading section of the test, students have thirty-five minutes to read four passages and answer ten multiple choice questions on each one. The ACT claims it is testing the ability to understand the ideas of a text, make inferences and generalizations, and see relationships among key points. A number of years ago, I asked a group of Honors College students at my university to look at a sample ACT reading section and tell me if they thought the test was valid, that is, that it really tests what ACT says it does. The students' conclusion was that the test did what ACT claimed. This result is anecdotal and from some time ago, but at the same time, it suggests that some students do see the test as an appropriate measure of key reading abilities. The ACT reading test is limited both substantively and practically for various reasons, but it does offer one approach to a few kinds of academic reading that a large number of students take. Many better measures, especially of reading in the context of writing, exist; some of these are discussed below.

The 2020 results show that 45 percent of students met ACT's benchmark score of 22, on a scale of 1–36 on the test. The ACT (2020, 3) explains its benchmark scores as follows: "A benchmark score is the minimum score needed on an ACT subject-area test to indicate a 50 percent chance of obtaining a B or higher or about a 75 percent chance of obtaining a C or higher in the corresponding credit-bearing college courses, which include English Composition, Algebra, Social Science, Biology, STEM and ELA. These scores were empirically derived based on the actual performance of students in college." Thinking through these results carefully suggests a few key observations. First, it seems reasonable to think that translated into any first-year college class, about half the students meet ACT's benchmark, but half do not. And the standard ACT sets for the benchmark is fairly minimal: earning a grade of B or better (50–50) or a grade of C or better (75% chance) if students hit the benchmark. These findings are not about first-year writing; they apply to the aggregate of all students in all classes going to all colleges across the country. Also, a score of 22 means that students who met the benchmark got a little more than half of the questions right. This says a lot about those abilities ACT rightfully claims (according to my own students) it is testing: only about half the students can grasp key ideas, draw inferences, and so on.

A closer look at what the test measures sheds more light on the kinds of abilities addressed in the ACT. Note that the ACT does not claim that it asks specifically for much critical evaluation of any text, so it is difficult to judge students' evaluation skills. The description on the ACT website shows that the reading test focuses on main ideas and details, including inference and conclusion (55%–60%); craft and structure, including vocabulary and point of view (25%–30%); and integration of knowledge and claims (13%–18%), including evaluating claims (ACT 2021). This description shows that the ACT offers a minimal look at students' critical reading ability. While little attention is devoted to critical reading and evaluation of texts, the test does assess some key components of reading. A very large number of students have taken this instrument, so it offers a broad look at high school graduates. On the other hand, it is a timed test with multiple choice questions that have only one right answer. Naturally, the passages are relatively brief and thus provide no insight on how well students can focus sustained attention to follow a fully developed argument or compare and contrast two texts on the same topic, evaluate credibility, or conduct other kinds of analysis required in high-level critical reading.

### SAT

Relatively recently, the SAT was redesigned, adding separate reading and writing sections to the test. Almost a decade ago, the College Board (2015) released a report on the redesign of the SAT in which it noted on the first page of the Executive Summary that 57 percent of those who took the SAT in 2013 were not prepared for college-level work. Here's how the College Board describes the test and what it measures: "The redesigned SAT's **Reading Test** is a carefully constructed, challenging assessment of comprehension and reasoning skills with an unmistakable focus on careful reading of appropriately difficult passages in a wide array of subject areas. Passages are authentic texts selected from high-quality, previously published sources. One notable feature of the test is its use of texts representing a range of complexities to better determine whether students are ready for the reading challenge posed by college courses and workforce training programs" (College Board 2015, 4–5). Other features are questions about one original document (such as part of the United States Constitution), analysis of graphic material such as a chart or table, specific questions about vocabulary, and the presentation of pairs of passages with questions relating to both.

Like the ACT, the SAT is a timed, multiple choice, paper-and-pencil test used in many high schools, now going all-digital. A number of colleges and universities have chosen to make standardized tests like the ACT or SAT optional, based on the claim that high school grades are as good or perhaps a better indication of students' likely success, as validated by a careful study in California with its very large community college system (Bahr et al. 2017). Even so, the SAT continues to be offered and is used by many colleges and universities to make admissions decisions. Like the ACT, though, it is to some degree a self-selected sample unless students take it as part of a state-mandated assessment. A recent report by the College Board (2024) shows the results for high school seniors who took the test in 2023, 1.9 million students in all. The reading section consisted of five passages; students were given sixty-five minutes to read the passages and answer ten–twelve multiple choice questions about each one.

On the reading portion of the ACT test, where the scaled score range is between 1 and 36, for the graduating class of 2023, 66 percent achieved the benchmark score of 22 (ACT 2024, 36). On the SAT Evidence-Based Reading and Writing (a combination of the Reading Test score and the Writing and Language Test, with a standard SAT scaled score range of 200–800), 62 percent achieved the benchmark score of 480 in the class of 2023 (College Board 2023, 4). As the report notes, "The SAT Evidence-Based Reading and Writing (ERW) benchmark is associated with a 75 percent chance of earning at least a C in first-semester, credit-bearing, college-level courses in history, literature, social science, or writing" (College Board 2023, 3). Thus, whether looking at ACT or SAT, somewhere between about 35 and 40 per cent of students do not meet the benchmark; moreover, the benchmark sets a fairly low bar for success.

Naturally, there is plenty of room for debate about the benchmark score, in terms of both its level and whether defining students' abilities in terms of grades earned in college courses is an appropriate way of setting a benchmark. For the purposes of the present discussion, these results give an indication of where a substantial number of students who have taken the SAT stand on this second standardized test, bearing in mind that the trend toward making the ACT, SAT, and other admissions tests optional means smaller numbers of students, not a large, representative sample of all students.

## NAEP

A third standardized test given to K–12 students is the National Assessment of Educational Progress (NAEP), often cited as "the Nation's Report Card." It is given this name because it is the United States Department of Education's carefully designed nationwide sample of students in all subject areas and at a variety of grade levels. High school seniors are not tested every year in every area, however. In addition, the NAEP was not administered in the 2020–2021 school year because of the pandemic. But in 2019, the most recent year for which high school student scores are available, the reading results show that 37 percent of students tested "proficient" (National Assessment of Educational Progress 2019). This result is no different from the outcome in

2015, the previous year in which seniors were tested. The implications of this result should be clear: based on this test, only four of every ten students in a first-year college writing class read well enough to do the work instructors expect. Again, however, it is important to keep in mind that the NAEP, like the ACT and SAT, is a standardized, timed, multiple choice, paper-and-pencil instrument, though by the post-pandemic time of publication of this book, NAEP had begun using tablets for the test on a trial basis in 2019. Assorted analyses, according to NAEP, were done to ensure that the digital and paper forms of the test were equivalent. The results have been thoroughly reviewed and critiqued by Diane Ravitch (2020), former United States Department of Education assistant secretary of education and New York University professor. The test, however, measures a true *sample* of students across the nation.

The description of the types of texts used in the NAEP includes both literary texts like fiction and poetry and informational texts such as arguments and documents. The test is intended to measure the ability to process texts of different kinds to "locate and recall" specific information, "integrate and interpret" through drawing inferences or identifying themes, and "critique and evaluate" for content and meaning (National Assessment of Educational Progress 2019). "Critique and evaluate" is just one of the three target areas for the NAEP reading test. The other skills measured by the instrument are certainly relevant and important for an overall assessment of students' reading ability. But the critical reading part is not the sole or major focus being tested, as is true of all the tests under discussion here. Of the three large-scale tests discussed thus far, all are exclusive to the United States, all measure similar sets of skills in a similar way, and all produce results suggesting that a majority of students do not read as well as they could and should, as measured by these tests.

## PISA

One more standardized test warrants review for the purposes of this discussion: the test from the Programme for International Student Assessment (PISA). PISA is a product of the Organisation for Economic Cooperation and Development (OECD), a group of about thirty mostly Northern Hemisphere countries that have joined forces for a variety of programs and activities, including testing a representative sample of students at age fifteen. Like the ACT, SAT, and NAEP, it is a timed, multiple choice instrument that has been translated as needed and administered every three years to students in the included countries. The last administration for which results are available is from 2018 (Programme for International Student Assessment 2018). The test is scored on a 300–600 scale. In the reading portion of the test, the US average (505) is above the OECD average (487), but it has been flat since 2000 according to the PISA Report (Schleicher 2019, 11). While US scores have not gone up, they have not gone down either.

PISA defines "reading literacy," the term it uses for students' abilities, as follows: "Reading literacy is understanding, using, evaluating, reflecting on and engaging with texts in order to achieve one's goals, to develop one's knowledge and potential, and to participate in society" (OECD 2019, 34). The test measures four specific abilities: "The PISA 2018 framework identifies four processes that readers activate when engaging with a piece of text. Three of these processes were also identified, in various guises, in previous PISA frameworks: 'locating information', 'understanding', and 'evaluating and reflecting'. The fourth process, 'reading fluently', underpins the other three processes" (35). In addition to finding materials, comprehending those texts literally, and drawing inferences, PISA measures critical reading with a specific focus on three areas: judging credibility, accuracy, and bias along with source authority; using prior knowledge to assess the quality and format of the text; and comparing and contrasting multiple sources to address conflicting information from more than one source (36). While this description suggests that PISA provides a solid focus on critical reading skills, the fact that American students have not improved in this area in over twenty years makes clear that much work remains to be done. There is clearly not less reading in anyone's future, and as access expands on screens, the need for stronger skills also expands. PISA gives a sense of where American fifteen-year-olds have been and are in the context of a global sampling. A stronger focus on the kinds of skills described by PISA is certainly in order.

The goal of reviewing these large-scale tests is not to compare them or the results they provide, as noted at the outset. In fact, the National Academy of Education issued a recent detailed report on a variety of issues that impact comparability of test scores, across administrations of the same test and across different types of tests. The report makes the following key points about differences in student background that might affect test performance:

*Students with different linguistic or sociocultural backgrounds should have the same opportunities to demonstrate their knowledge, skills, and competencies on assessments. When testing programs span diverse language or sociocultural groups, translated versions of tests may be used.* However, comparability across translated versions is far from ensured. Items often function differently between language groups, both within and across countries. Even in the same language context, such as in the United States, students from different sociocultural groups may speak structurally and semantically different varieties of the "same" language (e.g., indigenous students, African American students, Mexican American students, and students from nonmainstream socioeconomic backgrounds). The goal with translated tests must be measurement equivalence, including equivalence of construct, test, and testing conditions. The quality of adaptation to other languages is optimized when the assessments in the source language are developed with test adaptation goals in mind. (Berman, Haertel, and Pellegrino 2020, 8, original emphasis)

Student background is crucial in all kinds of testing programs and is essential to keep in mind in examining test results. However, in tests like the NAEP and PISA, the students who take them are not a self-selected group (as might be true of the ACT or SAT, taken by students who choose to go to college, to meet application requirements) but are part of a carefully designed sample, intended to reflect the larger population. Sampling is not perfect, but if a sample is well designed, the results will indicate the degree of certainty administrators have about the extent to which the sample represents the status of the entire population.

## *Other Issues Regarding Testing*

Other studies of the impact of students' socioeconomic status have shown for many years that college admission tests are skewed in favor of those from well-to-do backgrounds. A review of this research by two University of Minnesota economics professors, Nathan Kuncel and Paul Sackett (2018), shows clearly that students from wealthy backgrounds perform better on tests like the ACT and SAT than do those who are less advantaged. This finding is one reason many colleges and universities have gone "test optional," so students can present other data to support their application for admission. While high school course choices (such as taking Advanced Placement classes and tests), grades, interviews, and so forth provide useful background for college admissions, the tests *do* offer a standardized indication of students' skills. In their report, Kuncel and Sackett repeatedly mention the specific importance of students' critical reading ability as a key aspect of their background that is measured in some ways by the tests and plays a central role in overall success in college and careers. They write that "being able to read texts and make sense of them and having strong quantitative reasoning are crucial in the modern information economy" (4). These points are made with respect to college admissions tests, not the careful samples of the entire student population offered by the NAEP and PISA. These points about student background are important to the larger picture I am trying to present. My goal here is to show that in terms of these large-scale tests, whether we look at results from a self-selected sample of college-bound high school students or a careful national sample, the results are fairly consistent: roughly 50 percent or more of students do not read as well as they could and should, certainly not well enough to do the work college faculty expect.

There is one further point with respect to standardized tests. When we put these results showing that 50 percent of students lack effective and efficient reading ability next to the fact that about half of those who begin any kind of postsecondary education never complete it (National Center for Education Statistics 2022; also discussed in Oliveri, Mislevy, and Elliot 2020), those two facts warrant attention. Recent research by a nonprofit, nonpartisan research organization sponsored by 3,600 colleges and universities across the country (National Student Clearinghouse Research Center 2020) also shows that the rate of degree completion has been flat for a number of years. For this reason, among others, reading deserves much more attention than it has received for years, in writing classes and across the curriculum.

## *A Different Vantage Point: Students' Actual Research and Writing*

A broader model of critical literacy that involves all four language arts skills will be discussed as this book unfolds; the model includes the ongoing shift to all things digital. To explore both traditional and digital abilities, other kinds of data are needed. One option is students' own writing, especially writing that makes use of a variety of sources they have read or examined and that they use in research papers in college courses. The key ongoing study that provides data of this kind is the Citation Project work under the leadership of Sandra Jamieson at Drew University and Rebecca Moore Howard at Syracuse University. Their original data were collected in 2011–2013; the history of the Citation Project has been traced by Jamieson (2017). According to the project's website:

> Citation Project researchers studied researched papers written by 174 first-year students at 16 US colleges and universities and collected in the Citation Project Source-Based Writing Corpus (CPSW). Intertextual analysis of these students' work produced a data-based portrait of student reading and

source-use practices, presenting an image of students moving into their sophomore year of college while only sometimes demonstrating expert reading, summary, and citation practices . . . Analysis of the 174 researched papers found the students working from one or two sentences in 94% of their citations; citing the first or second page of their sources in 70% of their citations; and citing only 24% of their sources more than twice. (http://www.citationproject.net/)

The Citation Project has produced a number of different reports on students' reading of source materials, as reflected in their written work (Jamieson 2013, 2017). Because information literacy plays a key role in the ways students find and use source materials, librarians have also contributed to this work and have additional useful data and insights (Li 2020). Librarians themselves have also been working on students' critical reading skills in conjunction with information literacy; their work is discussed in more detail below.

In several publications (full disclosure: I was the guest editor for Jamieson's 2013 article on what the Citation Project reveals about students' reading status), Jamieson makes clear that students' weak reading abilities contribute to the likelihood that they will resort to patchwriting and plagiarism. In her careful review of the project data, she demonstrates that students lack key skills to engage fully with sources. Not only do they lack the skills to find appropriate sources (about which the librarians have much more to say), but they are also unable to go beyond basic comprehension to analyze and evaluate materials they do find for authority, accuracy, currency, relevancy, appropriateness, and bias. She writes, "Similarly, if they tend to work from sentences rather than extended passages, as do 93.7 percent of the 1,911 citations in the sample, we might conclude that students are less likely to be able to understand the larger concepts in the texts they read, or to be able to assess how an argument unfolds, how sources are in dialogue with each other, or how the author uses an accumulation of references and sources to further a position of his or her own, or support, challenge, or revise a position or interpretation presented by another scholar" (Jamieson 2013, 16). These are the kinds of skills students are missing, based on an analysis of the careful sample collected by the Citation Project researchers. Further examination of where cited material comes from shows that almost 83 percent of citations are from the first four pages of the source, chiefly from the first two pages. This finding in combination with the use of quotation rather than summary or paraphrase suggests that most students did not fully engage with the material they used (Jamieson and Howard 2013, 122–123).

In conjunction with the Citation Project, Janice R. Walker and other researchers have been developing related work in the LILAC Project (Learning Information Literacy across the Curriculum). Like the Citation Project, LILAC is also a cross-institutional project, examining students' information skills at various institutions. In results reported thus far, the researchers used "research-aloud" protocols, screen-capture recordings, and questionnaires to examine what students said about their strategies and what they actually did when conducting research. An early report on this work (Blackwell-Starnes and Walker 2017) focuses mainly on where students look for information when doing research and what they seem to know about how to do research online. The LILAC project focuses on information literacy rather than on reading per se, but it shows that students have limited knowledge of how to access valid and reliable information, since they rely largely on open web searches through Google or Wikipedia rather than on curated sources found through library databases or other appropriate resources.

Two other reports of the findings of the LILAC Project reveal what happens when multilingual students conduct research, providing further insights about the evaluation of sources found—that is, about students' critical reading abilities. The first of these (Mina, Bohannon, and Li 2018) provides additional insight into students' research behavior. The study involved fifty Chinese first-year writing students at an American university who completed an online survey about their research skills and then did a fifteen-minute research-aloud protocol, which recorded their comments on their search process and captured their actual work on the screen. A total of 650 minutes of screen capture and audio resulted from the data collection process. The research questions were chosen to investigate three of the Association of College and Research Libraries (ACRL) Framework points, but the one of interest for the present discussion is focused on evaluating search results and sources to establish authority and credibility. (The ACRL and its Framework are discussed in more detail below.)

Findings show that students have an array of problems when conducting research that requires strong reading skills: "The participants' plan for using the sources identified further confirmed this inclination: only two participants (4%) attempted to paraphrase the information identified; four (8%) indicated that they would copy and paste what they found onto their own papers; and none of the participants took the time to identify more specific sections to quote or to summarize, or to consider how relevant information from the sources can be integrated into their own writing" (Mina, Bohannon, and Li 2018, 259).

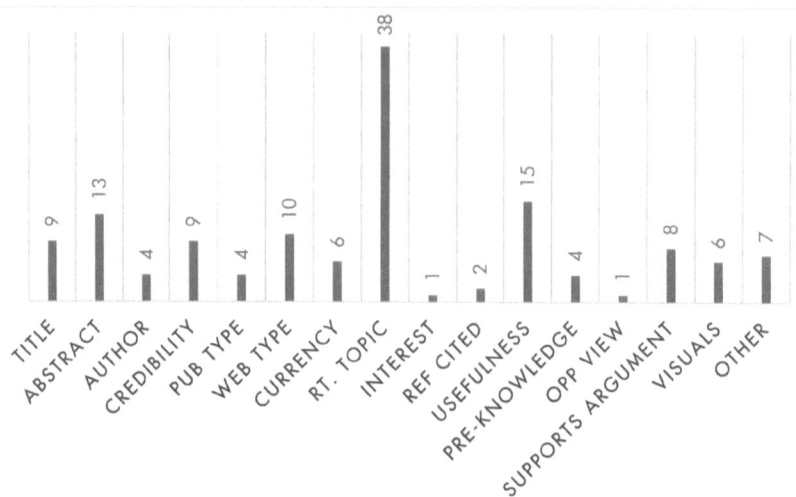

**FIGURE 1.0.** Criteria for evaluation of sources (Mina, Bohannon, and Li 2018, 261)

A more general overview of the criteria students use to evaluate sources appears in figure 1.1, drawing on the data from all fifty students. The authors point out that they did not have any direct insight from the students as to what constituted a judgment of relevance to their research topic. But it is clear to the researchers on this study that these students are novices at evaluating search results and then in evaluating the sources themselves. In summarizing the results of this study, the authors write: "Participants demonstrated narrow search scope and had difficulty accessing the information they needed for their writing projects. They also used limited search strategies without being able to refine or modify their searches. Further, most participants lacked strong search and source evaluation skills that resulted in their determining credibility randomly rather than systematically or consistently" (Mina, Bohannon, and Li 2018, 262–263). Reading challenges show up, this study shows, when students try to do research for their own writing projects. This kind of research provides a different perspective than the testing data because it looks directly at student work, in this case with a multilingual population.

The second report presents a different batch of data from the LILAC Project, with a larger multilingual population of 469 students. Like the previous study, this one entailed survey data and research-aloud protocols from typical college students, although the non-native speakers outnumbered native English speakers by about five to one. A sample of forty-five of the collected videos is included in this report (Li 2020). Although the students report fairly high confidence in their ability to evaluate sources, a close examination of their actual search behavior presents a different picture. They run too many searches and spend little time reading the sources they do find or evaluating them according to key criteria such as authority, accuracy, and currency. A marked flaw in their search strategies is the use of source-type phrasing along with content-based terms, such as "scholarly articles on global warming" (Li 2020, slide 14). Moreover, students' search terms are frequently general and do not seem to become more refined as they continue to search. Finally, with very few exceptions, students do not seem to understand that research involves a nonlinear process that draws heavily on prior knowledge. These points all apply to critical reading, of course, and so the LILAC Project findings provide further evidence of the reading challenges students face when they attempt to do research.

## *Information Literacy: Librarians' Look at Reading*

The LILAC Project, it should be clear, is closely connected to the Citation Project, using a similar approach to examine samples of actual student research and writing with an eye toward the information literacy skills students need to do research for academic and personal purposes. And information literacy is the key concern of library faculty. College and university librarians together with other kinds of research librarians constitute a separate section within the American Library Association, the Association of College and Research Libraries. The ACRL has developed its own Framework for defining and evaluating college students' information literacy (Association of College and Research Libraries 2016). This Framework document has given rise to a number of published reports. Among them, the most useful for the present discussion is the work of Project Information Literacy (PIL), a nonprofit research organization that studies information literacy at colleges and universities across the country. PIL is directed by Dr. Alison Head, currently at Harvard University. According to its website, "93 U.S. public and private colleges and universities, community colleges, and 34 high schools have participated in PIL's institutional samples during the past decade. PIL has produced 12 open access reports since 2009" (Project Information Literacy 2021). Its latest findings, as with all the other reports cited here, show students' difficulties in reading and evaluating all kinds of materials.

The work of librarians goes across all academic disciplines, since students who need help with research often go to the library regardless of the course topic or their specific major. The work of the ACRL and other library faculty, then, offers a wider lens through which to view students' abilities and needs. The Framework document and the studies done to date offer a compelling argument for much more focus on reading, not only in first-year writing courses but in every course in higher education. This goal has not been discussed in recent critiques of US higher education, like that of journalist Will Bunch (2022), but perhaps writers of these critiques will take up the idea. One writing studies scholar who has embraced the importance of reading is Ohio State University literacy historian Harvey J. Graff (2022), whose reasoning is discussed in chapter 5; others will surely follow in his footsteps, in writing studies and beyond.

Two studies from the librarians provide a useful picture of students' research behavior and their ability to evaluate sources. First, a study published in 2012 examines first-year students' research experiences, using a combination of online surveys of 1,941 high school and college students and interviews with 35 of them from six colleges and universities around the country (Head 2012, 11). Thus, the findings are based on students' self-report of their research experiences, not direct observation of actual behavior during research or writing. Still, the difficulties students report are revealing: 43 percent said they had a hard time summarizing material from different sources, 34 percent reported difficulty reading and comprehending sources, and 14 percent reported trouble evaluating sources for credibility (15). Summarizing these and other findings from the study, Alison J. Head writes: "Our findings suggest many freshmen were overwhelmed with the first part of the research process—finding—and were often relieved when they had some sources in hand. But other problems inevitably arose for most of them. They soon found themselves struggling with reading, comprehending, evaluating, and applying the scholarly sources they had found. These were the higher order thinking skills necessary for college-level research" (19). By taking all of the students' reports together, Head concludes that most of them had trouble with what can fairly be called critical reading.

The second, more recent study (Head et al. 2018) examined students' interaction with news sources of various kinds, seeking answers to questions about what they consider to be "news," what they actually do with news sources, and how good they are at critical evaluation of the materials they use. In this study, according to Head and her colleagues, "a sample of 5,844 respondents returned an online survey administered at 11 US colleges, universities, and community colleges. Thirty-seven follow-up telephone interviews and

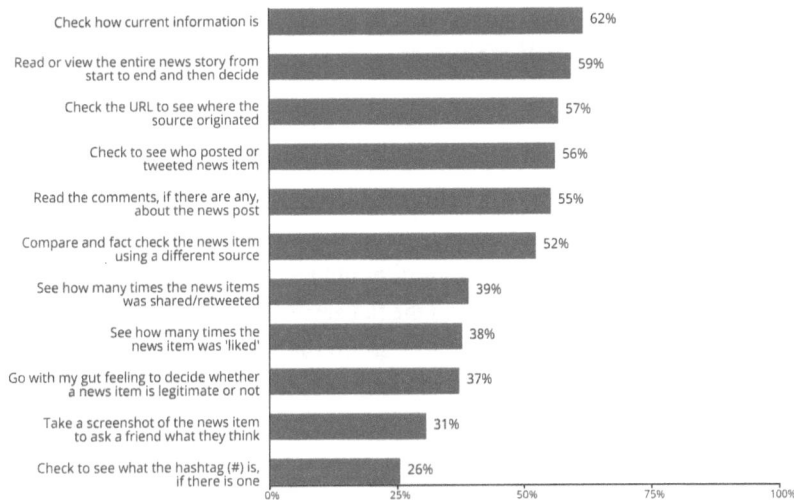

FIGURE 1.1. Information literacy source evaluation: student strategies

write-in responses to an open-ended question from more than 1,600 survey respondents provided qualitative data about their opinions and perspectives. A computational analysis of Twitter data from 731 survey respondents and a larger Twitter panel of more than 135,000 college-age persons provided observational data about news sharing behaviors" (3).

The study produced five key "takeaways" for educators and others (Head et al. 2018, 5–24), of which the last is most pertinent for the current discussion: "Takeaway #5: Traditional standards for evaluating news are increasingly problematic" (24). For the present purposes, the summary of source evaluation strategies in figure 1.1 is instructive (21).

These results show that 40 percent or more of students don't use any of the strategies listed here, suggesting their limited ability to evaluate material for authority, accuracy, currency, relevance, appropriateness, and bias. Further findings suggest that while students do use library databases to find sources of information, along with consulting their instructors and examining traditional sources like printed newspapers, for their personal lives they rely heavily on social media sources. A key finding is that students have limited ability to judge information coming at them from multiple sources, in great quantities, and at high speeds. When asked whether new studies confirm this result, Professor Head said she believed these findings have not changed over the past few years (personal communication, December 18, 2020). Given the results of other studies discussed in this chapter, this answer seems correct.

The librarians' work, then, also points to students' difficulties reading and evaluating source materials of all kinds.

## Online Reading

It isn't only librarians who are concerned about students' reading abilities, especially online. The famous or infamous "digital natives" are thought to be much better at reading all things digital online, including both alphabetic texts on screens large and small and the full array of visual texts, social media posts, and other kinds of materials. A group that has studied reading from this angle reports the same array of results as do researchers testing more conventional reading of traditional print texts. If anything, the picture that emerges is, according to investigators at Stanford University's Graduate School of Education (Stanford History Education Group 2016), "dismaying . . . [and] troubling" (McGrew et al. 2017, 5) in their description of their findings in a study of students in middle school, high school, and college working with an array of online materials. The researchers at the Stanford History Education Group (SHEG) have done two similar studies to explore students' critical reading in the online realm, obtaining similar results in both cases (Stanford History Education Group 2016; Stanford History Education Group and Gibson Consulting 2019). For the purposes of this discussion, the more recent of these two studies gives a better picture of students' abilities nationwide because it reports results from a national sample of US high school students.

To take a careful look at students' abilities, the SHEG researchers designed a study of online critical reading. They set up six un-timed tasks for students at the high school level, mostly juniors and seniors, requiring them to read and evaluate different kinds of online materials. Here is an overview of the kinds of tasks given to the students:

*Evaluating Video Evidence*
Evaluate whether a video posted on Facebook is good evidence of voter fraud.

*Webpage Comparison*
Explain which of two websites is a better source of information on gun control.

*Article Evaluation*
Using any online sources, explain whether a website is a reliable source of information about global warming.

*Claims on Social Media 1*

Explain why a social media post is a useful source of information about background checks for firearms.

*Claims on Social Media 2*

Explain how a social media post about background checks might not be a useful source of information.

*Homepage Analysis*

Explain whether tiles on the homepage of a website are advertisements or news stories. (Stanford History Education Group and Gibson Consulting 2019, 10)

It is easy to see that these tasks entail the kinds of materials students are likely to encounter and rely on for school assignments or for their own purposes. The 2019 report provides a detailed description of where and how the SHEG researchers administered these tasks to students, as well as the statistical analysis of the results. The study was done as follows: "From June 2018 to May 2019, we administered an assessment to 3,446 students, a national sample that matches the demographic profile of high school students in the United States. The six exercises in our assessment gauged students' ability to evaluate digital sources on the open internet" (Stanford History Education Group and Gibson Consulting 2019, 3). Thus, the study was carefully designed to show what a sample of students can do when reading online texts of different kinds, alphabetic and visual, with the sample drawn from sixteen school districts in fourteen states (7–8). The study was done prior to the presidential election in November 2020 and also prior to the pandemic.

The results show that almost 60 percent of the students could not do these tasks at all, and only thirteen students (0.038%) attained a perfect score (Stanford History Education Group and Gibson Consulting 2019, 23). The findings make clear the status of students' skills regarding online reading and the evaluation of texts. The researchers point out that efforts to help students read more effectively using a checklist—such as evaluating material for authority, accuracy, currency, relevancy, appropriateness, and bias—do not address the more fundamental critical literacy skills needed for effective evaluation of all kinds of materials, print or digital. They cite yet another study done by SHEG researchers that makes clear the kinds of skills expert readers have and use with all kinds of texts.

In the lateral reading study (Wineburg and McGrew 2017), the SHEG investigators compared the evaluation strategies of professional fact-checkers to those of faculty with PhDs in history and Stanford undergraduate students. While not a representative sample, this population does provide useful data on how professionals approach the verification of information, compared to students. The main findings of the study are that students and even people who hold PhDs are easily fooled by misinformation and disinformation from digital sources, chiefly because they rely entirely on vertical reading within a website; by contrast, professional fact-checkers read laterally, going from source to source as well as to other sites to check the accuracy of information. They were able to assess sources much more quickly and accurately through two strategies: lateral reading and taking bearings. The SHEG researchers define the lateral reading approach this way:

> When reading laterally, one leaves a website and opens new tabs along a horizontal axis in order to use the resources of the Internet to learn more about a site and its claims. Lateral reading contrasts with vertical reading. Reading vertically, our eyes go up and down a screen to evaluate the features of a site. Does it look professional, free of typos and banner ads? Does it quote well-known sources? Are bias or faulty logic detectable? In contrast, lateral readers paid little attention to such features, leaping off a site after a few seconds and opening new tabs. They investigated a site by leaving it.
>
> Paradoxically, a key feature of lateral reading is *not reading* . . . It requires knowledge of *sources*, knowledge of how the Internet and searches are *structured*, and knowledge of *strategies* to make searching and navigating effective. (Wineburg and McGrew 2017, 38, original emphases)

The study showed that the fact-checkers made quick and efficient use of lateral reading to investigate the sites they were given. They came up with correct evaluations significantly more quickly and more correctly than did the faculty with PhDs or the students.

A second key part of fact-checkers' strategy is what Sam Wineburg and Sarah McGrew (2017, 13, original emphasis) describe as "taking bearings," which they explain as "a concept borrowed from the world of navigation. Exploring an unfamiliar forest, experienced hikers know how easy it is to lose their way. Only foolhardy hikers trust their instincts and go traipsing off. Instead they rotate their compass's bezel to determine *bearings*—the angle, measured in degrees, between North and their desired destination. Obviously, taking bearings on the web is not as precise as measuring an angle in degrees. It begins, however, with a similar premise: When navigating unfamiliar terrain, first gain a sense of direction." This approach, as practiced by the fact-checkers, took them to other sites where they could get information on the source of the original site, check its claims with authoritative and independent sources, and find out what other verified resources might have said on the same topic, issue, or claim. The fact-checkers were 100 percent correct in verifying accurate information and in identifying inaccurate or misleading claims. The differences in performance between the fact-checkers on the one hand and the students and PhDs on the other were statistically significant in all cases. This further study by the SHEG researchers, then, shows clearly that the digital natives are no better at reading and evaluating material online than they are with traditional texts on screens or on paper. In the first of the SHEG studies discussed here (2016), 50 percent to 80 percent of the students were unable to evaluate the online materials accurately, with similar results in the more recent study (2019) of a national sample and the separate study of fact-checkers (Wineburg and McGrew 2017).

One additional study by the SHEG group provides further evidence of students' reading troubles and current or recent approaches to addressing them in the digital environment. In a more recent study, Wineburg and his colleagues (2020) asked 263 college students beyond first-year status at a large state university to perform two tasks: evaluate a satirical news website and then one that was a supposedly nonpartisan source run by a former lobbyist. The students were able to access the internet and were asked to evaluate the trustworthiness of both sites. They had been taught evaluation strategies such as the CRAAP test (currency, relevance, authority, accuracy, and purpose; cf. Breakstone et al. 2018), which, as Wineburg and colleagues point out, are based on print texts and their usual resources. However, as they write in a more recent study: "The basic assumptions of the CRAAP test are rooted in an analog age. Websites are like print texts. The best way to evaluate them is to read them carefully. But websites are not variations of print documents. The internet operates by wholly different rules" (Wineburg et al. 2021, 8). Results show the kinds of trouble students had with these tasks:

- OVER TWO-THIRDS never identified the "news story" as satirical.
- NINETY-FIVE PERCENT never located the PR firm behind the supposedly "nonpartisan" website.

Often students:

- FOCUSED exclusively on the website or prompt, rarely consulting the broader web
- TRUSTED how a site presented itself on its About page

- APPLIED out-of-date and in some cases incorrect strategies (such as accepting or rejecting a site because of its top-level domain)
- ATTRIBUTED undue weight to easily manipulated signals of credibility—such as an organization's non-profit status, its links to authoritative sources, or [its] "look." (Wineburg et al. 2020, 3, original emphases)

These results show that despite the widespread belief that the "digital native" students are adept users of the internet as well as critical readers, the Stanford group's work shows consistently that they are not. In an even more recent study, to be discussed in detail in chapter 7 (Breakstone et al. 2021), demographic variables show that a variety of personal and other factors also play a role in limiting students' ability. Moreover, as Wineburg and his colleagues (Wineburg et al. 2020, 6) observe, democracy relies on readers who can distinguish between fact and fiction, so there are much larger implications from this study and the others these scholars have conducted.

## *Summary*

Whether we look at the big, standardized tests of students' reading or very close analyses of their use of source materials in their own writing, the results are fairly consistent. Moreover, the results seem to apply to both self-selected samples of students who hope to attend college (and so take the ACT and/or the SAT) and careful national samples designed to represent all students. Whether we look at students' reading of traditional sources or their ability to judge digital resources of different kinds on screens large or small, the results are consistent there as well. It's the same story: all these studies make clear that students' critical reading skills are not where they could and should be. Clearly, not only writing teachers but all college and university faculty need to be paying much more attention to this issue. It is a fixable problem, but to fix it, a deeper understanding of the origins of approaches to reading is essential, as is a rigorous definition of critical literacy. I present a first sketch of that definition at the end of part 1, as it must reflect the current context in which students live and study; it will be expanded and enhanced over the course of the discussion. The history of the teaching of this critical literacy at the college level is largely untold. Literature faculty *have* given attention to reading, such as Louise M. Rosenblatt's widely respected proposal of "reader-response" theory, among other proposals that will be considered in chapter 5. In addition, a small group of writing studies scholars has been interested in reading and has recently managed to raise its profile. However, reading, taken together with writing, listening, and speaking, has suffered from inconsistent, uneven attention over the entire history of the field. In the chapters that follow, this history will be excavated from the roots of writing studies, beginning with English A at Harvard (instituted in 1885) through the Dartmouth Conference in 1966 to the present moment, as reading is variously integrated or supported through corequisite courses at community colleges and open access institutions or ignored in postsecondary settings of all kinds. Throughout the discussion, it should be clear that the focus here is on the field of rhetoric and composition/writing studies (United States Department of Education code 23.13), though *all* faculty, not just those in writing studies, need to pay much more attention to critical literacy as defined here.

# 2

# Varied Approaches to Reading

*Complexities and Equity*

I have two daughters who are formidable readers. The fact that one is a professional librarian accounts for some of this outcome, and surely the fact that both of their parents read a lot also has something to do with it. Their taste for reading started early as a by-product of being read to from infancy. But I know for certain that the older one toddled off to first grade one September not knowing how to read. She read *Hop on Pop* to me while I was cooking Thanksgiving dinner and could summarize the book, so she clearly learned to read in the first few months of school. The younger one was "reading" to her teddy bear (it was *Frog and Toad*, upside down and backward) at about age three and had figured out real reading before kindergarten. So, learning to read was not much of an issue for either of them. But even though they attended school in one of the best districts in the nation (based on all kinds of performance measures, these schools are well ahead in graduation rates, test scores, and so forth [MI School Data 2022]), after elementary school they had almost no instruction in reading; they both recently confirmed this impression. I motivated them to read with summertime book bets of this variety: "I bet you can't read 1,000 pages before school starts in September," with a monetary reward or a special outing or some such adventure; they recall this challenge, with ever-increasing numbers of pages required over the years, as highly motivating. Of course, they had English language arts classes through high school graduation, and they did a fair amount of reading in all their classes as well as in some AP courses offered at their high school, but this experience included limited instruction on comprehension and note taking, with little attention to critical reading and almost nothing about material found online. The younger of the two graduated from high school in the class of 2000, when online research was in its infancy. My daughters' literacy experiences contain many of the key components that lead to strong reading ability and academic success. Many students are not as fortunate, as they begin postsecondary education still working on foundational skills, which accounts for a number of the results discussed in chapter 1.

The importance of critical reading cannot be emphasized too strongly, particularly as more and more of what many people read is online and less and less of it is reviewed by authoritative editors or curators as traditional texts might be, verified by fact-checkers, and so forth. Moreover, not only is more of what we read on a screen of some kind, but there is more and more of it, coming at us at an ever-increasing pace, as observed by Ohio State University literacy scholar Daniel Keller (2014). Under these conditions, critical reading skills are more necessary than ever. But they might be described as a moving target because the technology is constantly changing, so the skills need to be updated to keep pace. Recent research, as discussed in chapter 1, shows clearly that education is not keeping pace, at least not when 50 percent to 80 percent of high school students in a recent national sample could not evaluate the credibility of websites, social media posts, and other online material (Stanford History Education Group and Gibson Consulting 2019).

Before delving deeply into the history of writing programs' approaches to reading, it seems useful to look at how both public education and higher education are *currently* attempting to respond to students' need to be better readers. Assorted responses have been proposed at the various levels of education in four specific, albeit somewhat overlapping, areas. The first of these is the development of the Common Core State Standards (CCSS) for K–12 schools, a state-level initiative originally adopted by most states around the country when first developed but dropped or modified to some degree more recently. While the CCSS are controversial for various reasons, they do provide clear goals for critical reading instruction as students move toward high school graduation and postsecondary education. A second area of response to students' reading needs has been to examine and address inequities in resources and access to programs, including access to technology. The inequities were highlighted by the recent pandemic, which led to the rapid rise of remote learning, essential for the safety of both students and faculty.

A third venue of response arises from the view that many students are newcomers to an academic environment that requires a specialized set of skills most don't have, didn't have easy access to in their lives, or both. The language of academia is effectively a different variety, so even students with some degree of skill in ordinary reading, writing, speaking, and listening need to develop the expertise that academic work requires. They need to master not only the conventions of the written language but also the cultural and linguistic contexts of college. Finally, college-level writing programs, including those at two-year colleges and open access institutions (TYCOAs), have attempted to address students' reading needs in various ways with an array of different kinds of courses and programs in writing, all efforts to help student newcomers judged to need additional help with literacy skills. This chapter looks at these four ways of currently understanding and addressing responsibility for students' need to become effective and efficient critical readers.

## *A K–12 Response to Students' Reading Needs: The Common Core State Standards (CCSS)*

The Common Core idea was introduced in 2010 to address some of the issues mentioned here. As this book was being written, the program had experienced a mixed response across the country. Although initially adopted by a majority of states, some refused to take up the CCSS at all, and some accepted the program but subsequently abandoned it. Still others are in the process of rescinding the use of the CCSS in their schools. The independent, nonprofit, nonpartisan World Population Review (2021) offered these facts early in this decade: "*Common Core States 2021.* The education initiative known as Common Core was initially adopted, in some states, as early as 2010, with Kentucky being the first state. Originally, 46 states passed laws adopting the Common Core standards in their schools. Despite this almost universal ratification of the Common Core initiative, implementation has been challenging, and even though many states have adopted it, through funding or protest issues, many have not yet been able to implement it into their schools." The CCSS have been caught up in various political issues in the states, so the decisions for or against their use are made for these reasons. But a careful look at the standards themselves reveals that they set a high bar for the kind of critical literacy students will need, both personally and professionally. Respected University of Albany education scholar Arthur N. Applebee offers a detailed history of the CCSS, exploring their strengths and weaknesses (2013). Like Applebee, Fordham University political scientist Nicholas Tampio (2018, 2019), author of two books on problems with the CCSS, has suggested that there are issues with both the form and the content of the standards as well as with the ways they are implemented and assessed. Lawrence University government professor Arnold Shober (2016) agrees with this view, as does Diane Ravitch (2020), a Common Core and standardized testing critic and former government official.

Ravitch, who is a key resource by virtue of having worked in the United States Department of Education, notes that the scores on the National Assessment of Educational Progress (NAEP, discussed in chapter 1) are not truly related to the Common Core, even though the CCSS were proposed in part to address the lack of score improvements on the NAEP. Scores on the NAEP are also not related specifically to students' grade levels ("Intended Meaning of NAEP" 2022). Moreover, the validity of both the CCSS and the NAEP have been questioned by respected authorities such as the National Academy of Education (Berman, Haertel, and Pellegrino 2020, 235) and the National Academies of Sciences, Engineering, and Medicine (2017). Ravitch's (2020) recent book is a thorough look at the overall situation of US public education (K–12) as an ongoing conflict between the "Disrupters" and the "Resisters." The former have used political and financial power to work against public schools by supporting charter schools, as well as government programs like Race to the Top, the Common Core, and standardized testing. By contrast, the "Resisters" support public education and the authority of teachers and schools.

In their careful review of the book, emeritus Arizona State University education professors Gene V. Glass and David C. Berliner (2020) find Ravitch's argument to be strong, unbiased, and accurate. They show that Ravitch presents detailed evidence and demonstrates that the Resisters have been able to offset the influence of money and power wielded by the Disrupters. Ravitch makes the claim that, ultimately, public schools should be supported and left to do the real work of educating students. Glass and Berliner suggest that the Resisters will prevail, especially as they build on performance-based assessments that provide better information on student achievement and issues such as success in college and careers; New York, Texas, and other states offer important examples, according to Ravitch (2020, 95–97). In the aftermath of the pandemic, these problems and challenges have only become more obvious, so public education has much work to do as ordinary classroom instruction is restored, post-pandemic.

Even though the CCSS have led to diverse views among the experts, their substantive content is on target on many aspects of critical reading. The standards point to key issues in reading and mark an attempt to focus on elements essential for student success. Here, for example, is a quick summary of the grade 12 standards for English language arts—including both literature and informational text—focusing on content, craft, and structure: readers should be able to grasp main ideas and details and make inferences; follow the development of characters or ideas; understand vocabulary and analyze the structure of a story or argument through the author's style and point of view; evaluate content, claims, and reasoning in a variety of material, both digital and traditional; and compare and contrast multiple sources on the same issue or topic. They should also be able to summarize content and analyze different critical responses to a text. These abilities should be demonstrated in both literary and informational texts, including US foundation documents, works by Shakespeare, websites, social media posts, and a wide range of other kinds of texts—both print and digital (National Governors Association Center for Best Practices 2010).

As discussed below, the CCSS and most of the assessments discussed in chapter 1 do not address the need for context for any kind of material, especially statistics and claims about specific demographic or other groups. The editors of the highly regarded Routledge *Handbook of Reading Research* stress repeatedly in their editorial comments and in the organization and content of the chapters of the latest volume (Moje et al. 2020, 501–505) the importance of the context, background, and sociocultural factors that impact reading. The Common Core, despite its flaws, does offer a useful substantive list of skills students need for college-level work, in the workforce, and as citizens in a democracy. It is also yet another attempt to set a federal government policy concerning the teaching of reading or student reading performance—as noted by a number of scholars in the field, including Northwestern University education professor Cynthia Coburn and her colleagues (Coburn, Pearson, and Woulfin 2010)—focused on K–12 instruction. No similar policy statements exist for college-level reading, though the Conference on College Composition and Communication does have a recent position statement on reading in writing classes, discussed elsewhere in this book (2021).

While the political discussions continue, and while a number of states have abandoned the CCSS or modified their own standards in ways like the ones discussed here in place of the national standards (cf. Ravitch's Resisters), this list comprises a helpful compilation of the key abilities students should have attained by the time they graduate from high school and enter college; they are also abilities that warrant continued development across one's life span. This point is one on which most scholars agree that much more focus is needed. Thus, the CCSS are a substantive resource for improving students' reading abilities, albeit in the K–12 realm, but they have not been widely and effectively implemented to do much good.

## *Responding to Reading Needs with Resources: Equity and Access for Everyone*

The recent pandemic brought an assortment of issues to light that were probably already present but receiving little attention. Among other points, the inequities in school funding as well as access to the internet contribute to students' overall reading situation. The pandemic forced these kinds of barriers to reading into the limelight because they make a difference in education across the entire system, from pre-K to college. At the college level, the inequity arises in two ways. First, students are often placed according to their performance on standardized tests, which are skewed by socioeconomic factors and other kinds of bias. Second, once placed in these courses, students who do poorly on this biased testing are required to take courses that entail the usual costs but do not offer degree credit. While the goal of both is especially to help under-prepared students be successful, research (discussed later in this chapter) shows that many, if not most, students can succeed in college-level work with some kind of support that may or may not include help with reading. The need for greater equity and access to credit-bearing courses from the beginning of college entails these and other complex issues, as discussed in a special issue of the journal *Composition Studies* (Shepherd, Sturman, and Estrem 2020), where options such as corequisite courses are considered. However, neither this journal issue nor a highly respected book on social justice issues in teaching and assessing writing (Poe, Inoue, and Elliot 2018) mentions reading or critical literacy except in passing. Thus, as is true in the field more generally, reading is included inconsistently or not at all.

These comments are not meant as a wholesale condemnation of the field. Some scholars and teachers have paid attention to reading and see the need for a much more sustained and widespread focus on critical literacy, both in writing courses and elsewhere in academia. Some well-known scholars like Ellen C. Carillo (full disclosure: she is often my coauthor or co-editor, as we share a common interest in this issue) and Chris Anson (who occasionally publishes on reading matters), as well as younger researchers (whose work appears in Carillo and Horning 2021a, 2021b), are paying attention; they have done studies, developed courses, and written about equity, access, and reading issues. Scholars at the community college level are also paying attention, including Joanne Baird Giordano and Holly Hassel (2021). And there have been other edited collections (cf. Sullivan, Tinberg, and Blau 2017; 2022), along with the aforementioned Conference on College Composition and Communication (CCCC) position statement (2021), on the role of reading in writing classes. So, there *are* efforts toward equity and access, just relatively few and less strongly focused on reading than they might be.

### TECHNOLOGY RESOURCE ISSUES

Technology in and of itself also has underlying access and equity issues, as discussed by Princeton University African American studies scholar Ruha Benjamin (2019). She points out the various ways key aspects of technology are biased and foster inequity. Among other concerns, she points out that simply reporting data without context or narrative explanation can encourage discrimination instead of moving readers to the more equitable understanding of it that information technology can provide. She points to a Stanford University study of data on discrimination in police policy and sending African Americans to jail, showing that the data, presented without context, resulted in viewers supporting more rather than less punishment or other alternatives. What is needed, Benjamin says, is for those presenting information in a tech-based environment to provide "more context, challenge stereotypical associations, and highlight the role of institutions in producing racial disparities. And while this more holistic approach to framing is vital, the problem extends well beyond retooling social science communication. It calls for a justice-oriented, emancipatory approach to data production, analysis, and public engagement as part of the broader movement for Black lives" (192). Critical reading plays an essential role in the analysis and public engagement that Benjamin points out. While those presenting the data have this responsibility, those teaching the audience for these data must also help prepare them with skills in analysis, synthesis, and evaluation so they can make their own judgments about all kinds of information.

### LINGUISTIC JUSTICE

Another dimension of these approaches is the way they all address the issue of linguistic justice, which is deservedly receiving increasing attention as this book is being written. The movement to eliminate non-credit courses in college writing programs may have originated as a way to help students save time and money by moving them directly into credit-bearing courses, or it may have begun as a cost-saving approach by institutions unwilling to fund such courses. In either case, it moves toward an antiracist goal of allowing novice students, regardless of background, to earn degree credit for all their work. If extra time leads to student success, as these programs clearly do, it's a good outcome regardless of the original motivation. Michigan State University education professor April Baker-Bell has discussed linguistic justice in several articles (2013, 2020a) and a book (2020b). She defines it this way:

> Linguistic Justice, the book and the framework, is about Black Language and Black Liberation. It is an antiracist approach to language and literacy education. It is about dismantling Anti-Black Linguistic Racism and white linguistic hegemony and supremacy in classrooms and in the world. As a pedagogy, Linguistic Justice places Black Language at the center of Black students' language education and experiences. Linguistic Justice does not see White Mainstream English as the be-all and end-all for Black speakers. Linguistic Justice does not side-step fairness and freedom. Instead, it affords Black students the same kinds of linguistic liberties that are afforded to white students. Within a Linguistic Justice framework, excuses such as "that's just the way it is" cannot be used as justification for Anti-Black Linguistic Racism, white linguistic supremacy, and linguistic injustice. Telling children that White Mainstream English is needed for survival can no longer be the answer, especially as we are witnessing Black people being mishandled, discriminated against, and murdered while using White Mainstream English, and in some cases, before they even open their mouths. (7)

In the classroom, using the preferred term *Black Language*, Baker-Bell argues that teaching students about this language can work toward an antiracist pedagogy and against the linguistic racism inherent in White Mainstream English. Drawing on her own teaching experience in a leadership academy program in Detroit, Baker-Bell shares her lessons on the history of Black Language as well as its grammatical structure and rules. She engages students in examining the rhetorical forms commonly used by speakers of Black Language. These lessons lead to a consideration of the ways language is used to exert power and to discriminate. Thus, these lessons, by addressing linguistic racism directly, can further the goal of antiracist teaching and learning (Baker-Bell 2020b, 63–92).

Baker-Bell (2020b, 100) makes a broader point about this kind of teaching and why it is important for all students, again regardless of background:

> *Linguistic Justice: Black Language, Literacy, Identity, and Pedagogy* is designed to give Black students the tools to liberate themselves from oppression. However, let me also point out that the Antiracist Black Language Pedagogy that I outline in this book offers ALL students and their teachers a critical linguistic awareness of Black Language and windows into broader conversations about anti-Blackness, language and identity, language and power, language and history, linguistic racism, and white linguistic and cultural hegemony. These critical capacities are just as important—if not more important—for white students as they are for Black students and other students of color, as white students are more likely to perpetuate Anti-Black Linguistic Racism and uphold white linguistic hegemony by way of their privilege, power, and lack of awareness of language varieties other than their own. And although an antiracist Black Language education and pedagogy are specific to the linguistic and racial needs of Black students, the principles and pedagogy can be adjusted and applied to benefit other language groups.

This view of teaching linguistic justice fits well with the trend toward giving all novice students a potentially more equal starting point toward earning a college degree. The message is clear: regardless of where students are when they start, postsecondary work can and should support the goals of linguistic justice for all, setting aside discriminatory terms like *remedial English* and respecting the historical background and current varieties of spoken and written language found among different groups of speakers. The model presented here proposes that critical reading is best viewed in this same, broader sociocultural and linguistic context. The model also shows how critical reading can and should be integrated with writing, speaking, and listening—with the goal of providing equitable access to critical literacy, technology, and linguistic justice for all students.

## *Responding to Reading Needs of Academic Newcomers: Language and Culture*

Since I published *Teaching Writing as a Second Language* (Horning 1987), I have been thinking of academic writing as a distinct linguistic system. In that book, I argued that because it is effectively a foreign language for many students, formal academic prose must be studied and learned more or less the same way a second language is learned: through classes, exposure in the environment, help from technology (though that was not part of the discussion in 1987 the way it is now), and so forth. But for formal academic writing, unlike French or Spanish, the input can only come one way: through reading. I believed that in 1987, having taught writing in English to second-language learners and having worked with basic writers as well. But aside from academics and perhaps others working in the professions, government service, or libraries, most people—including most students—don't live in an environment of formal academic prose. So, reading that kind of material is the only "environment" in which students can be exposed to it. It is not the world of Instagram, TikTok, and Twitter (now X), where students do have significant linguistic and rhetorical knowledge and expertise. As almost all second-language learners know from experience, it is much easier to learn a language in the place where that language is spoken than it is to learn it in a classroom or from a book. Traditional-age undergraduates attending residential colleges and universities enter the place where formal academic language is spoken, but this situation is less and less common generally and particularly among first-generation students who are more likely to be living off campus and working while going to school or to be nontraditional students with their own families.

The various bits and pieces of this argument have been transformed by more recent research over the years since my book, an early entry in CCCC's Studies in Writing and Rhetoric series, was published. Among the relevant concepts are Michael Silverstein's (1979) proposal of linguistic ideology and Suresh Canagarajah's (2012) concept of translingualism. These scholars' basic idea is that a dialect or variety of a language is an integral part of its social, economic, and political situation and status; some of its features may be common across languages or dialects. To the extent that academic English represents the academic community—with its hierarchy and authority figures of faculty, administrators, and others—students and especially first-generation, bilingual, and novice college students are acculturated or invited into this realm through reading and writing. It is not their native language or situation, so a lot of work is involved, even if there are common features across languages. A careful Harvard University education dissertation study, recently published as a book (Gable 2021), discusses the situational differences between first-generation students and those who come from families more familiar with academia.

The students' reflections and insights show that their adjustment to academic life includes not only key critical literacy skills but also a wide array of other issues and factors. One of the outcomes of the challenges these students face is that they are less likely to graduate, according to national data on six-year graduation rates which show that 56 percent do not complete a degree in this time frame (RTI International 2019b), although rates have recently begun to show some improvement (Complete College America 2022). These family or intra-personal factors are addressed by Peter Adams (2020b, 732–748) in his textbook, discussed in detail below, because his work with Accelerated Learning Program (ALP) students shows that they are at higher risk of leaving school because of these issues.

A focus on first-generation college students is relevant here for several reasons. First, according to a national fact sheet from the student affairs organization NASPA (National Association of Student Personnel Administrators), a majority of current students (56%) are first-generation students, and even more (59%) are the first child in their family to attend (RTI International 2019a). So, the odds are that half or more of the students in the average college class are first-generation students. They are in a country that is foreign to them. And they are joined by a vast majority of nontraditional students, around 75 percent according to recent national data reported by college referral site Best Colleges' editor Hannah Muniz (2020); these are students over age twenty-five who often have full- or part-time jobs and families of their own. These claims are updated and further supported by the Complete College America report (2022). These students are also in academia in a foreign country in which they don't speak the language and may or may not take up residence.

The specific linguistic work involved for nontraditional and first-generation students can also entail working across language boundaries, the point at which translingualism is relevant. This point is made by Joanne Baird Giordano (2020) in her experience creating an integrated reading and writing course built on her prior experience as a TESOL teacher; she also sees the relevance of second-language learning for students who are crossing an assortment of linguistic and social boundaries into the foreign country of academia. Others have made the same point in a variety of different ways; it has salience for those teaching in TYCOAs, often a kind of first "field trip" for students visiting what is for them the foreign country of academia. Holly Hassel (2020, 140) describes her experience, first as a student and later as a teacher, in her discussion of her work with TYCOA college students: "Students in open-admission and two-year colleges often have educational experiences that are not well matched to the demands of college writing, perhaps because they went to schools that emphasized literary analysis in their English courses; [are] nontraditional students who have a gap in their education; [are] home schooled students; [are] students with non-college-prep coursework, and [because of] many other circumstances."

Hassel (2020, 139–141) further points out that these kinds of students have particular needs as they move into this new territory: "rhetorical adaptability," or the ability to use a variety of styles and techniques as needed by the rhetorical situation; "structured opportunities to course correct," or opportunities to develop self-awareness and make changes as needed; and "critical reading skills," or the exposure to challenging texts of all kinds so they can use critical and information literacy skills for analysis and synthesis. Similar observations are offered by Brett Griffiths (2020) and student Lauren Sills (2020). Griffiths writes about the diversity in her student population at Macomb Community College, in a county immediately northeast of Detroit, where the students might be African Americans; immigrants from anywhere, but most commonly from the Middle East or South Asia; and others for whom not only college but also the United States is a foreign country. For them, Griffiths (2020, 75) says, "the very process of education is itself fraught with cultural, linguistic, and social roadblocks."

A clear example of these kinds of "visitor in a foreign country" experiences is captured by Alyssa G. Cavazos, a bilingual first-generation student when in school and now a writing studies faculty member. She began college at a school on the US-Mexico border. In first-year writing, she used some Spanish words in an English essay, with this result:

> I was instructed to assimilate into the dominant discourse regardless of my purposeful attempts to merge languages in my writing. My attempt to write while illustrating what Gloria Anzaldúa refers to as a "tolerance for ambiguity" through the coexistence of languages failed. If my writing teacher would have encouraged me to reflect on my translingual attempts to make meaning of a nuanced environment that directly opposes the university space, I could have further developed critical thoughts on the implications of living, studying, and using language in a border region. While the teacher shunned my use of Spanish, the essay nonetheless represents my desire to develop a healthy dialogue between the bordered and translingual spaces I was attempting to negotiate—my home and academic communities. The teacher's feedback was a critical moment in my college experience, especially as a first-generation college student. (2019, 39)

In these very tangible ways, then, as well as in less obvious ways, writing teachers are asking students to read and write a language they don't speak in a country in which they don't live and a place in which they don't necessarily want or expect to spend much time as their futures unfold. It is no wonder, then, that both reading and writing are challenging. However, it is in this context that we try to teach reading with writing, so it includes not only getting main ideas and details but also understanding the entire rhetorical situation from which a book or an article might arise. The parlor metaphor comes to mind, but it only skims the surface of students' actual experiences.

Contemporary students don't speak this language and do not necessarily hope or expect to be part of the "country" in which it is the common language. The goal of instruction instead might fairly be described as "communicative competence," a phrase coined by sociolinguist Dell Hymes (1964). Hymes was trying to capture the idea that language is always part of a social environment that plays a role in how the language functions. My larger view, then, is that critical reading of extended academic prose is not just a reading task but a task that entails students learning by coming to the "country" in which that language is used and being able to understand it fully (i.e., through reading) and use it themselves for their own goals (i.e., through writing). In an early formulation of the relevant aspects of communicative competence, Hymes builds on the discussion of linguistic competence and performance proposed by linguist Noam Chomsky. But he proposes that beyond language per se, the ability to communicate in a functional way requires much more than sentence structures:

> It is rather that it is not linguistics, but ethnography—not language, but communication—which must provide the frame of reference within which the place of language in culture and society is to be described. The boundaries of the community within which communication is possible; the boundaries of the situations within which communication occurs; the means and purposes and patterns of selection, their structure and hierarchy, that constitute the communicative economy of a group, are conditioned, to be sure, by properties of the linguistic codes within the group, but are not controlled by them. The same linguistic means may be organized to quite different communicative ends; the same communicative ends may be served by organization of, or by focus upon, quite varied means. Facets of the cultural values and beliefs, social institutions and forms, roles and personalities, history and ecology of a community must be examined together in relation to communicative events and patterns as focus of study (just as every aspect of a community's life may be brought selectively to bear on the study of a focus such as kinship, sex, or conflict). (Hymes 1964, 3)

This explanation is only one of a number of formulations of the idea of communicative competence or ethnography of communication that Hymes published in the 1960s. The key points for the present discussion are the ideas that there are patterns in the way communication occurs in practice and that context is crucial to producing and understanding meaning.

In a later paper, Hymes gives a useful example of why the overall situation in which language occurs is so important. The sentence "He decided on the floor" could have a variety of meanings, including what and where, depending on the context (Hymes 1972 [1971], 278). To address these possibilities, additional language is needed to make the meaning clear, but the entire situation in which the sentence occurred might also be relevant. The system of analysis Hymes created makes use of a mnemonic device in the word *speaking* to capture the elements of context, very much still in use today, discussed in detail in a well-respected textbook in sociolinguistics: setting and scene (S); participants (P); ends or outcomes (E); act sequence, or the form and content of the language (A); key, or the tone of an exchange (K); instrumentalities, or the channel through which the language is conveyed, including both written and spoken forms (I); the norms or behavior expected (N); and the genre or type of language used (G) (Wardhaugh and Fuller 2015, 232–234). It is easy to see how these various categories of analysis apply to the situation of students trying to learn to write academic English. It's also easy to see that this kind of language largely appears only in the written form: even writers of scholarly journal articles and books don't speak in a "scholarly" way.

Related insights arise in the detailed analysis of student writing in both first-year and upper-level college courses, according to an examination of "scholarly" or formal academic prose by University of Michigan rhetorician and linguist Laura L. Aull (2020). Using corpus analysis tools from linguistics not available to Hymes, Aull explores key features of student writing at each level, focusing on both argumentation and explanation. The characteristics Aull examines include civility, defined as "diplomatic evidentiality . . . blending open-mindedness with well-informed conviction" (6), which appears much more in upper-level writing than in first-year papers. A second rhetorical feature is cohesion, which involves "a range of cohesive ties that draw attention to how parts of a text relate . . . [that] help create a shared understanding between readers and writers . . . an attentiveness to the reading needs of an audience" (7). Finally, Aull points to compression, "the use of dense, phrasal detail" (7). She notes that this feature makes academic texts difficult to read and write: "Compressed detail can also obscure grammatical relationships, and cognitively, it is more taxing to read. Compressed phrases make academic writing unlike the English language use that students encounter most in conversation and informal writing" (7). While Aull does not go on from these insights to discuss how reading with attention to these features in published texts or the absence of them in less formal prose might help students develop flexible writing appropriate to different genres and situations, the data she provides do help show how students might benefit from an approach that applies her findings to both reading and writing. Some useful pedagogical applications do appear in her afterword (146–171).

The work of this kind using insights from Hymes, Aull, and others involves vocabulary and syntax as well as simply the idea of reading an entire book or a full-length journal article or other kind of material. It requires that students go beyond what the Citation Project scholars call "quote mining" (Howard, Serviss, and Rodrigue 2010), or selecting a few passages to quote in the typical ten-page research paper assignment, to being able to read and fully follow a complete argument through an article or a book. It is the opposite of tl;dr (too long; didn't read), requiring more attention and time than even the expanded 280 characters of Twitter's (now X's) tweets. So, the question becomes what to do with novice students in the foreign country of academia, who need to become efficient and effective critical readers and writers who can use academic language for their own purposes, in school and beyond. The related issues have to do with how postsecondary institutions are changing their approach to students who are unprepared for college-level work; in too many cases, these students never make it past the required basic courses, as Mya Poe, Jessica Nastal, and Norbert Elliot (2019) demonstrate. The whole idea of developmental or basic coursework is in a state of transition, with equity, economics, enrollment pressures, and assorted other factors driving institutions' decisions about reducing or eliminating such courses, partly in response to the recent pandemic. Different approaches in response to these factors are discussed in more detail below. But even before the pandemic, there was pressure on colleges and universities to change their treatment of novice students. Understanding and supporting students as newcomers to the academic environment offers another area where work on reading might help but is often missing.

## *Responding to Reading Needs in College Writing Classes and Programs*

### IN THE CLASSROOM: UNDER-PREPARED STUDENTS

Perhaps since the beginning of higher education and certainly since English A was first offered at Harvard University (see chapter 4), writing teachers have been aware of the need to work with all students, since many arrive at college at a novice stage in developing their ability to write—except perhaps those who have been lucky enough to go to good schools or had Advanced Placement or dual enrollment experiences with academic writing at the postsecondary level. Part of the reason some students come as novices has to do with the Common Core and related government initiatives discussed earlier, which are still under discussion or in dispute. Meanwhile, writing studies faculty at TYCOAs and all four-year institutions have the challenge of teaching the vast majority of novice students—especially under-prepared students—to write, to support their success in and beyond the first year. Various approaches have been tried over the years, with mixed success. On the one hand, from a historical perspective, community college scholar and teacher Patrick Sullivan (2017) shows that developmental courses have helped many students succeed at community colleges in particular, using national statistics and his own institution, Manchester Community College near Hartford, Connecticut, as a case study to support this claim. On the other hand, more recent research shows that in some ways developmental courses do more harm than good, holding students back from credit-bearing courses that lead to degrees or career-focused credentials. The array of developmental courses—often prerequisites—generally includes courses on reading, although increasingly they have been removed from the curriculum.

A careful analysis of the widespread use of basic or developmental courses for under-prepared students shows clearly that they have little impact on student success rates, assuming that success is measured by graduation rates. Maria Elena Oliveri and Robert J. Mislevy, former ETS (Educational Testing Service, which does testing for the College Board including the SAT and other tests) psychometric researchers, along with emeritus New Jersey Institute of Technology English professor Norbert Elliot, show that students who take more developmental courses are less likely to graduate; therefore, they say, "it appears that remediation is not having the desired effect on graduation rates" (Oliveri, Mislevy, and Elliot 2020, 349). This claim is based on the research of Xianglei Chen (2016) for the United States Department of Education, discussed in chapter 1. They also point out that there is much more need for ongoing feedback than for standardized testing, much more need for the development of "complementary skills" like collaboration, and, I would argue, much more need for critical literacy and thinking. In some places, changes are under way, as Oliveri and colleagues say: "Institutions have provided for-credit options for underprepared students in various ways, ranging from offering corequisite models (concurrently delivered basic instruction) to emporium models (computer-lab–delivered instruction)" (2020, 368). In addition, the shift away from standardized testing in particular may be accelerating as a by-product of the challenges of the recent pandemic. Meanwhile, there seems to be agreement about the need to rethink developmental work but not a clear understanding of where reading fits in this picture. It should already be clear that reading is not a set of skills that only some students lack or need to develop. It is an issue for all students in all courses, so perhaps an entirely new view is needed, as suggested by the model proposed in this book.

**REFORM EFFORTS**

A recent study on placement of community college students confirms the effectiveness of the approach that uses multiple measures to place students in college-level courses and not in developmental courses for both English and math. The study appeared in 2023 as a working paper by the Center for the Analysis of Postsecondary Readiness, which is part of the Community College Research Center (CCRC) at Teachers College Columbia in New York City. Students at seven community colleges in New York state were randomly placed in English and math either on test scores alone or on test scores, high school GPA, and other factors—the multiple measures approach. Of the 13,000 students in the study, those placed in college-level courses based on multiple measures performed much better than those who went into developmental work. They completed these courses as well as their degrees. The multiple measures approach—especially when coupled with other support through corequisite courses, advising, and tutoring—made an important difference to student success (Kopko, Daniels, and Cullinan 2023).

The CCRC took a careful look at the entire situation and prepared a report recommending five specific principles for changes in developmental education at TYCOA schools (Bickerstaff et al. 2022), based on a review of a large number of studies. The recommended changes begin with an approach to placement, giving entering students immediate access to college-level courses rather than holding them in developmental or other kinds of non-credit courses while providing additional support. A second change is for TYCOA institutions to provide both academic and non-academic support, in the form of corequisite courses, advising, and other kinds of help. The curriculum also needs to be modified as a third change, giving students more experience with the kinds of tasks they are likely to be assigned beyond the first year and more student-focused approaches that allow them to have more input into classroom activities. The last two recommended changes are steps to be taken across the entire institution: first, working to address any residual inequities for Black, Indigenous, and people of color (BIPOC) students and, finally, offering comprehensive support for students' academic and non-academic needs beyond the first year, all the way to graduation. Thus, there are two main approaches for students who appear to be novices, unlikely to succeed without several different kinds of extra help. These approaches coalesce into two options currently in use: placing students directly into an integrated reading and writing course that offers direct and explicit instruction in reading as well as writing or placing students into a regular first-year writing class and requiring an additional course to provide supplemental instruction that includes specific help with reading, support services, advising, and whatever else might be needed to ensure student success; this corequisite approach is also supported by Complete College America (2021).

The now widely adopted approach to placement and advising that seems most helpful in getting students into the right courses is called Guided Pathways, an approach meant to help students from entry to exit that has substantial research support and actual use in its favor. Its history is captured by the chancellor of one of the largest community college districts in California, Bryan Reece (2022), who leads the Contra Costa Community College District with 52,000 students at three TYCOA schools. This TYCOA group serves a diverse and historically underserved community on all its campuses. Reece explains that the idea of a comprehensive approach to program choice and progress for students began in the early 2000s with grant funding from Gates and Lumina, with research on various attempts provided by the CCRC.

In 2015, the CCRC published a useful report on Guided Pathways by Thomas R. Bailey, Shanna Smith Jaggars, and Davis Jenkins (2015; Reece 2022, 117). Instead of multiple choices for courses and programs, Guided Pathways addresses four key needs students have as they start college, take courses, and graduate: to see various distinct paths to completion through coursework, to choose a path to follow, to get help with staying on their chosen path or, if changing paths, how to maximize achieving a revised goal through advising, and finally, to help students invest in the work required in all their courses for degree or program completion, again through support services and advising, as needed. Guided Pathways can also help address the complications of transfer to universities; many states have adopted a standard transfer agreement to simplify this part of a complicated situation. Research shows that Guided

Pathways has significantly helped improve student success rates (Community College Research Center 2021).

Other research shows what has been happening in the entire area of developmental education, with many changes in approaches to placement, curriculum, and advising. Surveys at different points make clear the focal points of attention; in developmental education, there has been a great deal of attention to writing courses but less explicit attention to reading as a separate issue. An older study by D. Patrick Saxon, Nara M. Martirosyan, Rebecca A. Wentworth, and Hunter R. Boylan (2015) appeared in the *Journal of Developmental Education*, showing that at that point an integrated reading/writing approach seemed to work best, citing the ALP approach discussed below as a successful model. More recently, a nationwide survey of TYCOA institutions (Saxon and Morante 2021) confirmed wide use of the integrated approach, which sometimes includes specific attention to reading (cf. ALP, discussed in more detail below, and Blaauw-Hara, Tebeau, and Borowiak 2020), although many programs do not include reading specifically.

## Understanding Community College Complexity

The work of Hassel, Giordano, and other scholars highlights the need to expand the view of the field, specifically to include students at two-year and open access institutions. The population at two-year colleges (TYCs) specifically is much larger than most readers might think. According to the latest information from the United States Department of Education as this book was being written, about 40 percent of all US undergraduates were enrolled at community colleges (Digest of Education Statistics 2023). Those national statistics are reported for two-year and four-year schools without separating out "open access" or defining that term, which usually refers to institutions that admit nearly everyone who applies.

David Levinson, a community college president and sociologist, wrote a useful history of and status report on TYCs for ABC-CLIO, the publisher of a series of reference works on major educational topics. In tracing the history of community colleges, Levinson (2005) begins his chronology with a survey of developments in the history of higher education, beginning in postrevolutionary times and leading to the founding of the first community college, Joliet Junior College, in 1901. With the development of other community colleges, a professional organization was begun, changing its name from the American Association of Junior Colleges to remove "Junior" in 1920–1921

(45) and later adding "Community" to the name. A second major twentieth-century development, according to Levinson, was the report by the Truman Commission in 1947, which cited the need for education as a civic responsibility, to be provided by "a network of low-cost community colleges throughout the nation" (45). The report is well-known and often cited, not only because of its size and scope (six volumes) but also because of its recommendation of free or low-cost postsecondary education. The numbers of community colleges exploded in the twentieth century according to Levinson, from virtually none to 1,200 in the year 2000 (47). As this book is being prepared, there are 1,038 community colleges in the US, according to the American Association of Community Colleges (2023).

Levinson devotes a full chapter of his reference volume to the complicated nature of TYCOA institutions (2005, 117–147). He uses the word *conundrum* multiple times, for many good reasons. There are varied and opposing trends and goals within these institutions, the most basic of which is the fact that they offer both standard academic preparation for students who hope or expect to transfer to four-year institutions to earn a bachelor's degree as well as an array of different kinds of vocational training/certification programs (auto repair, nursing, tech support, and many other career fields). Drawing on other research, he provides this list of roles TYCOA institutions might fulfill:

- Academic preparation for transfer or terminal academic degrees
- Second-chance remediation
- English language development for non-native students
- Public job training for disadvantaged clientele
- Occupational preparation for public or private credentialing, licensing, and certification
- Worker-initiated short-term training and individual development
- Customized training and certification for employers and equipment vendors (141).

It is easy to see why the role of TYCOAs is complicated. If students are unsure about what goal they want to achieve, that adds further complexity to the overall situation, with shifting perspectives for both institutions and students. Critical reading is essential for all community college students regardless of their goals. This complicated history and status reveals the backdrop against which the array of approaches to reading is currently playing out.

## EVIDENCE OF VARIED APPROACHES

As the discussion to this point suggests, writing studies as a field pays inconsistent attention to reading. An examination of the research gives a sense that a kind of "don't bother me with facts when I've already made a decision" approach prevails, or perhaps faculty are simply overwhelmed or unsure about where to start, since plenty of data support a much greater focus on reading in higher education than is in effect at the moment. Part 3 of this book offers specific steps and strategies useful for faculty in writing and all other disciplines. In K–12 education, the data are more consistent, but the findings—especially those for high school that offer clear guidance for postsecondary institutions—do not seem to carry over. Even programs at the college level that show the usefulness and relevance of reading instruction in helping students write better don't seem to be widely acknowledged, despite clear evidence of a positive impact. Or such programs are accepted or adopted but then are lost, as they are usually part of a move to eliminate basic or developmental work rather than approaches that would benefit all college students. This situation seems strange in the face of the array of data presented in chapter 1: no matter how reading ability is measured or assessed, it is clear that most college students are not the efficient, effective, critical readers they should be to ensure their success in school, in their personal and professional lives, and in their roles as citizens. While none of the assessments discussed in that chapter offer a direct measure of student success on these dimensions, additional research points to effective steps faculty members can take to make a real difference.

## INTEGRATED READING AND WRITING VERSUS COREQUISITE VERSUS HYBRID (ALP)

A first example of this kind of investigation supports integrated approaches to reading and writing instruction across educational levels. Steve Graham, a highly respected and widely published Arizona State University education professor, presents the results of several major meta-analyses on reading-writing relationships in K–12 schools. The findings show repeatedly that when reading and writing are taught together, the result is better student performance in both areas; these persuasive findings, admittedly in the K–12 arena, can and should carry over to postsecondary instruction. After grade 12, after all, those students will appear in postsecondary classrooms. Two recent reports illustrate this situation clearly, both published by Graham and a team of researchers in 2018.

In one meta-analysis, the team looked at forty-seven studies of reading and writing taught together and published over the last several decades (Graham et al. 2018a). The reports were focused on the impact of programs in which reading and writing were taught together, with neither skill receiving more than 60 percent of instructional time. About half of the studies in this project involved students in middle school or high school. The results demonstrate that both reading and writing improved (using various measures of spelling, reading comprehension, observations of students' knowledge of content in discussion, substantive content in student writing drawn from readings, and other indicators) when the two skills were taught together. This first meta-analysis appeared in a top journal in the field, *Reading Research Quarterly*, the flagship journal of the International Literacy Association; a follow-up review appeared in 2020, as discussed below.

The second meta-analysis presented by Graham and colleagues also appeared in 2018, in the *Review of Educational Research* (Graham et al. 2018b). In this second report, Graham and his team reviewed ninety studies involving about 8,000 students over the previous two decades and again across the K–12 spectrum. They focused specifically on the impact of reading instruction on students' writing ability and found significant positive effects on writing quality, length, and spelling that were maintained over time. While this second meta-analysis focused mostly on elementary-level students, some secondary student studies were included. Moreover, Graham and his colleagues point out that most of the studies examined for this report were true experiments that appeared in published papers rather than technical reports or other kinds of materials. In terms of overall conclusions, they write:

> Increasing students' interaction with text improved their writing performance. When preschool to high school students were directed to interact with words or text or observe others doing so (e.g., watching a student read text to carry out a science experiment), 18 out of every 20 studies produced an immediate positive effect, resulting in meaningful improvements on composite measures of overall writing performance as well as specific measures of writing quality and spelling. More particularly, reading individual words, increasing the amount of reading students did, reading and analyzing text produced by others, and observing other readers interact with text enhanced students' performance on one or more measure[s] of writing (mostly involving spelling or writing quality). (2018b, 269)

Finally, the authors point out that the findings show the importance of teaching reading with writing; however, writing must still be taught directly:

> Although there is still much to learn about reading and writing connections and how and when they are mutually supportive, available theory and evidence justify the use of writing and writing instruction as a means for improving students' reading and vice versa. This is not a radical recommendation, as others have argued that reading and writing instruction should be integrated. Such instruction appears to have been relatively uncommon, however, based on survey and observational research conducted in the area of writing. In reviewing this literature, I found that most teachers were not adequately prepared to teach writing and that they devoted little time to writing or writing instruction . . . Reading and writing instruction is not effectively integrated when one of the ingredients occurs infrequently . . . It is unlikely that current reading and writing practices will change to accommodate more connected reading and writing activities if the importance of these practices is not understood and advocated by all constituents. (Graham et al. 2020, S42)

Graham makes clear the research agenda that is needed to move reading and writing closer together. While he doesn't comment specifically on the needs in higher education or on the ways equitable access or skewed testing might have an impact on the integrated approaches his research advocates, the discussion in this chapter demonstrates that these needs apply at both the K–12 and postsecondary levels. One approach at the college level that follows Graham and his team's recommendations is Peter Adams's ALP program, which includes an integrated reading and writing course and is a hybrid because it also entails the use of corequisite coursework, as discussed in the following section. Adams (2020a) has evidence showing that his approach confirms Graham's ideas. Because the ALP program does focus on both reading and writing explicitly and in depth, it warrants detailed examination.

### ACCELERATED LEARNING PROGRAM (ALP)

Among the most successful approaches to the recommendations of the CCRC report, which had been in operation for a number of years prior to its publication, is the Accelerated Learning Program (ALP) developed by Peter Adams at the Community College of Baltimore County (CCBC). In a recent paper, Adams (2020a) (now a national consultant on ALP) traced the history of the program and provided statistics that demonstrate its substantial success. The program entails having students who do not place into regular first-year writing enroll for it anyway but concurrently enroll in a supplemental class that provides both academic support and resources to address students' personal issues that may lead them to drop out of or have problems passing the writing course. The class is a kind of hybrid of integrated reading and writing and the corequisite approach, since students take a regular English 101 writing course that integrates reading and writing but must also take a corequisite course that provides various kinds of support. For many of these novice students, weak reading skills contribute to their problems, so one dimension of the ALP supplemental course is work on reading. Adams (2020c) explains, in a detailed discussion of his own teaching, how it became clear that the students struggled with reading substantive materials in each unit of the course. He modified his approach to allow time for students to develop and use active reading, annotation, summarizing, and evaluation skills to think carefully, read effectively, and write, over time, on the topic at hand. Adams reported that success rates for students in ALP are double those of students who take the traditional developmental composition course without the ALP supplement (2020c).

It is no surprise that Adams (2020a) is a superstar in the field as a result of the extraordinary success of the ALP program, now widespread nationwide. Essentially, Adams's approach sets aside the blame game; ALP doesn't really care why students show up at college as novice readers and writers. ALP starts with students where they are and moves them ahead with instruction and support to achieve their own goals. Help with reading is a key component of this successful approach. In a Zoom conversation with me (February 23, 2021), Adams discussed the way ALP courses are structured to require students to probe the reading they do so they understand sources' ideas and arguments on a particular topic. The courses use a theme-based structure, with three multi-week themes that entail students reading multiple sources and reviewing other materials that might be in videos or online. They have small-group discussions and complete short, informal writing tasks, culminating in a longer, more formal paper at the end of each unit. In this approach, then, reading and writing are integrated, so students go beyond basic reading comprehension to synthesize, evaluate, and use what they have read in their writing. Adams used the phrase *novice experts* to describe students' status at the end of each unit, with no prompting from me about this terminology (he also used this phrase in his reflection on his evolution as a teacher in this program [2020c, 264]). But it is easy to see that while ALP students become "experts" of sorts on each theme they work on, they are still novice readers and writers, developing their skills.

To facilitate that development in all sorts of corequisite courses, Adams (2020b) published a textbook that includes a distinct section on reading. The book is designed for use in ALP courses and therefore offers in its main chapters a fully integrated approach to reading and writing, with texts and assignments on topics likely to be of interest to students. The core of the book is divided into a series of projects, and the idea in the course structure is that a course might delve into some appropriate number of these projects but would not entail students staying on the same topic for the full semester. Each project includes texts for students to read, online material, exercises of various kinds, and writing tasks—both formal and informal. But in addition, the second half of the book offers chapters on key topics in writing and reading, such as editing and revising.

More than fifty pages are devoted to effective, efficient critical reading. While Adams evokes well-established strategies like paying attention to vocabulary, annotation, and summary, he also offers solid guidance on evaluating materials that is vital to the critical reading and thinking skills students need to develop. It is particularly noteworthy that he asks students not only to preview the material but also to focus on the rhetorical situation of the writer of any given text, whether traditional or digital. Students are guided to consider the writer's credentials and other aspects of credibility that are essential to judging the trustworthiness of a source. It should be immediately obvious that this approach taps into the integrated reading and writing advocated by Graham and other scholars. More recent research on ALP and other programs like it provides further support for this approach (Jensen forthcoming).

The three chapters in the textbook that concentrate on reading are intended, as Adams described them to me, to be a resource for students as they work on the projects in the first part of the book. This skillful arrangement of the material allows the instructor to keep the class's focus on integrated reading and writing in each topic used in the course. But where students might need specific kinds of help with reading, the reading sections are available for use, either by students on their own or as assigned by the teacher. Moreover, Adams points out in the preface that the book specifically supports the highly respected statement on outcomes for first-year writing set forth by the Council of Writing Program Administrators, the national organization of faculty who direct writing programs (WPA 2014). The outcomes document is quoted in detail in Adams's list of the specific parts of the book that can help students achieve each of the stated goals. And additional material for faculty on the topic of reading is provided in the Instructor's Manual. This last item is important: it is clear from Ellen C. Carillo's (2015, 32) research that a majority of college writing teachers believe they lack the training to help students with reading. My own research shows that current graduate programs for those preparing to teach college writing do not offer any training on teaching reading, with a handful of exceptions (Horning 2021b). Thus, overall, Adams's textbook and the ALP program provide a key approach that can help improve students' critical reading abilities.

## RELATED APPROACHES

While evidence suggests that ALP works well in many classrooms, an assortment of other strategies to help students with reading and writing together have been tried over time. Another kind of approach for novice writers is offered by the "stretch" program, the history of which was sketched by Gregory R. Glau (2007) at Northern Arizona University (NAU). In this approach, the standard first-term, first-year composition course is stretched over two terms, to give novice students additional time to develop the necessary skills. It can fairly be described as an integrated reading and writing approach (IRW). According to the report Glau published after ten years of the program (2007), it was clear that the additional time led to substantially better pass rates and student retention, evidently due to the positive impact of additional time to develop their literacy skills.

The other key feature of the stretch approach is that students receive degree credit for the courses, unlike other kinds of basic writing courses that often do not provide credit toward graduation. But an interesting point: reading played a limited role in the placement of students in the program, which was done by SAT verbal or ACT English (but not reading) test scores, and there is nothing in the more recent reports about exactly what the program offers in terms of reading instruction in its two-semester extended version of first-year writing. Still, the success of the program in terms of students' performance in the rest of the writing program and their retention in the university made the stretch approach seem useful. More recently, NAU has found other ways to provide novice students with academic support through its writing center, its Introduction to the University course, and online resources and thus has stepped away from the extended, extra course/stretch approach.

Different institutions have various versions of the stretch idea, as reported, for example, by Thomas Peele (2010) at Boise State University, but most share NAU's original plan, with the same basic characteristic of an additional semester of work for novices to develop their skills. A version of the stretch idea was used for a time at the City University of New York (CUNY), as discussed by Karen Uehling (forthcoming) in her review of the history of that program and of much basic writing instruction. CUNY's Barbara Gleason pointed out to me that the stretch approach never enjoyed the widespread adoption and success that ALP has garnered recently (email communication, August 2, 2023). The few published reports say little about the role of reading in placement or curriculum. Other institutions have tried different approaches, some with an overt and specific integrated reading-writing focus, like the one at San Francisco State University (SFSU) discussed by Sugie Goen and Helen Gillotte-Tropp (2003). That federally funded pilot program produced convincing results, showing the positive impact of teaching reading and writing both explicitly and together on novice students at SFSU.

Given Graham's research on the positive impact of teaching these skills together across the K–12 spectrum, this outcome is not surprising. Yet another example comes from the work of respected community college teacher and scholar Patrick Sullivan (2021). Sullivan's approach includes features specifically for community college students he has taught that address the inequities BIPOC students have often faced in getting to and staying in college. Sullivan provides the assignments he uses in both the class he teaches for underprepared students and in other, more advanced classes; all of them reflect an integrated reading-writing approach. While Sullivan's classes do not use a stretch format, the book shows how the integrated approach is used in actual courses he has taught.

This discussion surveys the range of approaches to address student needs taken by TYCOAs and other institutions with populations of under-prepared students. A number of different strategies have been tried, as this review demonstrates. In general, there is not nearly enough focus on reading, with the successful ALP program the notable exception. What distinguishes that program is the specific focus on reading, including Peter Adams's (2020b) textbook that includes sections on critical reading designed for all students who need to develop their skills. Given the clear evidence for the value of incorporating reading into writing courses, especially for under-prepared students (as well as all others), the ALP results provide a clearly useful approach.

## Summary

This chapter has provided an overview of the various ways students' reading challenges have been addressed, with relatively more or less attention and success, across the different levels of education. The Common Core might be the most direct effort, albeit limited by political difficulties and variations in different states. Its advantage is that it is specific about the key critical skills in reading that students should acquire through their K–12 educational experiences. The problem is that the CCSS have not been universally adopted and realized in the classroom. The second area in which students' needs have been recognized but not necessarily addressed as fully as they might be includes inequities in access to resources, including technology. Linguistic justice plays a role here, as is now addressed by scholars like April Baker-Bell.

From a broader perspective, faculty in writing studies and across all disciplines must be aware of the fact that many students at both TYCOAs and all four-year institutions are newcomers to the academic environment, trying to learn the language and culture of this new situation. Ever since my 1987 publication, I've been suggesting that academic language is a distinct variety that can only be learned through reading that variety, since very few people speak it, especially as a native language. Finally, there is the complexity of the TYCOA situation, where students' need for help with critical reading, writing, speaking, and listening may be most clear. While a number of different approaches have been tried and there is solid evidence of success in the ALP program that includes both integrated reading and writing in credit-bearing courses and corequisite support for personal issues, including stronger reading skills, a far-reaching focus on reading is very much needed.

An important question is why the mainstream absence of reading persists for both novice and more capable students at the postsecondary level, given these varied efforts. One answer, certainly, is that integrating reading instruction involves more work on the part of writing programs and writing teachers as well as the rest of the faculty. Another is that writing teachers in particular and the faculty across all disciplines in general are unprepared to teach students the necessary skills (cf. Carillo 2015). A further crucial point is that students' need to develop essential skills in critical reading is not only true of novice students but also of the purportedly competent student population generally, as discussed in chapter 1. A further answer is the absence of faculty preparation to teach critical reading; one of the very few examples of such preparation is the graduate certificate in teaching postsecondary reading offered at SFSU, described on its website (https://english.sfsu.edu/content/certificate-teaching-postsecondary-reading). Although this program does not explicitly address linguistic justice and other larger contextual issues, it does, along with the few others like it, focus on training instructors for two-year college teaching. Many more expanded programs of this kind are needed to prepare all college and university faculty to help students at all kinds of institutions develop the critical reading skills they will need for college and beyond. Finally, the array of issues and approaches discussed here shows that integration of reading and writing, together with the thoughtful awareness of students' backgrounds and language varieties, can help them move into and through postsecondary education to a degree. Reading has not been but needs to be at the center of this work. This chapter has provided an overview of the various ways students' reading challenges are currently addressed, with relatively more or less attention and success across the different levels of education.

# 3
## More Reading Now Than Ever

*The Current Reading Landscape*

While many faculty members teaching at the college level will quickly confirm that there is a reading problem among current students, a competing narrative says that students are reading and writing now more than ever because of their use of social media. It is easy to understand this view, given the popularity (corporate troubles notwithstanding) of Facebook, Instagram, and Twitter (now X)—the latter of which lifted its length constraints some time ago. So sure, young people are doing more reading and writing. However, the substance of the material is problematic, since much of what appears is short, prone to misinformation and disinformation, and not the kind of extended nonfiction prose readers will need to comprehend and evaluate for personal and professional purposes. Journalist Nicholas Carr (2020) gained considerable attention for his discussion of these kinds of problems created by the impact of the internet. Carr (2020) makes this observation:

> Several studies, including an extensive series of experiments at Yale, have documented this "misattribution" phenomenon, revealing that as people gather information online, they come to believe they're smarter and more knowledgeable than they actually are . . . That unhappy insight probably helps explain society's current gullibility crisis, with its attendant plague of propaganda, dogma, and venom. If your phone has blunted your powers of

discernment, you'll believe anything it tells you. And you won't hesitate to share deceptive information with others . . . When we constrict our capacity for reasoning and recall, or transfer those skills to a machine or corporation, we sacrifice the ability to turn information into knowledge. (237–238)

Thus, what students are reading, tweeting, blogging, and posting suggests that there are real underlying problems with critical reading, defined below, and not only for students but also for the population at large. We continue to ignore these problems and fail to teach an integrated model of all literacy skills needed at our peril. For this reason, the model I propose here includes not only reading and writing but also speaking and listening.

A careful look at the problematic reading landscape is needed, beginning with an exploration of what "reading" might mean these days when we spend so much of our time looking at screens and doing what people now call reading. Though the nature of reading might seem obvious, it is not. And it is especially not obvious now that people are looking at so many different kinds of materials, using different kinds of devices. People read at different times and in different venues using different devices, so reading ranges from traditional alphabetic texts in paper books with pages turned by hand to visual displays on screens large and small to no screen at all (i.e., audiobooks), across languages and language varieties. And who decides what counts as or constitutes reading? Ultimately, with this array of questions, we come to this issue: given the misinformation, disinformation, fake news, conspiracy theories, and other troubles, how do we define critical literacy? A working definition will need to consider two broad sets of factors in the backdrop: first, the focus of these activities must include not only "reading" as conventionally seen but also writing, speaking, and listening; second, the impact of sociocultural factors must be included to provide an awareness of the context in which literacy occurs. Once we have that definition and the rest of the backdrop, the goal here is to consider the who, what, when, where, why, and how of contemporary reading by students and others, setting up a trip back in time (in part 2 of this book) to see how writing studies has only occasionally attended to critical reading/literacy.

## Defining Critical Literacy

Choosing what heading to put on this section of this chapter gives me pause: do I just call it reading? Critical literacy? Critical reading? Deep reading? Many choices. This issue used to be easier to address. Over the past few years, in the talks and workshops I have given at colleges and universities around the country, I was variously the keynote speaker, the workshop leader, or a panelist for a discussion on reading issues. In my presentations, I usually use a definition like this one as a starting point: reading is the psycholinguistic process of getting meaning from print. Using these terms as the launch point, I go on to discuss the psychological and linguistic character of reading, exploring key aspects of the definition such as prior knowledge and its impact on reading speed along with how the eyes and brain work together to predict, minimizing the need to look at every word (the psycho part). Then I talk about the linguistic part, which pertains, in part, to vocabulary and syntax, the language of the display. Using assorted exercises, I next demonstrate how readers make meaning, pointing out that if readers just run their eyes over lines of print and cannot say what they have read, that activity would not constitute "reading" as defined.

Recently, a more focused definition has seemed to be necessary, since the texts we are reading might be traditional alphabetic print, but increasingly, they are quite a bit more than, and different from, straight alphabetic text. Pictures, sound, animation, color, light, and many other features are part of what readers might be processing when they read. Moreover, readers using screens are not confined to a full-sized desktop computer, as digital texts of all kinds can now be viewed on laptops, tablets, phones, and watches. So, in a study of novice and expert readers, I defined academic critical literacy (or what I mean by reading) this way: "Academic critical literacy is best defined as the psycholinguistic processes of getting meaning from print or putting meaning into print and/or sound, images and movement, on a page or screen, used for the purposes of analysis, synthesis, evaluation and application; these processes develop through formal schooling and beyond it, at home and at work, in childhood and across the lifespan and are essential to human functioning in a democratic society" (Horning 2012, 14). This definition is more detailed, attempting to capture both the reading side (getting meaning from print) and the writing side (putting meaning into print) and attempting to address the fact that not all texts consist of alphabetic print. I also intended to capture the uses of this literacy and the notion that it is learned and used both in and beyond school, over a lifetime. I wanted to keep the definition current, integrating all the ways the reading landscape has changed as a result of new technology.

Ultimately, for the purposes of clarity and consistency in this discussion, *reading* alone is going to be the term of choice, even though the phrase *critical literacy* appears in the title. These terms should be treated as interchangeable, but critical literacy is quickly going to become awkward. Readers of this book will understand and keep in mind the meanings I have laid out thus far and explore in more detail in the rest of this chapter. The basic idea of getting meaning from a visual or audio display of some kind probably captures the relevant essence of reading—past, present, and future. Further exploration will sketch out the contemporary reading landscape. Only some of the present situation will be directly relevant to the history in the next two chapters, since reading when English A was created in 1885 or even when the Dartmouth Conference occurred in 1966 was not what reading is now at either of those points or anywhere in between. But it is useful to understand current reading as the backdrop for the historical review and for the purposes of formulating plans for the future. The uneven attention to reading in writing studies is consistent across the decades, then and now, as will become clear.

The phrase *reading landscape* came to mind as this project developed. A quick Google search to see if it had been used before yielded an unexpected result. Most of the references in Google and even in Google Scholar led to sources on geography, plants, natural history, and the like—that is, landscaping real property and the environmental issues in doing so. However, Google also points to an area of inquiry called "discard studies," which focuses on what people throw away or give away. A quick look at this field shows an area of inquiry that is very much like critical reading, in that both fields draw from a wide range of different areas of study to address key questions. What is surprising is that in this field, key areas of study are readily identified; it includes academic scholars, a professional conference (https://wp.nyu.edu/thediscardstudiescollaborative/discard-studies-conference/—postponed in 2020), a website (https://discardstudies.com/), cross-disciplinary publications, and so forth.

The area defines itself this way: "*Discard Studies* was founded in 2010 as an online hub for scholars, activists, environmentalists, students, artists, planners, and others who are asking questions about waste, not just as an ecological problem, but as a process, category, mentality, judgment, an infrastructural and economic challenge, and as a site for producing power as well as struggles against power structures. We produce and host monthly research-based articles on discard studies; compile a monthly report on recent articles, jobs, and calls for participation relevant to discard studies; and maintain a repository of definitions, bibliographies, and syllabi as resources" (Discard Studies 2024, original emphasis). Drilling down into the site, several different categories of research appear that seem pertinent to any kind of landscape—physical, psychological, or psycholinguistic—just like reading. The researchers in this field explore the role of waste of all kinds in "society and culture, including social norms, economic systems, forms of labor, ideology, infrastructure, and power in definitions of, attitudes toward, behaviors around, and materialities of waste, broadly defined" (Discard Studies 2024). While pursuing the various research trajectories of discard studies wanders away from reading, the phrase *reading landscape* in the discard studies field captures the point here: reading reaches into and touches on a wide range of issues. The goal here is to keep this discussion focused on how reading has been treated in writing studies, with the broader reading landscape providing the context for examination of the past.

A number of books on reading provide definitions, of course, and some level of consensus exists about the points raised in the proposed definition for this book presented earlier. Definitions come from researchers who have done extensive studies on reading of various kinds. University of Wisconsin psychologist Mark Seidenberg (2017, 102), for example, offers a definition of a "certified skilled reader," as well as of a "master reader." His definitions include knowledge and the ability to use letter-sound relationships, vocabulary and interpretation, syntax, text structure, strategies for dealing with difficulties, background knowledge of many topics and issues, and awareness of flexible approaches for different types of texts. The "master" level entails more skill in inference; analysis of meaning, style, and genre; and knowledge of the particular field of the material being read. He cites both the National Assessment of Educational Progress (NAEP) and Common Core standards to capture additional areas of expertise, such as understanding the author's purpose and using evidence to support interpretation of a text (103).

Similarly, Maryanne Wolf (2018, 68), an award-winning reading scholar and researcher who directs a dyslexia center at the University of California at Los Angeles (UCLA), has a neat illustration to reveal the complexity of reading as she defines it. The illustration includes the two hemispheres of the brain, both of which contribute important elements to the reading process. Among other things, the right side of the brain contributes abilities to deal with elements of language per se: phonology, morphology, syntax, semantics, orthography, prediction, and inference. The left side of the brain offers integration, associations, retrieval of prior knowledge, problem solving, evaluation, and insight. Naturally, both sides work together when readers engage in "deep reading" (35–68). One of the key results of the interaction of all these abilities in reading is the development of empathy, which may be lost as fewer people read less and especially less deeply.

This outcome is the result, Wolf says, of the loss of "cognitive patience" that relates to both poor thinking and poor writing, and it has huge implications: "Just as earlier I described how a lack of background knowledge and critical analytical skills can render any reader susceptible to unadjudicated or even false information, the insufficient formation and lack of use of these complex intellectual skills can render our young people less able to read and write well and therefore less prepared for their own futures . . . How our citizens think, decide, and vote depends on their collective ability to navigate the complex realities of a digital milieu with intellects not just capable of, but accustomed to[,] higher-level understanding and analysis" (94–95). Wolf's definition is particularly helpful for the present discussion because she makes this direct connection between reading and writing. She makes clear not only that they are related but also the impact of the connection for students and for our democratic society. Even if reading is a highly complex activity that is difficult to define, these scholars agree with the essence of the definition offered at the outset: getting meaning from visual or aural input and being able to evaluate and use that meaning for various purposes.

The core of the model of critical literacy that will unfold in the rest of the book, then, looks like this (figure 3.1). This core suggests that reading must entail getting the ideas of the text (through analysis) and seeing the relationship of the content to other material (synthesis). Critical evaluation based on the listed issues is the key element that makes critical literacy *critical*. The entire enterprise requires the array of skills and awareness of context as proposed by all the scholars whose work has been discussed thus far. These points are explored in more detail in the rest of this chapter.

Who reads what; when, where, and how reading occurs; and why people read, taken together, explicate this view of critical literacy, providing a contemporary context for the historical discussion to come. What follows, then, is an attempt to sketch the current reading landscape, the backdrop against which the rest of the discussion will occur. To avoid the many other areas of inquiry that reading might touch, as suggested by discard studies, it quickly became clear that the argument's narrow focus must be sharply defined. Numerous books are being written about the overall reading situation in contemporary times: they include Jenae Cohn's *Skim, Dive, Surface: Teaching Digital Reading* (2021), along with Seidenberg's and Wolf's research as mentioned, plus Daniel Keller's *Chasing Literacy* (2014), to name a few from recent years.

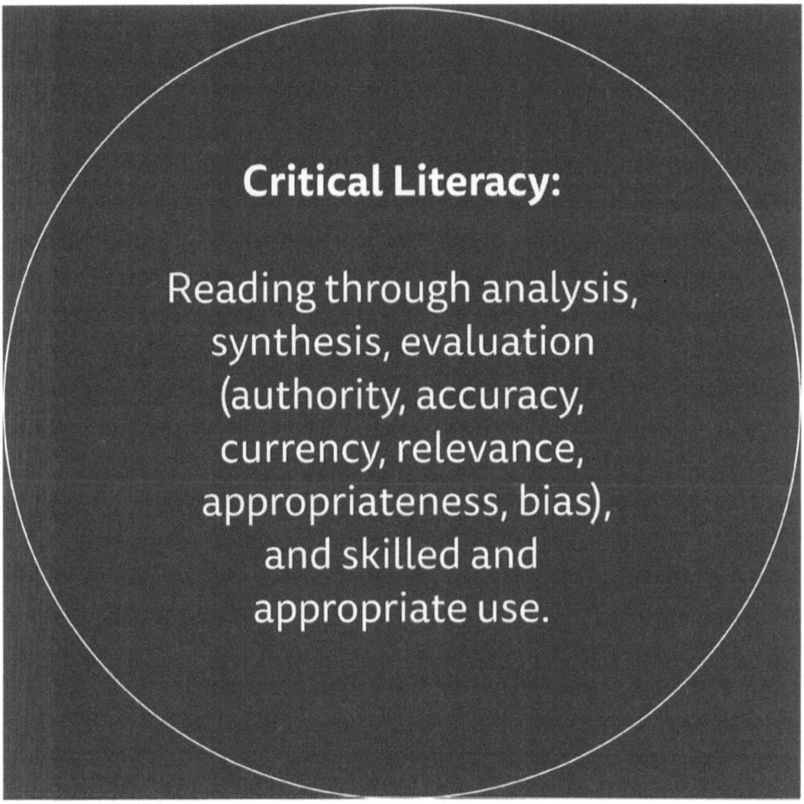

**Critical Literacy:**

Reading through analysis, synthesis, evaluation (authority, accuracy, currency, relevance, appropriateness, bias), and skilled and appropriate use.

FIGURE 3.1. Core definition of critical literacy

These titles give a good sense of the array of books that address reading; they are accompanied on the writing side by books like Deborah Brandt's *The Rise of Writing* (2015) and Mike Rose's *Back to School* (2012). There's no shortage. But the discussion here is focused on the field of writing studies in higher education and what has happened to reading within the field over the course of its development. Only by understanding the past treatment of reading can we gain an accurate picture of where things stand now and how students (and ultimately the population at large) could be better served through substantive attention to reading in writing studies and beyond.

## Who Is Reading?

In looking at the research that has been done on reading and its role in higher education, it is essential that the focus be on studies and samples of nationally representative groups of students. So, the data here and throughout the book are drawn as much as possible from national studies to obtain the broadest and most accurate picture. Also, the picture will be more accurate if the data use objective measures rather than self-report. An example appears in the carefully done Citation Project research, where the findings are based on the work of students drawn from a national sample. The Citation Project examines the use of source material in a representative sample of students' actual work, evaluated on objective criteria and not reliant on students' reports of what they did and how they did it (Jamieson 2013, 2017; Jamieson and Moore Howard 2013; Li 2020). While useful data might come from more selective samples, such as the Stanford Study of Writing done years ago by respected writing studies scholar Andrea Lunsford and her colleagues (data collected in 2001–2005 or 2006), to obtain a clear picture of the reading landscape, national studies will be more helpful. In particular, the role of community colleges in helping students develop their literacy abilities must be included because of the sheer numbers of students—roughly 40 percent of all undergraduates (*Digest of Education Statistics* 2023)—who begin higher education in those institutions, as discussed in detail in chapter 2.

So, who are the students under discussion here, enrolled in all types of postsecondary institutions across the country? One key feature is their status as first-generation students, that is, the first in their families to attend college. These students were described in chapter 2, but here it is useful to note that they constitute a large portion of the current student population, as shown in the earlier discussion. Although reports provide a range of numbers, some estimates suggest that more than half of current students are the first in their families to attend college. Moreover, as more colleges have stopped using standardized tests as part of their admissions requirements, the diversity of the student body has increased. In 2021, the *New York Times* reported on this trend—which developed at least in part as a by-product of the pandemic—for colleges to drop the requirement of test scores; specifically, in May 2021, the University of California announced that all of its schools were becoming "test blind," with SAT or ACT results used only for placement in some courses and for other limited purposes if students choose to present them. This outcome is the result of a lawsuit by students alleging racial discrimination (Del Rio 2021, 26). When schools used high school records and grades, enrollments showed clear increased percentages of first-generation students as well as more students of color (Hartocollis 2021, 1). Whether the trend will continue as the pandemic wanes remains to be seen, but admissions counselors at a variety of schools report that the "test-optional" approach is likely to be more or less permanent, according to the *Times* report (Del Rio 2021).

Joanne Baird Giordano and Holly Hassel (2019) discussed other key characteristics of current students in their plenary address at the Council of Writing Program Administrators' national conference in Baltimore, Maryland, that year and made these observations based on a variety of sources:

> Recent higher education research from the Pew Research Center, Higher Learning Advocates (HLA), and the federal government illustrates the diversity of college undergraduates in the United States in the last two decades:
> 
> - The share of students who are in poverty has increased . . .
> - The proportion of college students who are students of color has increased throughout higher education . . .
> - Just over half (55%) of students are financially independent, but a greater percentage of self-supporting students live in poverty . . .
> - Fewer students attend two-year colleges than 20 years ago, but the students who do attend two-year schools are more likely to be low income and to be students of color . . .
> - Greater numbers of veterans and students of color attend for-profit institutions . . .
> - Only 13% of first-year students live on campus . . .
> - Most students (58%) work while going to school: of these, 40% work more than 30 hours a week, and about 25% work full time . . .
> - About one in three college students (34%) are the first in their family to attend a higher education institution . . .
> - About a quarter of students (26%) are parents . . .
> - Two in five students (40%) are older than 25 . . .
> - Almost two in five students (39%) attend part-time . . .
> - Only about one-third of students at public institutions finish a bachelor's degree in four years. (Giordano and Hassel 2019, 36–37)

This information gives a very different picture of current students than the view many readers might have that the hypothetical average students come directly from high school, are uniformly well prepared for college work, and live on campus while attending a four-year institution full-time, from which they will graduate in four years. The data provided by Giordano and Hassel do not support this common view of "typical" students. Students' financial situation, including time spent working and on family responsibilities, has important implications for how much time they can spend on schoolwork and on reading. The phrase tl;dr (too long, didn't read) is not just a cynical view of students' willingness to do assignments; it may simply be a practical response to the reality of their lives. These data do not address the language status of current students, which may also have implications for their college success generally and their literacy work specifically, as well as other sociocultural factors discussed later in this chapter. Moreover, Giordano and Hassel's point about the preparation of these first-generation college students and others who are nontraditional by any measure also speaks to the likely variability of their levels of reading skill.

More recent data appear in a book by Santa Clara University sociologist Laura Nichols (2020). She points out that the profile of first-generation students, along with that of students considered to be Generation 1.5 (native-born but who speak a language other than English at home), is complex. Among other factors, these categories need to consider that the students included may be full-time or part-time at two-year or four-year institutions, both public and private. In a careful analysis of recent studies, Nichols shows that the first-generation definition needs to include not only parents' educational status and economic factors but also "cultural factors such as family knowledge, expectations and values" (30). Her research shows that first-generation students report feeling like outsiders, "moving between two different cultures and worlds" (31). She points out, in addition, that much of the research that has been done on first-generation students centers on those at selective four-year universities, even though many more attend two-year institutions or less selective public colleges and universities, so the data are skewed and do not reflect the full picture (32).

Further observations by Nichols offer pertinent insights to understanding the status of first-generation students as a "transitional generation." This phrase captures several important points. First, all students face a series of transitions as they move through the educational process: elementary school, to middle school, to high school, and then, if doing postsecondary work of any kind, to the next level. But first-generation students may experience additional transitions as the result of moving to a new place or leaving school temporarily, perhaps due to family responsibilities or some other kind of change that is a by-product of immigration status. Some rely on religious institutions as a path to academic success. Finally, for many, though not all, there is the personal transition to adulthood that happens while students are attending whatever postsecondary institution they choose. So, being a first-generation student has many different implications, all of which may have an impact on student success, persistence, and degree completion (Nichols 2020, 26–47).

A better picture of who the students are, including first-generation students and all others—at least for those at two-year institutions—comes from the American Association of Community Colleges (AACC) (2023), which publishes a profile of students on its website. The most recent data as this book is being written show that 66 percent of students were attending part-time, with an average age of twenty-seven, and the population at two-year schools was predominantly female (59%). The data also show the diversity of the two-year student population, with 27 percent Hispanic, 12 percent African American, 45 percent white, and 6 percent Asian or Pacific Islander; the remaining 10 percent consist of students of multi-racial or unknown backgrounds (2023). The AACC reports 30 percent of current students as first generation, though the fact sheet does not give an explicit definition of this complex category, as described above.

The other side of the "who" question concerns the faculty who are teaching this diverse pool of students. The makeup of the faculty is as complicated as that of the students, if we consider the professoriate at both two-year and four-year schools and the full range of public and private colleges and universities, historically Black colleges and universities (HBCUs), and all others. Moreover, at issue is not only who is standing at the front of these classrooms but also whether and how they are prepared to help students become effective and efficient critical readers. Good, current data about the postsecondary teaching faculty are not readily available. Recent data from the federal government from 2018, reported in the *Digest of Education Statistics* in 2021, show that of 832,000 faculty members at degree-granting institutions, roughly 24 percent are members of a minority group (de Brey et al. 2021, 299). These numbers are consistent with other government sources reported by Pew Research Center scholars (Davis and Fry 2019).

Considering who is doing the teaching, their preparation to teach reading is also relevant. My informal survey of graduate programs in writing studies was done for another project (Horning 2021b). Using the list of graduate programs on the Conference on College Composition and Communication (CCCC) Consortium of Doctoral Programs website, which includes more than eighty programs (as of March 2022), I looked at the program descriptions and the websites of about a third of them, chosen more or less at random. I found that none required or offered a course in reading theory and pedagogy, and only a small handful had a course on literacy, usually historically based. Thus, faculty who have earned PhDs in current writing studies programs are generally unprepared to work on reading with first-year writers or students in other writing courses. This finding is consistent with the self-reported responses of faculty who volunteered to answer a survey conducted and reported by Ellen C. Carillo (2015).

While some of those participants said they used a specific approach to reading in their classes, such as "rhetorical reading," "critical reading," or "reading for analysis" (Carillo 2015, 30), a majority felt unprepared to help students improve their reading ability. My informal survey findings are also confirmed, in general, by a task force of the Two-Year College English Association, which published guidelines for the preparation of faculty to teach in two-year colleges. The guidelines specify the need for coursework in reading, among other areas (Calhoon-Dillahunt et al. 2017, 558). Moreover, this task force report is only a set of guidelines, not requirements, to help prepare faculty to teach reading, despite the fact that the report acknowledges that most two-year college students are novices who need help with reading and other basic skill areas (552). The fragmentation of critical literacy into different specializations that seldom have contact with or encourage sharing of students or course recommendations persists, also despite research showing the benefit to students of the integration of reading and writing (along with speaking and listening) in both teaching and learning.

There are, of course, exceptions. At the master's level, some programs prepare faculty to work on reading, usually those planning to teach at the two-year college level. A quick search turned up six such programs, including two in California that meet a state requirement for certification of community college teachers to teach reading at the postsecondary level. The programs all include courses in reading theory and practice, with some attention paid to issues like diagnosing reading disorders, the needs of English language learners, and language variation as well as the interaction of reading and writing for adult students. Thus, a small number of programs do prepare people to teach reading in postsecondary settings, so theoretically, those in a PhD program could have some preparation to teach reading if they happened to have taken a master's certification program before entering the PhD program at one of the Consortium of Doctoral Programs schools. It is impossible to get an accurate idea of how many faculty might be in this group, but it is surely not a large number. The overall point here is that the faculty in most colleges and universities is clearly more homogeneous than the student body, is overwhelmingly white, and is generally unprepared to improve students' reading ability. These are more or less current statistics that provide a sense of the current landscape.

## *Who Is Reading: A Broader View*

Other factors need to be considered with respect to the students and, to some degree, to the faculty in the reading landscape, including the array of special needs of students who might have a disability or other kinds of personal concerns and the sociocultural factors that frame readers' interactions with texts. Texas Woman's University rhetorician J. Logan Smilges explored some of these matters in a discussion of "neuroqueer literacies." Smilges (2021, 106) notes that "literacy includes reading but is not limited to it," supporting the language arts view my model proposes. In the model of critical literacy I am offering, as Smilges says, critical reading is central; but writing, speaking, and listening also play essential roles. Smilges (112–117) focuses attention on "meaning making" as a way to think about literacy, allowing for the inclusion of neurodiverse individuals and others who might make meaning with or without necessarily using alphabetic print. Such an approach opens space for all students to make meaning, using a wide range of options to do so, including multimodal approaches. Michigan State University rhetorician Crystal VanKooten (2020) has shown in her work that students not only do well using such approaches, by choice or necessity, but importantly, they more readily transfer multimodal literacy skills from class to class and beyond classes to work environments. So, the *who* needs to include all students, considering those who may make meaning in a variety of ways, given their own needs and interests.

A second aspect of who is reading, not yet discussed, is the inclusion of the sociocultural factors in the context in which a text is produced and understood. Defining these factors is not an easy task, but those interested in literacy development generally agree that they are integral to a full picture of the text and are certainly relevant to the history to be discussed in the next two chapters. One compilation of sociocultural variables that play a role in literacy is presented by Washington State University education professor Stephen B. Kucer. He offers this list: culture/ethnicity, socioeconomic status or class, gender, organizational membership, occupation, religion, psychological background, nationality, family, age, and sexual orientation (Kucer 2014, 233). While not definitive, this list seems to capture many of the factors that come to bear on literacy development in terms of who is doing the reading. Naturally, these factors pertain to both students and faculty and to first-generation students and all others as well.

A further broad consideration concerning who is doing the reading relates to the language per se that is used in the text. Readers' native or non-native language, along with their chosen variety in each context in which a text is encountered, is also part of who they are. Current discussion of linguistic justice by education scholars such as Michigan State University's April Baker-Bell (2020a), for example, points to these matters, as noted in chapter 2. Linguists might refer to these points, taken together, as the discourse community in which the exchange of meaning happens. A discourse community might include the choice of language, choice of a specific variety of the language used by readers, and the other sociocultural factors enumerated by Kucer. Other scholars have taken up these issues at various educational levels and in a variety of contexts. Canadian education scholars Sunny Man Chu Lau and Saskia Van Viegen (2020), as well as Simon Fraser University education scholar Kelleen Toohey (Norton and Toohey 2010), have written extensively on the issues of power structure, sociocultural context, and critical literacy, for example. From another perspective, University of Nebraska English professor Stacey Waite has considered gender and identity with respect to literacy. Waite's (2017) work makes clear that reading is also shaped by gender, so "teaching queer" entails raising critical questions from many different perspectives.

Two other angles on who is reading warrant further consideration, possibly related to these matters of the diversity of who is doing the teaching as well as who is doing the learning. One of these angles is about who has the authority to determine what is read at the postsecondary level, and the other is a broader question about linguistic justice that might play a role in the choices of, among other things, common reading programs, banned books, writers included in survey courses, and other pedagogical issues, as discussed by Baker-Bell (2020a, 2020b). Since these choices depend on who is making them, they seem pertinent here. Common reading programs can serve as a kind of template for some of these issues.

In my own experience, for example, the writing program I led for ten years had a common book in first-year writing classes for many of those years. The idea was that students in all sections of the first course would read the same book, hear from the author, and write about some aspect of the topic in their classes. I formed a committee to help choose the book for each year, including a student or two, someone from the library, and full-time and part-time faculty members. The book had to be fairly current, available in paperback, little more than 300 pages (preferably shorter), and on a topic the group thought was likely to be of current interest to students. Other institutions make the choice in different ways, but it is rarely made by a single person. Indeed, publishers have created promotional materials for a number of books, and there are lists of options that have been chosen at other schools. A 2019 report on the array of choices at the time gives some sense of the titles chosen (Hazelrigg 2019) and the rationales for many of the selections. The post-pandemic choices are likely to be similarly diverse and will certainly address social justice and other contemporary concerns.

Common book programs may or may not fit into any particular course in the curriculum. To respect academic freedom, participation is generally voluntary, at least for the faculty. The choice of books to include in, for example, a required survey of British literature might not be as flexible. That raises the question of authority. Are the works included part of the agreed-upon "canon" and, if so, who says what is on that list? Can faculty members choose other works or other authors if they wish? Can one have a proper survey of British literature without Shakespeare? Without James Joyce? Without Zadie Smith or Reni Eddo-Lodge? And who says so? This issue bears on many kinds of courses and many kinds of reading. Underlying these questions are the larger issues of linguistic justice, discussed in more detail in chapter 2 and also in the following section. It should be clear that a full picture of who is doing the reading that is the focus of this book is a complicated question. It will be important to keep this and the other parts of the reading landscape in mind in the following chapters on the historical development of the field, since the teachers and learners at the time of English A and the Dartmouth Conference were a different group than the students and faculty of today.

## *What Are Students Reading?*

Another broad question about the current reading landscape concerns what students are reading. Some people think the only reading that should count is the reading students do for school and that audiobooks, social media posts, TikTok videos, and everything else that entails getting meaning from a visual display or an audio text should not "count" as reading. This approach is part of the reason for the focused definition given at the beginning of this chapter.

The kind of reading I mean for the purposes of this book is effective, efficient critical reading of extended, content-rich texts, as suggested by my definition. While the text readers take in might come in through audio or visual input, the goal is always for them to make sense of that input. However, it will be important to consider the full array of reading options now available, as well as those—surely much more limited—in the past. Today, readers have a huge array of choices. Some immediate reading options come to mind. For example, do audiobooks "count" as reading? When my daughters were small and read "series" books, tossing off 80–100 pages of a novel in a few hours, did that "count" as reading? How about when my non-reading six-year-old went off to first grade in September not knowing how to read and read *Hop on Pop* to me at Thanksgiving? Did her accurate oral rendering of the text and full summary "count" as reading? Did the *Archie* comic books I read as a kid "count"? Do blogs and graphic novels "count"? Or is reading the old-fashioned alphabetic texts printed on paper pages becoming what Nicholas Carr (2020, 227) called a "quaint pursuit," perhaps still the only activity that counts as "reading"?

I don't have a good answer to any of these questions, but I am sure that teaching students the skills to understand and evaluate all kinds of textual input is the basic and essential goal that is urgently needed. I also think that probing the matter of audiobooks might be a useful way to approach the definition question. The history of audiobooks has been explored in depth by British literature scholar Matthew Rubery (2016). His comprehensive discussion begins with Edison's phonograph and traces the history through to Audible and its commercial relatives and their success, seeking to show that the recording of books started out as "a way of reproducing the printed book and as a way of overcoming its limitations" (3).

Like other scholars, he points to the complexity of reading and the need for both visual and auditory skills in processing texts (14–16), whether the reader is looking at print or listening to a recording. Talking books came into their own during and after the 1930s, developed mainly for soldiers injured in war (21). When the commercial market first picked up talking books, they were on records; one of the first was Dylan Thomas's *A Child's Christmas in Wales*, produced on an LP by Caedmon (which I myself owned) (23). Books on Tape soon led to Audible as technology improved. Now, because of the development of speech synthesis along with alt text (verbal descriptions of images on a screen), screen readers offer audio versions of any text that can appear on a screen—a huge boon for people with written language challenges that interfere with traditional reading of alphabetic texts (271–275).

One term that has been used in various reports is *mobile reading* to capture the idea that listening to audiobooks can be done on the move, say, while walking or doing housework or engaging in other kinds of activities. Danish communications scholars Iben Have and Birgitte Stougaard Pedersen (2020) write about whether those activities interfere with the reading of audiobooks and conclude that they do not. They also make the case that audiobooks are both a remediation of printed books and an entirely different medium, independent of the traditional printed book. After careful consideration of the key issues in both fiction and nonfiction audiobook reading, they conclude that mobile reading *is* indeed reading, in the sense of the term used in this book. It might also be useful to think of audiobooks as continuing the long history of an oral tradition of texts and storytelling that goes back to the Greeks, Romans, *Beowulf*, and other cultures of earlier times.

Have and Pedersen's view is supported by brain research which shows that the same parts of the brain that are activated in traditional reading of a print book on paper are also activated by mobile reading. The brain science is reported by University of Virginia cognitive psychologist Daniel Willingham (2017). Willingham points to studies showing that certainly for adults, the brain activity involved in both listening to a book and reading one is essentially the same. A further study by neuroscientists at Berkeley supports this claim. Fatma Deniz and colleagues (2019) used fMRI to study brain activity as people either read or listened to the same stories. They wrote that "although the representation of semantic information in the human brain is quite complex, the semantic representations evoked by listening versus reading are almost identical" (7722). While relatively few participants were involved in the study (a total of nine), the number of brain images was large, and the results were very clear. So, it is fair to say that listening to audiobooks provides the same experience as traditional reading of print on paper, based on the albeit limited research to date. Similarly, it seems fair to say that getting meaning from a visual display—whether it is alphabetic text printed on paper or on any of the many kinds of texts in digital form, or an audio presentation, or anything in between—constitutes reading. As we explore the past, the reading most scholars were referring to until very recent times is ordinary processing of alphabetic text on the printed page; it will be important to keep this perspective in mind as we look back from a significantly expanded idea of what constitutes "reading."

Willingham makes some further points on this issue. He reports data showing that computers expose the average American to huge numbers of words (meaning, admittedly, spoken and written words), and the data he reports were collected before widespread computer access. But he points out that this kind of "incidental" reading (Willingham 2017, 169) does not produce better readers because it is not the kind of material that provides broader background knowledge on a topic that is "content-rich"; instead, it is derived from games, text messages, and social networking. Such reading may improve reading fluency; Willingham says this angle has not been studied (170). So, when a report from the Pew Research Center suggests that young people in the millennial generation are reading more than older adults, that's not the full story:

> Millennials are quite similar to their elders when it comes to the amount of book reading they do, but young adults are more likely to have read a book in the past 12 months. Some 43% report reading a book—in any format—on a daily basis, a rate similar to older adults. Overall, 88% of Americans under 30 read a book in the past year, compared with 79% of those age 30 and older. Young adults have caught up to those in their thirties and forties in e-reading, with 37% of adults ages 18–29 reporting that they have read an e-book in the past year. (Zickuhr and Rainie 2014)

So, young people report book reading, but a book a year is likely doing little to support and improve the kind of critical reading under discussion here. Taken together, all this research suggests that reading in the sense meant here happens when readers take in an audio or a visual display of a text—whether print or sounds, images, animation, and so forth.

Book reading, of course, is not the full story of what students are reading; indeed, the findings discussed thus far suggest that complete books are a very small part of what students read. In a recent discussion with a group of retired faculty, I was describing this book. One of them pointed out that students don't read "the paper" in the sense that faculty might think of it, that is, a printed newspaper of national scope like the *New York Times* or the *Washington Post* read in its traditional paper form with separate sections devoted to news, features, sports, and so on. The Project Information Literacy (PIL) research study on how college students take in the news, discussed in chapter 1, shows clearly that students lack effective strategies for getting or evaluating not only news sources but all kinds of other content, online and off, as well (Head et al. 2018). PIL director Alison J. Head's (2021) more recent reflections on her own research and that of others provide further support for this view. One possible explanation is that without a paper version, they lack the traditional signals that would help with content and evaluation, as the following experience suggests.

My colleague's comment reminds me of a teaching experience with students in a developmental reading class. I asked them to find a printed newspaper published that same day. The campus had free copies of the *New York Times* and *USA Today*, and I suggested they might also bring in the local papers: the Detroit *Free Press* and the Detroit *News*. We ended up with four or five papers and put them on the front desks. The students quickly noticed the variations in the lead stories, but the concept of stories "above the fold" and below struck them only when they saw the physical papers. The same kinds of surprise resulted from looking inside the papers and at the editorial pages. It was an eye-opening experience for these students, many of whom didn't read a newspaper (even online) or had almost no experience with a printed paper. I concluded the lesson by making clear what the layout, sections, and other features of the paper meant—especially the distinction between the news and editorial pages—and how they could try to determine those meanings when reading digital forms.

Finally, in terms of what students are reading, questions of "linguistic justice" arise, as discussed earlier. As part of her argument, Baker-Bell suggests that White Mainstream English should not be considered the only option for success in education or careers for people who speak other varieties of English; surely, what students read or what is required reading for all students should reflect this view. Thus, students can and should be reading a wide range of texts in the many varieties of English (or any other language, for that matter). Baker-Bell illustrates this point with a detailed discussion of the book *The Hate U Give* to reveal the kind of linguistic racism found in assigned readings and the need to rethink what students are reading for school. All the reading students do in conjunction with the development of efficient and effective critical literacy must include the kind of "content-rich" material that will build those essential skills, including, as needed, full consideration of the sociocultural context in which a text or an input occurs.

## *When, Where, How? Time Spent on Reading on Varied Platforms*

While we accept the idea that reading on any sort of platform or display (or lack of the same with audiobooks) is reading, or "counts," it is important to keep in mind that in a big-picture sense, time spent on reading does seem to be declining. Recent data from the United States Bureau of Labor Statistics (BLS) show the trend in a very general kind of way, using self-reported data. The BLS American Time Use Survey asks Americans about time spent on

**TABLE 3.1.** Trend in time spent reading for personal interest, 2009–2019

| American time use | | | |
|---|---|---|---|
| Original data value | | | |
| Series ID | TUU10101AA01006315 | | |
| Not seasonally adjusted | | | |
| Series title | Average hours per day—reading for personal interest | | |
| Type of estimate | Average hours per day | | |
| Activity | Reading for personal interest | | |
| Type of days | All | | |
| Age group | Fifteen years and over | | |
| Years | 2009–2019 | | |

| Year | Period | Estimate | Standard Error |
|---|---|---|---|
| 2009 | Annual | 0.34 | 0.009 |
| 2010 | Annual | 0.30 | 0.010 |
| 2011 | Annual | 0.30 | 0.010 |
| 2012 | Annual | 0.33 | 0.010 |
| 2013 | Annual | 0.32 | 0.011 |
| 2014 | Annual | 0.32 | 0.010 |
| 2015 | Annual | 0.32 | 0.010 |
| 2016 | Annual | 0.29 | 0.009 |
| 2017 | Annual | 0.28 | 0.009 |
| 2018 | Annual | 0.26 | 0.010 |
| 2019 | Annual | 0.27 | 0.010 |

Source: https://data.bls.gov/pdq/SurveyOutputServlet.

"reading for personal interest" in average hours per day. The data are drawn from 210,000 interviews with a nationally representative sample of the population, but they rely on what participants report and thus do not constitute an objective measure (United States Bureau of Labor Statistics 2021). The results for the years 2009–2019 appear in table 3.1. As this book was being written, the BLS reported that it was unable to update or include 2020 data due to the impact of the pandemic and loss of data collection during the related shutdown (Cody Parkinson, BLS, email communication, April 12, 2021).

Furthermore, the broader definitions of what constitutes "reading" suggested above might also limit the usefulness of these findings. It should be clear that the trend in terms of time spent on "reading for personal interest" is clearly downward, notwithstanding the limitations enumerated here.

But even in the best of times (pre- and post-pandemic), when perhaps much more reading was a common activity, the venues for reading are much different now than they were in the days of English A at Harvard University (1885). Today, reading can entail looking at alphabetic text on a printed page (the only option in the late 1800s), but current alphabetic and non-alphabetic texts can appear on screens of all sizes or on no screen if an audiobook is the text of choice. Plus, beyond these options, there is also the matter of the speed of the texts coming at readers from every kind of source. So when, where, and how reading happens are not trivial questions concerning the current reading landscape.

The importance of the acceleration of information was pointed out in a useful study of high school and college students' research and writing done by Daniel Keller (2014) at Ohio State University at Newark, where he is a digital media and literacy scholar. Keller did a close study of nine high school students on their way to college and followed four of the students into their first year of college. Using a case study approach, he looked at students' reading in and beyond school, describing how they dealt with the increasing accumulation of material (drawing on the work of University of Wisconsin literacy scholar Deborah Brandt) and the acceleration of the demands for reading, understanding, and using texts of various kinds. He found that the students used a variety of strategies to cope with their reading work: oscillation, or moving back and forth between deep and superficial reading, and foraging, or picking up and choosing useful parts of materials for closer reading at a later time (117–118). These are strategies the students developed on their own, but two key points about them are useful to keep in mind: first, they are consistent with research studies of expert readers (discussed by Hayles [2007], among others), and second, they should be taught to students explicitly to help them become efficient, effective critical readers.

The problems associated with the speed of incoming material have other messages for teaching that are reflected in a growing body of evidence that the brain "prefers paper" for comprehension and recall (Jabr 2013). Both Ferris Jabr, a senior writer for *Scientific American*, and UCLA reading scholar Maryanne Wolf (2018, 79) report that people read alphabetic text on paper more effectively and efficiently than they do on screens. Jabr (2013) says:

"Paper still has advantages over screens as a reading medium. Together, laboratory experiments, polls and consumer reports indicate that digital devices prevent people from efficiently navigating long texts, which may subtly inhibit reading comprehension. Compared with paper, screens may also drain more of our mental resources while we are reading and make it a little harder to remember what we read when we are done" (50). And the more reading is done on screens, the more these problems appear.

Furthermore, Wolf (2018) points out that in the absence of the deeper reading that happens on paper, readers have a harder time developing the essential human ability to empathize with others, contributing to the increasing divisiveness of contemporary society. She says that the empathy that develops through reading done the old-fashioned way has much larger implications: "It involves our leaving past assumptions behind and deepening our intellectual understanding of another person, another religion, another culture and epoch . . . It may also be our best bridge to others with whom we need to work together, so as to create a safer world for all its inhabitants" (53). The when, where, and how of the contemporary reading landscape, then, point to a number of challenges coming from the push toward technology. Students need to be taught how to deal with these challenges, which will continue and will also continue to change with new technologies. The English A students at Harvard may have been facing heavy reading assignments in their classes, but their books were not competing with the endless, specifically curated content on their phones. Writing studies can and should address these challenges in every class; focused, evidence-based strategies for doing so appear in chapter 7.

### *Why Read?*

When thinking about youngsters learning to read, the commonplace is that reading is reading is reading. If kids read books on paper or on a Kindle, comic books, graphic novels, YA (young adult) fiction, or TikTok posts (or whatever is the latest popular technology), as long as they are getting meaning from a visual or audio display/input on any sort of platform, they are reading. To develop speed and vocabulary to get meaning from these sources, they need to do a lot of such reading. However, these activities can all fit into the category of "learning to read," as distinct from activities that entail "reading to learn" or the kind of reading meant here. At some point, usually around fourth grade, the transition from learning to read to reading to learn takes place in school as a natural transition (Allington and Johnston 2002, 16). The transition does not mean that kids read fewer graphic novels or Instagram posts, but it does mean that at least in school, there is a much higher demand for substantive reading in all subjects. The transition to reading to learn is one of the answers to why students read at all. A lot of school reading is reading to learn, of the "read this chapter and answer the questions at the end" (or post your thoughts to a discussion board or some such) variety. While some students can and will do this kind of reading, a number of them can't and won't, and this lack of "reading compliance" is part of "tl;dr" (too long; didn't read), a lack of what Maryanne Wolf (2018, 92) calls "cognitive patience" (see also Baron 2021, 45).

But there are assorted rationales for reading, whether school assignments or otherwise. For postsecondary educational purposes, the Conference on College Composition and Communication has a rationale for reading in its position statement on the role of reading in the teaching of writing: "College-level reading varies depending on the reader's primary purpose, and different reading approaches each have their own emphasis: 'rhetorical reading' and 'reading like a writer' suggest reading texts for the purposes of understanding the impact of writerly choices, 'close reading' is focused primarily on textual interpretation, and 'active reading' and 'mindful reading' suggest a type of mindset or orientation toward a text" (CCCC 2021). This position statement captures the key academic purposes for reading: understanding content, implications, and context as well as rhetorical choices (full disclosure: I was co-chair of the task force that developed the position statement). But the rationales for reading go well beyond these aims, whether the reading is done for school, work, pleasure, or any of a number of other reasons. The question of why people read has been explored from a variety of angles, producing a variety of answers.

In her study of adult literacy learners, for instance, Eastern Connecticut State University rhetorician Lauren Rosenberg discusses the motivations of the four participants she followed as they learned to read and write. They offered the commonplace views of the value of "education, economics and moral self-improvement" (Rosenberg 2015, 9), but in addition, these adults sought the freedom and independence that comes with reading and writing ability. Coming at the "why" question from a different direction, University of Exeter (UK) literature scholar Helen Taylor has looked at women's reading of fiction and opens her book with this list of reasons for reading that she found: "Reading as escape; a joyous connection with the world beyond the self; a challenge to the imagination and intellect; a solitary luxury; an activity in special shared times and places with people close to us; a life-enhancer and lifesaver in many situations." (2019, ix) She points out that women vastly outnumber men as readers of fiction, borrowers at libraries, and members of book groups (3–4). Novelist Francine Prose (2018, 14) has a similar list of reasons for reading: amusement, emotional sustenance, information, protection, consolation. So, a vast range of rationales exists for reading of all kinds.

## Summary

The object of this chapter has been to sketch the current status of reading among college students and others to provide a backdrop against which the history of writing studies can be examined. The issue of critical literacy is important not only for the field but also for higher education and for the future of the United States more generally. The impact of critical literacy is made clear in the recent film *Trust Me: Are You Being Manipulated?* (Belic 2020); it is only one of many explorations of the implications of the lack of critical literacy in the population at large (cf. Carillo 2018; Carillo and Horning 2021a, 2021b; Lockhart et al. 2021). The movie's producers make the case for media literacy by showing that conspiracy theories, fake news, misinformation, and disinformation flourish when readers lack critical skills. While writing studies isn't the only field responsible for teaching these skills, it might be fair to say that it has a larger share of the responsibility for doing so because it offers the courses nearly all college students take at nearly all institutions. Although many colleges and universities have had basic courses in reading, there are fewer of them now; even where they still exist, they are often not part of writing studies (as in, they are offered through a tutoring center or something like an Upward Bound or other bridge program; cf. Appatova and Horning 2023).

Thus, ways to address students' reading difficulties could be described as fragmented. Critical literacy bears on all parts of the curriculum, so faculty across all disciplines could benefit from working closely with the library, for instance. Thinking about who the students are as well as the faculty who teach them reveals their true current identity: students are more diverse than they have been in the past and faculty are much less diverse, with wide ranges in every demographic category among the students and little diversity among the faculty. Technology has brought a similarly wide array of "stuff" to read, books and beyond. The when, where, and how angles show that reading is not only curling up on the couch with a good book but a vast array of different kinds of activities in different venues and on different devices, with much of it coming faster and faster. Finally, students and others deal with all this "stuff" for many different reasons. The complexities of who reads what, as well as the when, where, how, and why of contemporary reading, make clear the challenges of current teaching and learning. These points provide a frame of reference for looking back to a simpler time for reading to understand what has happened to it over time in college classrooms and in society at large.

PART 2

# The Lost History of Reading in Writing Studies

Turning to the history of reading in writing studies, chapters 4 and 5 trace the ways reading has been integrated in the field, to a greater or lesser degree. These chapters sketch a focused history of reading issues in the field of writing studies as it has developed over the decades, from its beginnings in the 1880s. These chapters are not intended as a comprehensive history of the field, taking instead a narrower view of the ways reading has been treated over time. Some larger educational and academic issues necessarily come to the fore during the discussion; there is not complete agreement even about the correct starting point of the field itself. The discussion begins with English A at Harvard University in 1885, following major trends to and through the important conference at Dartmouth College in 1966 and on to the present day. The uneven attention paid to reading during its history will emerge clearly from these chapters.

Figure 4.0 adds elements to the model under discussion throughout the book. It does not reflect the fully developed language arts model for critical literacy (previewed at the outset) that will ultimately provide a more comprehensive, contemporary view that includes reading integrated with writing, speaking, and listening. Critical literacy here is initially and chiefly realized through skilled reading as the definition suggests, though over time, technology will add writing, speaking, and listening. From a traditional vantage point, the kind of reading that is in focus here is the conventional reading of extended nonfiction prose texts, including, for example, books, full-length articles (like a *New York Times Magazine* cover story several thousand words in length), scholarly journal articles, research reports, white papers, and various other kinds of extended texts—usually published in paper or PDF form by publishers, government agencies, research organizations, and other recognized purveyors of information. Such texts typically have been edited and checked by either recognized experts or professional fact-checkers. Even so, readers, in this view, are capable of understanding such texts through analysis and synthesis, relating them to other texts on the same topic or issue. Readers may have some of the critical evaluation skills enumerated in the definition; once applied, these skills together allow readers to use the texts for their own purposes in an accurate and ethical way.

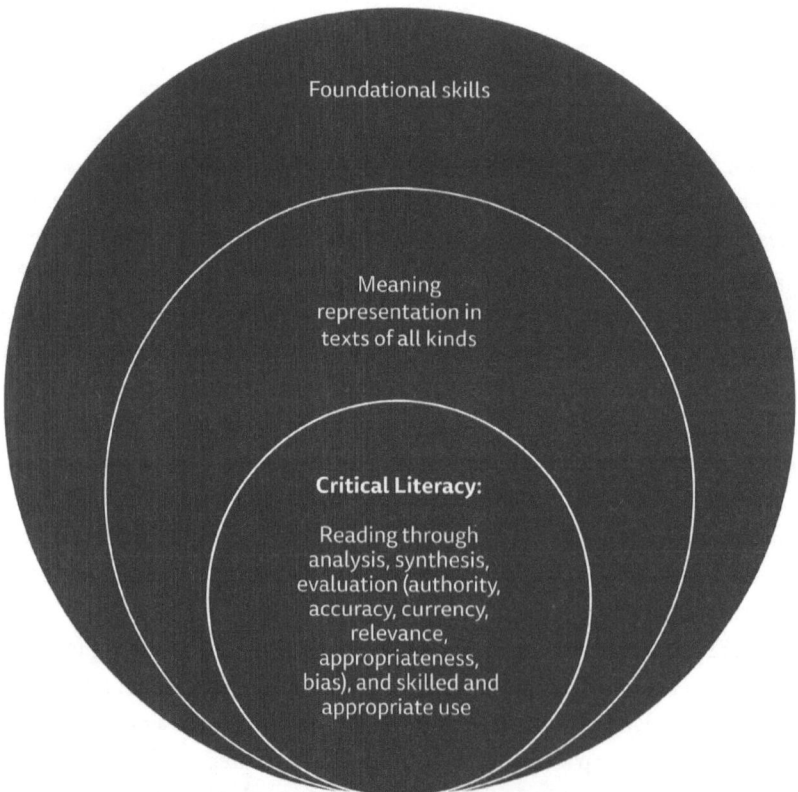

FIGURE 4.0. Partial model of critical literacy

# 4
# How We Got Here Part 1

*Early History*

I'm lucky to have Anne Ruggles Gere as my intellectual fairy godmother who has served as a generous and terrific sounding board and resource for several of my writing projects. Among other things, we share a deep interest in the period 1880–1930, the focus of two of my recent books (Horning 2018, 2021a) and of her book on women's clubs that engaged in literacy activities during that period (Gere 1997). In a conversation about this period, Anne told me about something called the "uniform lists" at Harvard University around the time it instituted a course called English A. The creation of that course might fairly be seen as the start of the field we now call writing studies (as I am calling the field in this book). Anne told me that Harvard instituted the lists as guidance to high schools preparing young men for college, to provide consistent readings and curriculum for the students. The lists also served as the basis for an admissions essay test for those applying. Harvard found that students, even if they were well prepared in other ways, did not write well; the English A requirement was set up to address this problem. English A comes down to us variously named and numbered as English 101 or first-year composition, required in some form or another at most postsecondary institutions. This chapter traces that history, with a focus on the reading expected of students and subsequent developments up to the time of the conference at Dartmouth College in 1966.

While my intention in this book is to focus on what is going on in college writing classrooms and the limited attention to reading, it is impossible to delve into the history without looking at high school reading and writing work. This is not surprising: in 1885, relatively few people went to college, and the majority of those who did were men who could afford the cost in both time and money. But most young people did go to high school and graduated. So, it is impossible to ignore what happened in high school classes in English, not to mention that doing so would omit much of the history of the writing-reading relationship or lack thereof. It might also be pertinent to point out that the classroom situation around the 1885 institution of English A at Harvard fits into the Modern period I have defined and discussed elsewhere (Horning 2018). It was a period of intense change in many aspects of US society, including education at both the K–12 and postsecondary levels.

The present discussion begins in this period and continues past it to 1965, just prior to the Dartmouth Conference (discussed in chapter 5). This includes both world wars and many changes in the field, such as the development of the major professional organizations for teachers of English—the National Council of Teachers of English (NCTE, in 1911), the Conference on College Composition and Communication (CCCC, in 1949), and the Modern Language Association (MLA, in 1883)—plus related developments like the founding of the International Reading Association (IRA, in 1955), the start of the community/junior college movement, and the first administration of the SAT (in 1926). These developments reveal what was going on in the field, helping to shed light on how reading was addressed in postsecondary classrooms.

## *The "Uniform Lists" from Harvard and English A*

Harvard already had an assortment of exams for entry into Greek, Latin, mathematics, and other programs when it added an English composition exam in 1873–1874. According to Iowa State University rhetorician David R. Russell (1991, 48–51), writing about the history of writing in the disciplines (now writing across the curriculum [WAC]), there was widespread and general concern about students' poor writing at Harvard and elsewhere, revealed in part as a result of changes in the curriculum there at the time. To get an idea of students' skills at entry, the target of the test was the correctness of the students' writing, with little attention paid to topic or content. The effort to teach students the kind of writing thought necessary was led by Adams Sherman

Hill, a journalist appointed to the Harvard faculty by then-president Charles Norton Eliot. Hill worked for ten years to have a composition course, English A, moved from later in the curriculum to the first year. Upper-level writing courses were overseen by the departments (Russell, 54).

To prepare for the entrance exam in writing, Harvard published "uniform lists" of readings for high school students hoping to attend. The nature of these exams and students' performance on them has been studied through an analysis of the actual data on the results by historian of rhetoric John C. Brereton of the University of Massachusetts at Boston. In his discussion, Brereton suggests that the test and the institution of English A in response to the results might be seen as the start of the field of writing studies, for three specific reasons. First, the faculty were shocked by the test results; second, this was the initial use of an entrance exam on writing, which had not been done before at Harvard or elsewhere; finally, the institution of English A marks the start of first-year composition course requirements that were soon instituted everywhere (Brereton 2012, 32). For the purposes of the present discussion, some of Brereton's other observations are also pertinent. He points out, for instance, that while the test was based on readings, the questions called for fairly superficial understanding of the relevant texts. Little critical analysis is called for by the instructions from the 1879 exam:

> Write a short composition upon one of the subjects given below. Before beginning to write, consider what you have to say on the subject selected, and arrange your thoughts in logical order. Aim at quality rather than quantity of work. Carefully revise your composition, correcting all errors in punctuation, spelling, grammar, division by paragraphs, and expression, and making each sentence as clear and forcible as possible. If time permits, make a clean copy of the revised work.
>
> I. The Character of Sir Richard Steele.
>
> II. The Duke of Marlborough as portrayed by Thackeray.
>
> III. The Style of "Henry Esmond."
>
> IV. Thackeray's account of the Pretender's visit to England.
>
> V. Duelling in the Age of Queen Anne. (qtd. in Elliot 2005, 11–12)

Although we don't have the scoring criteria, the test's correctness target is clear (using the same analytical criteria applied in chapter 1 to analyze large-scale tests like the SAT).

The method in this entrance exam was actual student writing, but the students had just one hour to write, under test conditions. While recent scholars have claimed that half the students failed the test, the actual Harvard report shows the failure rate to be more like 25 percent and similar to failure rates on entrance exams in Greek, Latin, algebra, and other topics. Brereton (2012) further points out that the uniform lists consisted of large numbers of works to prepare, so the students most likely limited their efforts to the longest pieces. Moreover, what was meant by preparation is not clear: should the students read just enough to do a plot summary, or did they need to be able to do more than that? Who read the tests and how they were scored are also not clear in the record. The dean's reports that Brereton reviewed suggest higher failure rates in other areas; it should be clear that the actual results and their meanings are contested. Some students were admitted conditionally based on the test results, but no remedial course in English was put in place until 1885, when English A was first offered. If a number of students needed remedial English, there are no data to support that. And since Harvard relied mainly on tuition and a solid endowment to stay afloat, it could not raise its standards and risk losing enrollment because of higher expectations, suggesting a lower level of prestige (a possibly familiar view, even now). The outcome, even given these various issues, is that beginning in 1885, all students were required to take English A at Harvard.

Eleven years later, in 1896, Harvard published a report on the complete situation with respect to reading and writing. The report is a compilation of several articles written by faculty members Adams Sherman Hill, Lyman Briggs, and Byron S. Hurlbut about the tests and requirements. Very little is said about reading or students' preparation; moreover, the reading is largely, though not entirely, drawn from literature, with only passing reference to the fact that all of the students' entrance exams in all subjects would have been considered part of the English exam in terms of the clarity and correctness of the writing. Following are excerpts from the pamphlet, beginning with this one from the chapter by Hurlbut (1896, 52) on the then-extant requirements and his experience with them: "This [approach], however, was not the most serious fault of the method of teaching then in vogue. Pupils were not taught to assimilate the books they studied. Neither do the teachers of to-day insist on this as they should. In my own school experience a premium of high marks was actually set upon a mere rote repetition of the statements of the textbooks." And from the appendix:

In the Catalogue for 1893–94 teachers are explicitly told how to deal with the prescribed reading:

> "The candidate is expected to read intelligently all the books prescribed. He should read them as he reads other books; he will be expected not to know them minutely, but to have freshly in mind their most important parts. Whatever the subject of the composition, the examiner will regard knowledge of the book as less important than ability to write English."

In conformity with the recommendations made at a meeting of teachers held at Philadelphia in 1894, a change was made in the requirement. The new requirement was optional in 1895, but is prescribed for 1896 and subsequent years. As stated in the Catalogue for 1895–96 it is as follows:

> *English.*—English may be offered either as a Preliminary or as a Final subject. In 1896 and thereafter the examination will occupy two hours.
>
> "The examination will consist of two parts, which, however, cannot be taken separately:—
>
> "I. The candidate will be required to write a paragraph or two on each of several topics chosen by him from a considerable number—perhaps ten or fifteen—set before him on the examination paper. In 1896 the topics will be drawn from the following works:—
>
> "Shakspere's [sic] Midsummer Night's Dream; Defoe's History of the Plague in London; Irving's Tales of a Traveller; Scott's Woodstock; Macaulay's Essay on Milton; Longfellow's Evangeline; George Eliot's Silas Marner.
>
> "The candidate is expected to read intelligently all the books prescribed . . . As additional evidence of preparation, the candidate may present an exercise book, properly certified by his instructor, containing compositions or other written work.
>
> "The works prescribed for this part of the examination in 1897, 1898, and 1899 are as follows:—
>
> "In 1897: Shakspere's [sic] As You Like It; Defoe's History of the Plague in London; Irving's Tales of a Traveller; Hawthorne's Twice-Told Tales; Longfellow's Evangeline; George Eliot's Silas Marner.
>
> . . .
>
> "II. A certain number of books will be prescribed for careful study. This part of the examination will be upon subject-matter, literary form, and logical structure, and will also test the candidate's ability to express his knowledge with clearness and accuracy."

The books prescribed for this part of the examination are:

"In 1896: Shakspere's [sic] Merchant of Venice; Milton's L'Allegro, II Penseroso, Comus, and Lycidas; Webster's First Bunker Hill Oration.

. . .

"No candidate will be accepted in English whose work is seriously defective in point of spelling, punctuation, grammar, or division into paragraphs.

"In connection with the reading and study of the prescribed books, parallel or subsidiary reading should be encouraged, and a considerable amount of English poetry should be committed to memory. The essentials of English grammar should not be neglected in preparatory study."

The English written by a candidate in any of his examination-books may be regarded as part of his examination in English, in case the evidence afforded by the examination-book in English is insufficient. (pp. 210–211 of the 1893–1894 Harvard catalog)

(Harvard University 1896, 56–57, original emphasis)

So, the lists of readings are clearly prescribed, and the target and method are clearly spelled out. The discussion in the pamphlet makes clear that the test was considered unsatisfactory—too many failures—but still insisted on correctness. Nothing was said about more focus on how students were to do the reading or anything about critical reading, however defined. This approach is still largely true today, as shown in a large-scale study of writing assignments across the disciplines by University of California at Davis rhetorician Dan Melzer (2009). In this large review of 2,100 writing assignments from a national sample of institutions and courses in the full range of disciplines, Melzer examined the kinds of research and writing students are asked to do. According to his analysis, little to no critical evaluation of source materials was required, even in research writing of various kinds. But then and now, these sources show that while students have been expected to read, little attention was then or is now paid to critical reading, as defined in chapter 3 of this book.

However, some attention was paid to reading in English A itself, once students were on campus. A book by Charles Townsend Copeland and Henry Milner Rideout (1901), two instructors who taught the course, provides a full summary of English A, along with a discussion of the use of readings and how they were to be handled. The book appears to be a kind of guidebook for instructors, including the requirement that the students write daily themes, meet with their instructors individually, follow common topics and reading assignments, and so forth; but it was a regular book, published by academic publisher Silver Burdett. In the final substantive chapter, the authors begin by noting that the students should read an array of different kinds of material because they are novice readers with limited reading experience. The suggestion of a range of reading is made so students can distinguish good from bad and see models of what to do and not to do in their own writing. In addition, the study of the rhetoric text is meant to give students more tools for analysis and for their own work. So here again, it should be clear that reading was not ignored entirely, but it wasn't the main focus of English A and no specific teaching strategies are offered; sample assignments and student responses give some ideas of what must have been discussed. The focus was not on the reading but on the correctness of the writing students presented.

At Radcliffe, according to feminist rhetorician Joanne Campbell's (1992) close examination of the writing of three students around the time English A was instituted, the focus was on correctness, just as it was for the men at Harvard. Campbell makes no comments about the role of reading in English A for Radcliffe women, and she does not suggest that reading was a focus of attention in the course. Her article does not take up entrance exams for women at Radcliffe, but she makes clear that as an institution, Radcliffe was at the outset a small add-on, not a full-fledged institution.

In the same issue of *College Composition and Communication* in which Campbell's study of Radcliffe's English A appeared, Kansas State University rhetorician Donald Stewart (1992) had a long article exploring Harvard's impact on the teaching of writing from the beginnings of English A. He sketches some of the rationale for the composition/literature split and the criticism of Harvard's approach to the teaching of writing by Fred Newton Scott at Michigan. But none of this discussion includes reading. There's no mention of the uniform lists as reading tasks or any exploration of how the lists could have been used to help students develop their reading ability as the basis for writing or for any other reason. It's not clear: did these early teachers and leaders take reading for granted, assuming that students knew how to read and that no further instruction was needed? Did they think reading literature would provide students with sufficient analytical skills to cover all their needs? Did they think there was enough nonfiction on the lists to take care of whatever reading help students might need to develop their critical faculty? Or was critical reading as defined here not on the radar of compositionists, literature teachers, or anyone else? No clear answers appear in the materials from Harvard.

What *is* clear is that other groups were forming to address some of these questions, notably the MLA in 1883 and the NCTE in 1911. As these and other organizations have come down to contemporary times, there is some division of the field among them. The MLA is the key organization for teachers of literature in English and other languages at the college level. The NCTE has become the organization for teachers of English language arts, K–12, though it also has a college section and a section devoted to English education (i.e., K–12 teacher preparation). It added a section devoted specifically to the teaching of writing at the college level in 1949: the Conference on College Composition and Communication.

Here and in the following discussion, it's fair to ask what all this history tells us about the treatment of reading in the field, notably at the college level. The uniform lists and entrance tests appear at the crossroad between high school and college, with the colleges effectively dictating what to teach in high school to prepare students for college. The lists and instructions do not point specifically to reading as defined here. But students are expected to read the items "intelligently" and to pay attention to, and presumably be able to write about, "subject matter, literary form, and logical structure." Thus, reading was surely expected—albeit almost exclusively the reading of literature—with attention to form and structure but no explicit focus on critical skills. There is also no mention of listening and speaking skills. It is important to see that reading, albeit not critical reading, was very much a part of the curriculum and expectations in these years.

The inconsistent attention to critical reading persists now with respect to the Common Core State Standards (CCSS), discussed in chapter 2, along with the tests used to assess students' skills in terms of the standards. The standards themselves are good with respect to reading; many of the points addressed in the CCSS appear in my proposed model of critical literacy because they are fairly comprehensive, capturing its key elements. However, as Indiana University writing studies scholar Christine Farris (2020) points out: "Students' success in college is often a matter of how well they can write in terms of the ideas in what they read in college-level texts. How closely and critically they engage with, not just one, but a number of multigenre texts in conversation can determine the quality of their writing in English and other courses" (129). She argues for much greater integration of high school and college curricula, especially for more attention to both reading and writing in high schools and colleges in ways not driven by the assessment instruments that resulted from the adoption of the CCSS. But her observations about the lack of integration of language arts skills also show the persistent lack of focus on reading from the time of English A to today.

## The Modern Language Association (1883)

In this same period, as Harvard was instituting its entrance exam in English and beginning the English A requirement for all students at both Harvard and Radcliffe, the MLA was formed by a small group of college professors of English, French, and German in 1883. The history of the organization is traced on a time line on its website (MLA History 2022), which begins with an account of the first meeting, in New York City, in early 1883. The proceedings of that meeting and the papers presented there are also listed on the time line. One of the first papers caught my attention: "The College Course in English Literature, How It May Be Improved" by James Morgan Hart of the University of Cincinnati (1884). The paper makes for fascinating reading. Hart argues that both logic and rhetoric should be excluded from English courses, where the focus should be exclusively on literature. He gives his own definition of the kind of reading that should happen in literature courses, beginning with why rhetoric should be separate. The result of the study of rhetoric, Hart says, is that "we shall be none the wiser in understanding an author, the influences that moulded [sic] him, his peculiar mission, his hold upon us. The proper object of literary study, in one word, is to train us to *read*, to grasp an author's personality in all its bearings. And the less rhetoric here, the better—in my judgment" (85, original emphasis). In a footnote, he accepts the usefulness of teaching rhetoric and composition but only after appropriate time spent on literature.

Hart passes quickly over prose of all kinds as he moves ahead with his proposal that literature be taught by time periods, sketching how to break its entire history into sections. He moves along to discuss the importance of background in history to provide the full context for literary works. This model is one my professor followed in my college survey of British literature: he had us read G. M. W. Trevelyan's *History of England* in three mind-numbing volumes, alongside the *Norton Anthology of British Literature*. The rest of Hart's suggestions include having students read the literature of other countries and having them own and use a book on meter in poetry to facilitate reading everything from free verse to epic poems. While not exactly an argument for critical literacy as I have defined it, Hart does at least give passing attention to the need for students to read literature in context, with some attention to structure and technique in poetry. Although hardly the definitive view of the MLA, this paper offers a snapshot of where the organization was in terms of its attention to reading, albeit focused largely on literature. This article also makes an early case for the separation of literature and composition. Finally, it is noteworthy that the MLA, from its beginning in 1883—similar to Harvard—did not ignore reading, but in this article at least, the focus is only minimally on context for the reading of literature and not on critical analysis of texts of any kind, literary or otherwise.

### Curriculum Review and Development: The National Education Association (NEA) and the College Entrance Exam Board (CEEB)

As the MLA developed as a functioning organization for college faculty in English and the modern languages, and as Harvard developed the uniform lists and then instituted English A in 1885, further developments in K–12 education were attempting to address the need for consensus about curriculum. The Harvard uniform lists and its entrance exam continued to have a substantial influence on high school English, though teachers were increasingly dissatisfied with this influence on what they were doing in terms of the curriculum, both in high school and throughout the entire K–12 program. Moreover, while some other colleges followed Harvard's lead, many did not, so there were different lists and exams for different colleges and universities. High school teachers found the situation chaotic and difficult, according to highly respected SUNY-Albany literacy scholar Arthur N. Applebee (1974, 32). In 1892, the NEA addressed the issues in English and all other subjects by appointing a Committee of Ten, made up of school and college administrators from around the country. This group, in turn, created conferences of ten other faculty to review curricula in each subject area, survey current offerings, and make recommendations about the requirements in each field (National Education Association 1894).

The Conference on English, as the subject-area groups were called, set out basic goals for the discipline: "The main direct objects of the teaching of English in schools seem to be two: (1) to enable the pupil to understand the expressed thoughts of others and to give expression to thoughts of his own and (2) to cultivate a taste for reading to give the pupil some acquaintance with good literature and to furnish him with the means of extending that acquaintance" (National Education Association 1894, 86). In this case, the NEA specifically points to reading, but it is reading focused on literature, with no mention of informational prose texts or critical reading. The goals do not explicitly say that "expression to thoughts of his own" includes speaking, but perhaps that aspect of a language arts model is implied. About the closest the requirements come to mentioning reading is the following, included in the list of proposed requirements and expanding on the idea that students should read some literature on their own—mostly complete works of literature—in addition to required books: "In connection with the reading of all these required books the teacher should encourage parallel or subsidiary reading and the investigation of pertinent questions in literary history and criticism. The faithfulness with which such auxiliary work is carried on should be constantly tested by means of written and oral reports and classroom discussion and the same tests should be applied to the required books read cursorily" (94). So, at least the requirements offered some suggestion that students should examine literary history and criticism, although not specifically that they should develop critical skills for themselves. There is some mention of rhetoric, but it is limited according to Applebee (1974, 34). Applebee concludes his discussion by suggesting that the Committee of Ten and the discipline-specific Conference on English were key developments in establishing the study of English as a subject in high schools, in clarifying the importance of literature, and in showing that the field should include language and composition in addition to literature for all students (38). He did not point out that there was no discussion of reading, as defined in this book.

Beyond or perhaps parallel to this internal review and discussion of the requirements for the discipline of English was the more general conflict in education between the goal of preparing students to go on to college and the goal of preparing those who might be moving on to work (i.e., leaving school entirely) or to technical or vocational training. The conference report (National Education Association 1894) proposed that all students should have the same preparation in English regardless of where they might be going after high school, but the conflicting goals continued to cause problems. Applebee and his colleagues later explain what led to the founding of the National Council of Teachers of English (NCTE) as a result. They write that at the 1910 meeting of the NEA, the New York State teachers' group raised a protest against the uniform lists and sought a revision of the entrance exams to focus on the two goals stated by the conference in its 1894 report: read and express. Ultimately, the protest and request for revision were not approved because the teachers wanted to eliminate the entire enterprise (Applebee, Langer, and Nachowitz 2010, 174–175). They stepped away from the NEA and formed the NCTE, which became the central organization for teachers of English beginning in 1911.

The NCTE continues to occupy this role, as does its important conference for college teachers of writing, the Conference on College Composition and Communication, which was formed in 1949.

The other important development around this same time was the formation of the College Entrance Exam Board in late 1899 and early 1900. It might be easy to get caught up in the full history of testing and the various groups of teachers, college admissions folks, and testing advocates, but the goal here is to keep the focus specifically on reading. So, the main goal in this period was to standardize the requirements for admission to college, with little to no direct focus on reading and certainly not on critical reading. Various regional associations were working toward this goal, as were the colleges themselves. According to Applebee, the president of Harvard, Charles Norton Eliot, had suggested that a college admissions board be formed to agree on the texts students should read and the questions to be used on the exam; the CEEB, with these goals, was thus formed. The other driving force in the formation of the CEEB was a request to the NEA from a group of schools, the Association of Colleges and Preparatory Schools of the Middle States and Maryland. According to the report that led to the formation of the group, two uniform lists of readings for students were proposed, as were general guidelines for standardized exams to be used by all the colleges (Plan of Organization 1900). This report, which has been widely quoted, built on the "uniform list" idea, offering two lists to serve as the basis for entrance exams.

One list was of works students should have read; the goal was that they have knowledge of the content and the author's background. The exam was to consist of writing a few paragraphs on specific topics related to the readings, with a broad choice of topics. The report makes clear the focus in this first part of the test: "Knowledge of the book will be regarded as less important than the ability to write good English. In preparation for this part of the requirement, it is important that the candidate shall have been instructed in the fundamental principles of rhetoric" (Plan of Organization 1900, 11).

The second list, for study, required that "the examination will be upon subject-matter, form, and structure. In addition, the candidate may be required to answer questions involving the essentials of English grammar, and questions on the leading facts in those periods of English literary history to which the prescribed works belong" (11). It should be clear that at least at the outset, the idea of the lists and exams for college entrance included consistency, a focus on correct writing, and some attention to reading per se. After specifying requirements for English classes at the various grade levels, the report states at the conclusion of the section on English instruction and testing:

> 7. That each of the books prescribed for study be taught with reference to
>    a. The language, including the meaning of words and sentences, the important qualities of style, and the important allusions;
>    b. The plan of the work, i.e., its structure and method;
>    c. The place of the work in literary history, the circumstances of its production, and the life of its author. That all details be studied, not as ends in themselves, but as means to a comprehension of the whole. (12)

While these points are not *critical* reading in the sense of this book, at the very least the CEEB was clearly setting the stage for instruction in careful reading in context and with attention to comprehension and some analysis. The CEEB's approach was widely accepted, albeit firmly dictated by colleges to the high schools.

There was still resistance to the domination of colleges in setting the requirements, even though the lists and other points presented by the CEEB did offer more consistency in what to teach and how to teach it. Schools overwhelmingly followed those lists and the advice on curriculum. They offered a substantive set of readings, almost exclusively of literature, but retained the use of the entrance exams. At the same time, however, particularly in parts of the country away from the East Coast, there was growing resistance to both the lists and the entrance exams. This resistance might be seen as an early forerunner of current resistance to all standardized testing in the name of equity. Applebee and his colleagues (Applebee, Langer, and Nachowitz 2010, 174) point out that at least some of the resistance to the uniform lists and tests arose from social reformers like Jane Addams, who saw the goals of education more broadly than simply college prep. At about the same time, this resistance led to a request to the NEA from the New York State English Teachers organization for a protest against the CEEB setup. Because the group asked for reform rather than elimination of the lists and tests, the request was rejected, but the NCTE was founded on a resolution to the NEA in 1911 to address the relevant issues (174–175), under the leadership of Chicago educator James Hosic.

The CEEB was not sidelined by the creation of the NCTE. Much later, in 1965, it convened a Commission on English to review the high school curriculum and make recommendations in the areas of language, literature, and composition. The resulting report does address reading, albeit in the section on literature rather than in the one on composition. The commission members were almost entirely university faculty, with only a few high school teachers in the group. The recommendations focus the study of literary works around form (type of work, parts, and connections), rhetoric (speaker, occasion, audience), and meaning (vocabulary, context, intention, and so forth), along with some attention to personal response and quality (College Entrance Exam Board 1965, 58). These matters reflect an interest in helping students become attentive readers of literature; they offer little in the way of critical analysis for non-literary texts. Thus, again, there *is* attention to reading, but it comes from the vantage point of teaching works of literature, with no reference to extended nonfiction prose. Naturally, it was too early for the CEEB or anyone else to be thinking about non-alphabetic texts.

As in the other sections of this chapter, a comment on what these developments have to do with reading as defined here is in order. On the one hand, if the idea is that reading is reading, regardless of what is read and how, then it is important that reading was not ignored or mistreated through the uniform lists and entrance testing. Indeed, the approach of the CEEB, both early and much later, and its forebears captures some of the key goals presented by the contemporary Common Core (discussed in earlier chapters) and by reading teacher/scholars like Doug Lemov, director of the charter schools called Uncommon Schools (2022). Among other things, Lemov and his colleagues (Lemov, Driggs, and Woolway 2016) argue for having students read challenging texts, notably including nonfiction; engage in close reading (defined largely as thorough comprehension without critical evaluation included; 52–112); and write directly about what they have read—all points derived from the Common Core principles. On the other hand, while the Common Core and Lemov, as one of its advocates, do recommend that students read nonfiction, one key point is that the uniform lists are focused almost exclusively on literature. Moreover, there's little to suggest that the set of dictated requirements that arise from the lists and tests pay attention to other aspects of the language arts model in the current discussion, as no effort exists to help students develop listening and speaking skills in addition to reading and writing skills. Soon, the NCTE would move carefully in this general direction.

## NCTE (1911) and CCCC (1949)

### NATIONAL COUNCIL OF TEACHERS OF ENGLISH (NCTE)

Applebee (1974) offers a detailed account of the founding of the NCTE under the leadership of Fred Newton Scott, who served as the first president. The organization took shape following a thorough report by Hosic (1911), in which he proposed the new group and its constitution and organization and also suggested leadership. The NCTE had three major organizational features, set up by Hosic: sponsorship of local affiliates, resulting in nineteen such groups by the end of the first year; creation of specific committees on various topics or issues; and the founding of the *English Journal* by Hosic as the "official organ" of the NCTE (Hosic 1912; Applebee 1974, 52). The journal began publication in 1912 and continues to the present, along with an assortment of other NCTE journals such as *Research in the Teaching of English* and *College Composition and Communication*.

Commenting on the NCTE's influence on reading, Applebee (1974, 90–91) reports on various studies done in the early twentieth century and offers several key observations. First, in the face of increasingly "scientific" studies of reading, teachers were shifting attention to silent as opposed to oral reading to emphasize expression, thus perhaps stepping away from the language arts model proposed in this book. In addition, he reports a finding in a 1925 study on comprehension that will sound familiar: "Average reading comprehension . . . is so mediocre that it is very hazardous to proceed on the assumption that students in the ninth grade can read well enough to comprehend and appreciate literature merely by reading" (90). The result of this study and others, though, was to suggest that literature teachers should stay with their curriculum, with the idea that it would provide students with the needed reading ability. Ultimately, he observes: "NCTE['s] concern with practical reading skills continued, but except for occasional and short-lived flirtations, it soon became a separate concern from the teaching of literature. By the early thirties, with attention in reading studies shifting toward physiological defects in disabled readers and that in literature toward the provision of 'experience,' the teaching of reading in the high school had come to mean almost exclusively remedial work" (91).

Applebee makes no mention of the landmark psycholinguistic research of Edmund Burke Huey (1908) or its implications for teaching and learning. Even at the time of its publication and more so since, Huey's work was and remains recognized as the best compilation of everything known about the reading process to that point. Beyond merely compiling what was known about reading, Huey revealed the nature of eye movements in reading through the first studies of eye tracking; he also focused attention on the role of context and prediction in the reading process (1908). These findings had been preceded by the work of psychologist G. Stanley Hall (1886), which led to some statistical studies of reading, but ultimately teachers moved back to a variety of approaches to literature, according to Applebee (1974, 56–57). Given the view that for high school students, any needed work in reading was intended to correct individual problems, reading once again fell by the wayside as a teaching focus.

A different view comes from University of Georgia reading scholar Donna E. Alvermann, a widely published and highly respected specialist in adolescent literacy development. Alvermann (2010) offers a historical sketch on the NCTE past and present in which she discusses the impact of Huey's work on the NCTE and on the development of school libraries. She points to the same shift to instruction on silent reading, as well as the appearance of home reading lists in both schools and school libraries, a somewhat ironic development given that the NCTE had been founded in reaction to the prescriptive lists coming from Harvard University and elsewhere. These newer lists, however, reflect a broadening interest in having students bring their prior knowledge and experience to bear on their reading, including contemporary materials of all kinds. Furthermore, Alvermann points out that Fred Newton Scott, in his second NCTE presidential address, was encouraging teachers to develop students' ability to read sensationalist-prone newspapers using critical skills.

**FRED NEWTON SCOTT ON READING**

Scott's speech was published in the *English Journal* (1913) and is quite something to read. After chastising his colleagues for students' lack of skill in writing, reading, and appreciating literature, Scott explores newspapers as general reading for students and the rest of the population, as they had become popular with young people for more than the comics pages. He then takes the newspapers to task for failing to be polite, truthful, wholesome (i.e., not sensational), and well written. The quality of the writing and the lack of factual reporting particularly bother Scott: "The formal errors which the language of journalism tends to encourage, serious as they are, may be overcome by correction and patient drill, but the brutality, the boorishness, the spirit of faking, the condoning of indecency and vulgarity and sensationalism that manifest themselves in the modern newspaper and which are quickly absorbed by the young and sooner or later reappear in their habits of thought and expression—what manner of classroom procedure can pluck out these rooted evils" (8). So, that's the problem with newspapers' influence on the writing side.

To counteract the bad influence of newspapers that Scott finds so objectionable, he cites a rather overblown account of the *Titanic* disaster and follows it with information from an eyewitness so the problems with the newspaper account are clear. If he were the teacher, Scott says he would take a few specific steps, since newspapers cannot be changed, to prepare students to read them critically:

> Ask the pupils what attitude should be taken toward a writer or a corporation that in cold blood, for purely mercenary ends, fabricated such a story and applied it as an excitant to the already overwrought nerves of the community . . . I should point out examples of [newspapers'] prejudice, insincerity, and cowardice . . . I should put copies in [students'] hands and ask them to judge for themselves whether the newspaper accounts could be trusted. In particular, it would be well for a class to verify at first hand by personal investigation the truth of some newspaper story, if a story suitable for this purpose could be found. An exercise of this sort would have permanent value, both as a lesson in the difficulty of ascertaining the facts of any occurrence, and also as arousing a critical attitude toward news stories in general.
>
> Nor should the funny paper be neglected . . . By adroit questioning, however, and especially by a comparison of this depraved humor with that of the older caricaturists and the better modern cartoonists, a spirit of criticism might be aroused and a foundation laid for the cultivation of taste. (10)

In his concluding advocacy for critical reading, Scott (1913, 12) describes the newspaper as a metaphorical house guest: "A daily visitor who is courteous, tactful, and sympathetic, who never says anything which he believes to be untrue, who is scrupulously clean in thought and word, who is wise and tolerant and unselfish—what may he not accomplish for young people as teacher, guide and friend?" As mentioned, Scott was the first president of the NCTE and was elected for a second year, when this presentation was given. He thus set the focus and tone for the organization from its earliest days. But as Alvermann (2010) points out, over time, there was less for the NCTE to say about reading at the high school level, since most of the instruction had shifted to basic help for readers with disabilities or other kinds of reading problems.

## CONFERENCE ON COLLEGE COMPOSITION AND COMMUNICATION (CCCC)

The other major development in this organizational history was the formation of the Conference on College Composition and Communication after a conference on college freshman English was convened in 1949. The NCTE already had some college sections, and one of them requested this meeting, according to Julius N. Hook, who served as the organization's first executive secretary. Hook's (1979) history provides a detailed look at the organization's first sixty-seven years, including the beginnings of the CCCC. He writes that the NCTE organized the first conference, posting a note in *College English* about an April meeting in Chicago under the leadership of John Gerber of Iowa State University. The conference was a success, so the leaders asked the NCTE to make it a permanent organization with its own separate meeting, "magazine," and so forth (148). Hook comments briefly on the inclusion of the word *communication*, suggesting that it may have been the result of the influence of Harold Allen, an early leader, reflecting a major program at the University of Minnesota. It allowed for the inclusion of various issues and the role of all the arts, thus opening the door for the integration of speaking and listening as well as music, art, and other fine arts in the organization's work (149).

Hook makes no mention, however, of the role of reading in the CCCC or, for that matter, in the NCTE. In fact, based on the book's index, there are exactly two references to reading. One is to the development of *Lists for Home Reading*, which the NCTE created, at least in part, in response to the uniform lists for the entry exams at Harvard and other schools. The other is a passing reference to a Commission on Reading, which was formed much later. So, despite Fred Newton Scott's focused discussion on the importance of teaching students to read newspapers critically in 1913, there was no particular interest in critical reading at the founding of either the NCTE or the CCCC. It is true that the home reading lists were popular from their beginnings in 1912; they were eventually shaped into different lists for each grade level and were still in use, in updated form, when Hook was writing his history of the organization. But the list illustrated in Hook's book (24) was just that: a list of titles and authors. Alvermann (2010) also comments on these developments, pointing out the irony of the NCTE having been formed, in part, in response to the uniform lists from Harvard but also noting that the home reading lists were meant for students' pleasure reading; their development and maintenance was one of the tasks taken up by school librarians. Then and now, the NCTE does offer summer reading recommendations for students and teachers at all levels (Boehm 2020). Critical reading does not appear in any form in any of this early history.

## International Literacy Association (ILA) and the American Library Association (ALA)

Another way reading is ignored in college-level teaching appears in the focal points of the organizations nominally concerned with reading, such as the International Literacy Association (formerly the International Reading Association [IRA]) and the American Library Association—though the latter has a separate association for college and university librarians, the Association of College and Research Libraries (ACRL) as mentioned earlier. The histories of both organizations show their limited input into first-year writing at the college level, as well as their lack of contact with faculty across the disciplines. The ILA was originally formed as the IRA in 1956, as the result of a merger between the National Association for Remedial Teachers and the International Council for the Improvement of Reading Instruction, according to the IRA website (International Reading Association 2002). The names of those source organizations suggest an original focus on remediation and students with reading difficulties. In its current form, the ILA holds an annual conference, publishes six professional journals, and has thousands of members, according to its website (International Literacy Association 2022). The site shows that while some college faculty are involved in the work of the organization, including Steve Graham of Arizona State University, among others, their research is largely focused on reading in K–12 schools, not on the postsecondary level. Norbert Elliot, a reader of this book in draft form, suggested that rigorous, controlled studies can be done in the structured environment of K–12 schools; in the postsecondary realm, vast differences in students and curricula as well as optional faculty participation make such studies extremely difficult or impossible.

I have discussed elsewhere and at length the contribution of libraries to literacy in the population at large throughout this period (Horning 2018). Among other things, in the 1920s and early 1930s, the ALA developed its Reader's Advisor service. This service was provided by librarians, offering patrons advice on reading choices based on their interests and needs. In addition, in 1925 the ALA developed a program called Reading with a Purpose that produced lists on sixty-six topics, including an introduction and annotated recommended readings. These lists were sold to 850,000 readers (52). While not connected to college-level courses, the lists do suggest that there was considerable interest in reading and the use of libraries. Students going to college would likely have had library cards and would have spent time in their local public libraries.

This backdrop is still in place today, despite the impact of the internet. A recent study by economists from the Federal Reserve Bank of Chicago shows clearly that the 15,000 branches of public libraries in the US have important positive impacts on children's literacy (Gilpin, Karger, and Nencka 2021).

The work of the ACRL offers a pertinent perspective and somewhat positive picture of what libraries try to do to develop college students' critical literacy. The ACRL is the part of the ALA that specifically deals with postsecondary libraries, library instruction, information literacy, and related matters, along with working with research libraries not necessarily in or connected to colleges or universities. It created and subsequently revised information literacy guidelines now called the *Framework for Information Literacy for Higher Education* (Association of College and Research Libraries 2016). The six frames proposed in the guidelines explicitly address critical literacy: Authority Is Constructed and Contextual, Information Creation as a Process, Information Has Value, Research as Inquiry, Scholarship as Conversation, and Searching as Strategic Exploration (8). Here is a fuller discussion of the first frame that offers a focus on critical literacy, as discussed in the ACRL document:

> Define different types of authority, such as subject expertise (e.g., scholarship), societal position (e.g., public office or title), or special experience (e.g., participating in a historic event);
>
> use research tools and indicators of authority to determine the credibility of sources, understanding the elements that might temper this credibility;
>
> understand that many disciplines have acknowledged authorities in the sense of well-known scholars and publications that are widely considered "standard," and yet, even in those situations, some scholars would challenge the authority of those sources;
>
> recognize that authoritative content may be packaged formally or informally and may include sources of all media types;
>
> acknowledge they are developing their own authoritative voices in a particular area and recognize the responsibilities this entails, including seeking accuracy and reliability, respecting intellectual property, and participating in communities of practice;
>
> understand the increasingly social nature of the information ecosystem where authorities actively connect with one another and sources develop over time. (12–13)

These points provide attention to critical evaluation of source materials, surely providing evidence of and support for the view of critical literacy as used in this book. However, since first-year writing courses frequently offer only a single class session devoted to library instruction, it is difficult to convey these fine insights along with helping students learn to navigate the range of resources most libraries now offer. The librarians take the further step of telling faculty and administrators how to integrate the *Framework* document in their teaching (Association of College and Research Libraries 2016, 25–27), going beyond the single-session library instruction that is commonplace. Thus, while the ACRL is definitely not ignoring reading, having clearly taken up the challenge of critical literacy in the realm of information literacy, its efforts do not seem to reach the goal of building critical literacy among students. Research by Project Information Literacy (discussed in chapter 1) suggests that students lack the information literacy skills needed to be critically literate, despite librarians' attention and effort.

## Wars and Literacy

The two world wars come immediately to mind as major factors affecting critical literacy development when thinking about the period under study here. It is also important to keep in mind that the overall education situation in the US at large changed in various ways during those years: more people, especially more women, went to college; returning soldiers after World War II had access to the GI Bill, leading to huge increases in enrollments for men as well. In addition, the federal government land-grant program, which began in 1862 but had a second round in 1890, led to the establishment of many of the historically Black colleges and universities (HBCUs), among other institutions (Horning 2021a). All these changes shaped the landscape at large, though not necessarily with any direct impact on first-year writing courses.

The two wars did affect what was happening in colleges insofar as they made clear the importance of literacy for soldiers. The army urgently needed testing to help assign soldiers appropriately; those who could read were fit for different assignments than those who could not. In addition, for the soldiers themselves, being able to stay in touch with family was critical to their ability to function in the military. For this reason, the work of someone like Cora Wilson Stewart, the creator of the Moonlight Schools program in rural Kentucky that taught hundreds of people in that state and beyond to read, was a key contribution to the war effort in World War I (cf. Horning 2021a, 67–86). Similar needs in World War II gave rise to the movement toward standardized testing as we know it, traced in detail by Norbert Elliot (2005).

Julius N. Hook writes about what was happening to the NCTE and English teaching in general through the period surrounding both wars. With respect to World War I, he suggests that most of what happened involving English teachers was an effort to promote patriotism in the classroom in whatever ways they could, as well as to provide support for Americanization of the increasing immigrant population in the years after the war (Hook 1979, 60). Throughout this same period, the NCTE was working with the Hosic report that appeared in 1911, just before the start of the war. Between the two world wars, in terms of the teaching of English, there was a shift to the use of anthologies for high school English. As I discussed in detail in *Literacy Then and Now* (Horning 2018, 125–127), a leading exemplar of the anthologies was *Literature and Life* in four volumes (for grades 9–12), edited by Edwin Greenlaw. Greenlaw and Clarence Stratton (1922, 1–5) specifically address students' reading skills in the introduction to the second book, "Learning to Read," which makes clear that their goal is to help students develop critical reading and literacy skills. So, again, it is noteworthy that direct attention to reading was appearing, albeit in a limited way, not only in the organizational development of the field but also in its textbooks. The success of *Literature and Life* is clear from the fact that it remained in print until 1979.

With respect to World War II, the 1941 attack on Pearl Harbor occurred not long after the NCTE introduced the "Experience Curriculum" in K–12 schools in the mid-1930s. The idea was generally that experiences of all kinds could be presented to students vicariously through studying literature and improving their reading at all levels. This approach marked a change, according to Hook (1979, 117), because prior to the adoption of this curriculum, teachers in middle and high schools did not teach reading because it was taught in the lower grades. Hook notes that "since 1935, in part because of *An Experience Curriculum*, the high schools have been more cognizant of their role in bringing each student's reading skills to a higher level than before, and many high school teacher-preparatory programs have required a course in how to teach reading" (117).

The curriculum had a substantial impact on teaching in all K–12 schools, especially insofar as it moved the focus to silent reading and to reading nonfiction. Moreover, reading was seen as separate from literature (and presumably also from writing) because of the need to concentrate on students' reading. This curriculum and its attention to reading was the main focus of the NCTE and its teacher-members prior to and through the war period, though the justification of English as a topic was a challenge given its lack of direct relevance to the war effort (131). Hook also reports that there was a significant expansion of reading in general as a by-product of the war, resulting from the increased availability of inexpensive paperbacks, book clubs, and library use (136). Against this backdrop, as was true in World War I, the military needed to be able to sort literate soldiers from non-readers and give them enough skills to be able to fight.

## Community Colleges and Reading

While the period discussed in this chapter includes the time of the development of community colleges, beginning with the first "junior" college in 1901, the major growth in the number of two-year colleges occurred at about the same time as the Dartmouth meeting, in the 1960s. These institutions and their contribution to the development of students' reading ability were explored in chapter 2; the relevant historical developments are discussed in more detail in chapter 5. The origin of these institutions falls into the period of significant growth in higher education generally, according to the authors of one of the major studies of American community colleges, who are leaders of the Center for the Study of Community Colleges in Los Angeles (Cohen, Brawer, and Kisker 2014). It seems important to note community colleges' origins in this earlier period here because they play a substantial role in postsecondary education in general. Moreover, they pay a great deal of attention to reading; they did so particularly in their early years. Indeed, the Arthur M. Cohen and colleagues' volume devotes an entire chapter to the work on literacy and foundational skills, demonstrating that these institutions have focused on reading to a much greater extent than have four-year schools, as acknowledged in chapter 2.

Because community colleges have always accepted students with a wide range of preparation, it might be easy to say that they have needed to pay more attention to reading because they draw more students whose reading ability is not as strong as it could be or should be. But the earlier chapters demonstrate that currently, a majority of all college students don't, won't, and can't read in the ways faculty expect. Building on the discussion in chapter 2, the further exploration in chapter 5 will examine how community colleges have offered a useful and substantial focus on reading that might serve as a model for all institutions. The overall picture is more complicated, though. Recent research and changes arising from the use of remote instruction during the pandemic suggest that many students (at community colleges and elsewhere) are more capable than placement tests suggest and have better outcomes in terms of persistence and degree completion. These improvements result from updated approaches using multiple measures for placement directly in college-level courses or in corequisite courses (Barnett et al. 2020); changes in both demographics and students' interests and needs might also play a role. Chapter 5 provides a further look at the enrollment levels and impact of the teaching of reading in community colleges.

## *Summary*

This trip down memory lane through the early classrooms of high schools and colleges provides a look at the role of reading. While the field of writing studies, in its infancy, did not totally disregard reading, it did not offer much of a focus on it either. Limited evidence suggests that students were expected to read and be able to write about the texts they had read, but there is little demonstration of any direct teaching of critical literacy as defined in this book. The NCTE leadership was clearly aware of the issues; Fred Newton Scott would not have devoted his entire second presidential address to it otherwise. But the other professional organizations, such as the MLA, did not address reading issues at all. In all fairness, the MLA in particular has recently begun devoting important energy to improving students' reading ability, a positive sign that will be discussed in chapter 7. But in general, the picture is largely one of inconsistent interest specifically in developing students' critical reading skills.

# 5
# How We Got Here Part 2

*Writing Studies as a Distinct Discipline*

I'm dating myself, but I started college in 1967, the year after the conference at Dartmouth College—known officially, according to University of Pittsburgh rhetorician Annette Vee (2020), as the Anglo-American Seminar on the Teaching of English. Vee has written a detailed history of the Dartmouth Seminar (or Conference), as it was informally known, for the WAC Clearinghouse, and there are a number of books and articles on the meeting, which ran for four weeks in the summer of 1966. About fifty scholars and teachers from the UK and the US and from K–12 and postsecondary institutions were part of the meeting, the goal of which was to discuss English curriculum. While some scholars suggest that the field of writing studies began with the offering of English A at Harvard University, as discussed in chapter 4, others suggest that this conference at Dartmouth was the launch point for the field. The Dartmouth event is discussed in more detail below, but it probably made little difference to my experience in first-year English. The same is true, for that matter, of subsequent debates about the role of literature in writing classes, widely discussed by Gary Tate (1993) and Erika Lindemann (1993, 1995), among other scholars, several decades later.

The English classes I took (a two-semester sequence with fiction as a focus in the first term and poetry and drama in the second) were standard first-year writing courses at the time, involving composition and literature. These typical courses at four-year institutions were far from the important work being done by community colleges, where the focus was much more on ensuring that students could read well enough to do college-level work. There and elsewhere, much of the attention was given to students' reading difficulties and basic work on comprehension, vocabulary, speed, inferences, and other issues. A quick look at Mina P. Shaughnessy's (1977) landmark work shows the range of approaches as community colleges and four-year institutions of all kinds were coping with open-admissions policies as well as non-native speakers. Moreover, some attention was paid to reading as a part of attempts to integrate K–12 and postsecondary education, such as through the National Writing Project and, later, the Common Core project; at the same time, testing of various kinds separated reading and writing in problematic ways. But when we come down to the present day, post-pandemic, and despite all the evidence of college students' reading difficulties discussed earlier, reading—in writing courses and across the curriculum—is still receiving less attention than it should. These threads lead to the last chapters of this book.

Different events and programs were happening at different times and places or sometimes at the same time, making a strictly chronological discussion impractical, so this chapter proceeds through a series of focal points: developments resulting from the Dartmouth Conference in 1966 and its follow-up, the literature and composition split, the work of literature scholars on reader-response theory, significant divisions within higher education concerning developmental reading and writing at community colleges and elsewhere, a different kind of attention to reading in the broad-based critical literacy approach, and attention to reading from "other" directions (i.e., not first-year composition per se). The chapter ends with a review of the contemporary hit-or-miss presence or absence of reading in writing studies writ large, with a second look at the model of critical literacy presented earlier. The model is expanded but still incomplete as the field addresses reading today; an aspirational and more complete version will appear in chapter 7.

## *Dartmouth 1966 and Anniversaries*

We are close to sixty years past the Dartmouth meeting and almost ten years past the fiftieth anniversary, which was celebrated at Dartmouth University in 2016. According to Vee (2020), the original meeting had a substantial but largely indirect influence on the English curriculum. It has been difficult to track down material beyond the two published reports on the original meeting (Dixon 1967; Muller 1967), though some of the early planning documents are in a National Council of Teachers of English (NCTE) archive at the University of Illinois (NCTE Archive 2009). Vee and writing studies historians Cinthia Gannett and John C. Brereton have all been helpful, as has Kristen Ritchie at the NCTE who directed me to the NCTE archive. The picture that emerges suggests that while there was some interest in reading at the time of the Dartmouth Conference, it was focused mostly on traditional-age college students reading literature in writing classes, with little or perhaps no explicit discussion of critical reading as defined here or of the language arts model that provides the basis for this discussion. The meeting did produce, in addition to the two formal reports, a list of eleven Points of Agreement among the attendees, which appears to give a good sense of the general issues discussed:

1. The centrality of pupils' exploring, extending, and shaping experiences in the English classroom.
2. The urgency of developing classroom approaches stressing the vital, creative, dramatic involvement of children and young people in language experiences.
3. The importance of directing more attention to speaking and listening experiences for all pupils at all levels, particularly those experiences which involve vigorous interaction among children.
4. The wisdom of providing young people at all levels with significant opportunities for the creative uses of language—creative dramatics, imaginative writing, improvisation, role playing and similar activities.
5. The significance of rich Literary experiences in the educative process and the importance of teachers of English restudying particular selections to determine their appropriateness for reading at different levels.
6. The need to overcome the restrictiveness of rigid patterns of "grouping" or "streaming," which limit the linguistic environment in which boys and girls learn English and which tend to inhibit language development.
7. The need to negate the limiting, often stultifying impact of examination patterns which direct attention of both teachers and pupils to aspects of English which are at best superficial and often misleading.
8. The compelling urgency of improving the conditions under which English is taught in the schools—the need for more books and

libraries, for better equipment, for reasonable class size, for a classroom environment which will make good teaching possible.
9. The importance of teachers of English at all levels informing themselves about scholarship and research in the English language so that their classroom approaches may be guided accordingly.
10. The need for radical reform in programs of teacher education, both preservice and inservice.
11. The importance of educating the public on what is meant [by] good English and what is meant by good English teaching. (Document shared by Annette Vee. Press release by James Squire, NCTE, September 26, 1966, shared by permission.)

Point 5 seems to be the only one that says anything specific about reading, and it is clearly focused on literature, though point 8 suggests that books and libraries will help, albeit indirectly. Similarly, John Dixon's report (1967) on the seminar from the British point of view pays relatively little attention to reading in the chapter that deals with "activities in class." In this section, about twenty pages long, Dixon suggests that students should just have experiences with literature of different kinds and should have virtual (i.e., vicarious) experiences, with less attention to analysis and criticism. These points reveal Dixon's sense of how the reading of literature was seen at the Dartmouth seminar.

Herbert J. Muller's (1967) report, from an American point of view, published as a book as was Dixon's, captures the seminar experience. Muller was on the faculty at Indiana University. His report was supposedly meant for general readers as opposed to Dixon's, intended for professionals. Muller devotes a chapter to "The Uses of Literature" (75–94). He points out that most of the study groups at the meeting paid some attention to literature, albeit not to reading per se. The debate was over what literature to teach and how to teach it, focused mostly on the K–12 level, although he notes that "some held it was the best means to improving writing" (78). The main idea was that students should be given a wide range of books to read above and beyond what might be excerpted in textbooks or other publications that offer condensed or edited versions of novels, plays, or other literary works—chosen from English, American, and world literature. There was no prescribed list or interest in anything like a "great books" approach (79).

Evidently, literary criticism and history were proposed for omission in the K–12 curriculum, which participants felt should focus on students' experiences with literature (Muller 1967, 80–81). However, Muller reports differing views on the issue of critical judgment: "The problem, then, is to decide at what stage the formulation of critical judgment should start. The British, thinking of the youngster as a 'child' until he is fifteen or sixteen, seemed to think that it should be postponed until that age . . . Most of the Americans seemed inclined to start earlier and do more . . . Some explicit teaching about literary forms and critical vocabulary would make it more pointed, disciplined talk" (87). Furthermore, there was a general rejection of most of the ideas of New Criticism—an approach that entailed reading literary works with little regard for their context, historical or otherwise—since the participants felt it would take away from students' enjoyment and response (87). It seemed more important to encourage reading of all kinds, as students seemed not to be reading much beyond school—a familiar complaint then as now. Finally, Muller made comments on the importance of using literature to teach values or moral issues, which the seminar did not take up. He suggested that teachers should address conflicting values directly, as he himself would, but this issue was largely omitted from discussion. An important point to keep in mind is that Dartmouth was focused largely on English in K–12 schools, not on postsecondary classrooms.

It seems fair to say that, at least according to Muller's account, there was little focus on reading in the critical reading sense. In passing, as illustrated in the preceding quote, English teachers might present some critical terminology, but it would be about the literature that was the focus of most teaching. And again in passing, participants noted that students needed to be encouraged to read more or to read at all. A 1997 follow-up to Dartmouth by respected composition scholar Joseph Harris (1997, 23–52) reviews the history of the field since 1966. While he discusses voice, among other key ideas from Dartmouth and following conferences, he makes virtually no mention of reading. A more recent publication of reflections on Dartmouth 1966 from a group of British, Canadian, Australian, and American scholars shows the influence of the meeting long after its conclusion, with the British at least, in their 2007 English Programme of Study, adopting some key points about critical reading in the national curriculum.

These points included helping students learn about differing interpretations of a text and the need for evidence to support those views, rationales for choices of what to read and how to respond, the role of purpose in topics chosen, and how meaning is constructed in both traditional and multimodal texts (Connolly 2019, 186–187). In the same volume in which Steve Connolly's chapter appears, two other contributors mention the impact of wide reading for pleasure beyond the school curriculum, citing evidence from the Programme for International Student Assessment (PISA) studies (discussed in chapter 1) showing that more reading helps students be better readers and better students (O'Mara and Beavis 2019, 217). So, much later, the long reach of Dartmouth 1966 did extend to some aspects of generic reading, just not with a specifically critical focus and not in its immediate aftermath.

Around twenty years after the 1966 meeting, a conference intended as a celebration of the twentieth anniversary was held that followed a similar format to that of the original meeting. The three-week meeting was held at the Wye Plantation and Conference Center in Maryland and involved about sixty English and language arts teachers from elementary, secondary, and college levels. It was organized by the NCTE, the MLA, and several other leading organizations in the field. The report of the conference was assembled and edited by Richard Lloyd-Jones and Andrea Lunsford (1989). Of the various sections of the report, the one on college-level teaching, curriculum, and so forth is the most pertinent. Several key features emerge clearly from the discussion: participants saw English as a field that integrates reading, writing, speaking, and listening in substantive ways; they pointed to the need for extended time and focus for students to develop their abilities, using literary as well as informational texts. They recognized the importance of a wide array of media, speaking to the importance of students' language arts skills as crucial to their future roles as participants in a democratic society. While there is no explicit discussion of critical reading per se, a few passing references make clear that the participants saw it as a focal point for teaching and learning to a much greater extent than had those in 1966.

In 2016, a fiftieth anniversary conference was held at Dartmouth College. Dartmouth's Christiane Donahue was the chief organizer, but many highly respected scholars from the field were involved as plenary speakers or presenters at the institute that was part of the meeting. An eight-day institute was followed by a two-day conference at the original site. The website for the 2016 meeting describes the anniversary gathering: "A small, focused eight-day Institute, designed to recall the original 1966 event while looking forward to the future of writing research, will feature intense discussions of 'working papers' by authors including Chuck Bazerman, Deborah Brandt, Ellen Cushman, David Galbraith, Makoni Sinfree, and Clay Spinuzzi. These authors will work on their ideas in conversation with twenty Institute participants. These authors will present their new work as plenaries at the Conference; the Institute participants will respond to the plenaries and present their work in concurrent sessions" (Dartmouth Institute 2016). A review of the institute paper abstracts and the plenaries of participants at the following conference reveals little interest in reading per se (2016).

The only paper that takes up reading in any detail is the report on research by Rutgers University neuroscientist Paula Tallal (2016) using Fast ForWord, a computer-based training program to improve reading and writing skills among a small group of college students, including both native and non-native speakers of English. The program produced significant improvement in both reading and writing on two standardized tests: the Gates MacGinitie Reading Test and the Oral and Written Language Scales. No other presentations focused on reading processes, critical reading, critical literacy, or related topics, according to the website. While it is not surprising that virtually no attention was paid to reading, given that the focus of the institute was on the development of writing research from Dartmouth 1966 to the time of the anniversary, it does help explain the widespread lack of interest in reading per se at both meetings. The follow-up volume of many of the papers presented (full disclosure: this edited collection appeared in the Studies in Composition and Rhetoric series I edit for Peter Lang Publishing) reflects a similar lack of interest in reading (Blewett, Donahue, and Monroe 2021).

Vee noted in comments to me (email communication, August 19, 2021) that she didn't pay particular attention to reading in her review of the Dartmouth Conference materials, but given her detailed discussion of the original meeting, there was little to pay attention to in the seminar. This conclusion is also fair, given Harris's (1991) discussion of the 1966 conference. Part of the reason for this outcome, according to Harris, is that the American participants at Dartmouth mostly saw themselves as scholars, whereas the British attendees saw themselves primarily as teachers, with more focus on the classroom. Still, Harris writes that the goal of teaching English, based on the discussions at Dartmouth, might be as follows: "Rather than seeing the goal of study in English as helping students further develop certain skills they already have as writers and readers, such a view instead pictures our work as centering on finding and making differences in the ways they use language" (644). Such a goal might be useful to language arts teachers at all levels, but it says little about the role of reading in developing students' abilities in these ways.

Similarly, Christiane Donahue assessed the overall impact of Dartmouth 1966 in a 2015 blog post (written ahead of the 2016 conference), offering several key points that remain areas of focus for writing studies as a whole:

- The role of technology: A paper on technological advancement made claims about sweeping changes driven by technological advancements and their place in English.
- The attention to process: Writing pedagogy began to focus on student writers creating a text, rather than the resulting text. The British influence in writing studies helped to foster an environment that sought to understand how writers write, not just what they write.
- The interaction between speech and writing: Speech was presented as tightly linked to constructing meaning and to writing ("The Spoken Word and the Integrity of English Instruction," Study Group Paper 1).
- The shifting nature of "standard English."

In these notes and the rest of her summary, Donahue says little about the role or the teaching of reading, though she does say that another result was more attention to Louise M. Rosenblatt's transactional view of literature, discussed in more detail below. Meanwhile, reading per se was receiving some attention in two other programs developing at more or less the same time as the Dartmouth meeting (discussed as alternative approaches later in this chapter): the *Hooked on Books* program, developed at the University of Michigan, and the Great Books program, developed at the University of Chicago and Columbia University. These programs did pay direct attention to reading but went outside the realm of formal schooling, K–12 and beyond. Prior to discussion of them, a multi-year debate on the role of reading in college writing classes warrants consideration, as does related work in reader-response theory.

### The Tate-Lindemann Debate over the Lit/Comp Split

In the 1990s, changes in the field of writing studies opened the curriculum question yet again in a debate on the issue of whether first-year writing should be the kind of composition and literature course I had as a first-year student in the 1960s or should be focused exclusively on the rhetorical situation—including audience, topic, purpose, style, and related issues—using the then-current understanding of the writing process. The debate played out in journals and at professional meetings, notably in a shared panel at the Conference on College Composition and Communication (CCCC) in 1992. Erika Lindemann (1993), a University of North Carolina rhetorician, and Gary Tate (1993), then at Texas Christian University, subsequently published dueling articles in *College English*, the leading journal in the field. Lindemann was opposed to using literature in the course, while Tate's view was that literature along with a wide range of many different kinds of texts should be included in first-year writing.

For the purposes of the current discussion, it is important to note that neither side focused on reading per se. Lindemann seems to have characterized the debate correctly when she wrote to me that "the argument about whether or not belletristic literature belonged in a first-year writing class . . . became entangled with the larger political and structural issue of who controlled writing programs in English Departments, literature faculty or composition specialists" (Erika Lindemann, email communication, November 11, 2020). Two years later, Lindemann (1995) had what might have been the final word on the subject, in another piece in *College English*, in which she explored three different views of English 101. For the present discussion, these differing views offer distinct angles on the role of reading in the course.

So, a first view of English 101 (Lindemann's term for the course) sees writing as a product, with traditional approaches that entail students writing essays, usually about literature. Teachers, in this view, correct students' work more than they respond to students' views or understanding of the works involved. While there is attention to reading, again, it is not to critical reading per se but to the analytical reading of literature. A second view sees writing as a process, focusing on students' discovery of themselves as writers and thinkers. Although such courses might entail having students read literature or nonfiction prose texts of many kinds, again, the focus is not on critical reading per se. With students' attention directed to invention, pre-writing, revision, and other aspects of process, the reading is often the result of students reading one another's work as part of peer review. Imitation of literary forms or criticism is generally not part of this view. Students' practice and self-discovery are keys to the teaching of this version of English 101. The third view is of writing as a system, where students write to explore their role in the world and to have influence on it. Writing is not just across the disciplines (i.e., WAC) but above and beyond the curriculum. Community literacy projects, writing in prisons, and writing in other non-university settings allow diverse groups of students to develop their writing for a broader audience.

Literature is not necessarily relevant here; instead, the reading and writing call for detailed analysis of an array of different types of texts and materials, ranging from journal and magazine articles to books to other kinds of materials. Lindemann concludes that there is a need to find common ground among these views for the purpose of developing consistency in teaching and evaluating student work. Although she doesn't say so explicitly, a strong focus on reading could be a starting point for such common ground, as discussed in chapter 7 of this book. Lindemann's approach was also supported by respected Georgetown University rhetorician James F. Slevin (2001). He discusses the importance of students' reading directly, making the case for a direct relationship between reading and writing.

Slevin says that "critical literacy, literacy that is historical and contextual . . . helps students develop a clearer sense of writing not just as a process but . . . in historical terms, as related to larger cultural and social issues" (140–141). These arguments show that while reading did receive some attention, it was not specifically in the form of direct teaching of the nuts and bolts of getting meaning from print, with a focus on critical analysis of all kinds of texts. Much more recently, the idea of including literature reappeared, broadly defined as both literary and non-literary texts in the argument for a critical thinking approach to all kinds of reading advanced by Teachers College Columbia literacy scholar Sheridan Blau (2017). Drawing on a wealth of discussion by Louise Rosenblatt and other scholars who followed her, Blau suggests that deep critical reading can focus on an array of many kinds of texts.

A further analysis of this debate and its impact on reading scholarship appears in Ellen C. Carillo's (2015) landmark book on the role of reading in writing studies. Carillo and I met while she was conducting research for this book, under the auspices of a CCCC Research Grant. She did a survey but offered follow-up in-person interviews at the next available CCCC conference. Since then, I have been lucky to collaborate with her on a variety of projects. In one chapter of *Securing a Place for Reading in Composition* (2015), she sketches the rise and demise of reading as a focus of research in the field in the period 1980–1993, ending with the Tate-Lindemann debate. Her start point in 1980 relates to another publication on reading, a key article in *College English* by University of California at Santa Barbara researcher Charles Bazerman (1980). Among other issues, Carillo (2015, 76) notes that the articles, conference papers, and such throughout this period reflect definite interest in reading, but they result from "the struggle over disciplinary identity . . . [and] clashes—disciplinary, political, and others—that characterized English studies and departments at the time." She points out the merger of two terms, reading and literature, that results in the loss of an ongoing interest in reading, as discussed here.

In her close analysis of the publications throughout this period, Carillo (2015) finds that the focus of most work on reading devolved into discussions of literature and literary theory rather than of critical reading. The

Tate-Lindemann debate is just one example of this conflation of terms and approaches (85–86). Some scholars wanted to use reading approaches to improve the teaching of writing, such as eliciting students' responses to literature through double-entry notebooks or "difficulty papers" but the use of empirical methods and drawing on the history of rhetoric greatly concerned literary scholars (87–88). These issues, which date back to Dartmouth, are fundamentally about approaches focused on research/theory versus those on pedagogy. In this period, Carillo says there were some positive connections between reading and writing that scholars were writing about, such as viewing reading as an active process of constructing meaning, seeing reading as different from but a counterpart to writing, understanding reading as a complex process, trying to see how a text works to convey meaning, or using reading as a cognitive activity (92–95).

Despite these common threads, which did not arise directly as a by-product of Dartmouth and its aftermath, reading largely fell away as a focus in writing studies by the middle of the 1990s, as the various approaches to reading discussed here illustrate in detail. Texas A&M University rhetorician Richard Fulkerson (2005) offers a different perspective based on a wide-ranging review of the field, including the period Carillo focuses on and a much longer period. He concludes that more attention is being paid to reading (681) in all kinds of writing classes; at the same time, he makes clear that the attention is not on critical reading but rather is fitted to whatever approach the courses or programs might take (critical/cultural studies, genre-based analysis, argument, and others). Moreover, too much attention to reading results in a lack of attention to teaching writing, in his view (665). Also, readings might serve as sources for students' own writing or as models to be emulated, but again, no clear and consistent attention is paid to critical reading in any approach Fulkerson discusses (675). The developments discussed up to the turn of the twenty-first century provide further examples of the inconsistent and variable attention to critical reading that appears both early and late in the history of writing studies as a field.

### *Literature Scholars' Reader-Response Theory*

From a broader viewpoint, an overt focus on reading was offered by literature scholars, led by Louise Rosenblatt, the leading proponent of reader-response theory. The work of many reader-response scholars was carefully reviewed by Patricia Harkin (2005), who is a helpful source because she had a joint appointment in the Departments of English and Communication at the University of Illinois at Chicago and is the author of *Acts of Reading* (Harkin 1999), a textbook for reading and writing about literature that is focused on reading strategies and analysis. (The textbook is discussed in detail in chapter 6.) Harkin puts reader-response theory in context by listing some of the key texts that presented the theory, offering her view of why reader-response theory fell out of favor:

> Louise Rosenblatt's *Literature as Exploration* [1938] and *The Reader, the Text, the Poem* [1978], David Bleich's *Readings and Feelings* [1975] and *Subjective Criticism* [1978], Wolfgang Iser's *The Implied Reader* [1974] and *The Act of Reading* [1978,] Stanley Fish's *Is There a Text in This Class?* [1980], and Norman Holland's *Poems in Persons* [1973] and *Five Readers Reading* [1975]—[are] collectively known as reader-response theory... Reader-response theory, by contrast, is properly an effort to provide a generalized account of what happens when human beings engage in a process they call "reading." Such accounts are warranted in any of several disciplines—psychoanalysis, linguistics, semiotics, phenomenology, etc. Iser's *The Act of Reading*, a phenomenological account of the processes that occur in consciousness when human beings encounter literary texts, is an example (Harkin 2005, 411)... In all of these... reader-response theory was applied to nonliterary as well as literary texts, a reflection of the theoretical awareness both that the tenets we were using were as applicable to essays and newspaper articles as they were to stories, poems, and plays and that students need explicit instruction in reading all kinds of texts (418)... Discussions of reading have been so thoroughly conflated with discussions of teaching literature, of the purpose of English studies, of the future of the humanities, of the politics of general education, of the definitions and uses of literacy, and so forth, that a pedagogical or curricular decision not to teach literary texts in writing courses became or entailed a decision not to teach reading. That, I think, is what happened to reader-response theory. (421)

Thus, writing studies as a field turned away from both literature and reading, taken together, according to Harkin. (In her textbook, Harkin attempted to apply reader-response and other aspects of critical theory to reading for students; see chapter 6 for further discussion.) In addition, she makes a point of saying, in the course of her historical review, that a parallel development was the "professionalization" of composition or writing studies as a field.

This development likewise moved writing studies away from literature and thus also from teaching reading. One further issue to consider is that reader-response theory in its various manifestations was chiefly about reading and writing about literature. That's not a criticism, but it is important because while it meant the focus was variously on a novel, a poem, or a play, it was on imaginative literature and not on the full array of texts students have available now, as University of Maryland literary scholar Brian Richardson (1997) pointed out in an exploration of an array of approaches to reading this kind of work. Moreover, while it is always unfair to look back and criticize theory and practice in a different context and in hindsight, it is pertinent to point out that no evidence suggests that the leading reader-response theorists like Rosenblatt were discussing the issues of accuracy, currency, bias, and related matters most urgently needed now.

What reader-response theory offers, importantly, is a focus on the reader as distinct from and responding to the text, a different viewpoint than other theoretical perspectives, as sketched by different sources. Rosenblatt's biography and the origins of the earliest statement of her theory are offered in a thorough review by New Jersey Institute of Technology rhetorician Norbert Elliot (2008). A textbook review of a number of other critical theories show this specific reader focus clearly in the summary of reader-response theory offered by Grand Valley State University literary scholar Lois Tyson (1999). Before summarizing the reading process within the theory, she says "reader-response theorists share two beliefs: (1) that the role of the reader cannot be omitted from our understanding of literature and (2) that readers do not passively consume the meaning presented to them by an objective literary text; rather they actively make the meaning they find in literature" (154). Different reader-response theorists, according to Tyson, have a variety of views of how readers construct their responses, but a text is "an event that occurs within the reader" (157). Her analysis of Rosenblatt's approach shows that it consists of a transaction in which the text provides a stimulus for readers to respond to, offering a "blueprint" against which readers can check their reactions. The process, then, involves reading, responding to, and checking/correcting the responses by referring to the text (157–158).

To explore Tyson's analysis more thoroughly, Rosenblatt's own reflections on her transactional theory as part of reader-response reveal its focus. Writing in 1993 in *College English*, which publishes work on theory and practice in both literature and writing studies, Rosenblatt offers the key points of her theory years after the publication of her two key works (1938, 1978). She begins by tracing her professional career path, including her move from teaching English in a traditional department to a position in a School of Education that ultimately developed a full graduate program more closely aligned with her own "unorthodox stance" (Rosenblatt 1993, 379) about theory and practice. She describes the continuum of reader-response:

> The efferent stance (from L. efferre, to carry away) is involved primarily with analyzing, abstracting, and accumulating what will be retained after the reading. Examples would include reading to acquire information, directions for action, or solutions to a problem. In the aesthetic stance, attention is focused primarily on experiencing what is being evoked, lived through, during the reading. Moreover, I stressed that there was not an opposition, a dichotomy, but a continuum between the two stances . . . The difference lies in "the mix," the proportion of public and private aspects of meaning attended to during a reading. In readings that fall somewhere in the efferent half of the continuum, the reader selects out predominantly more public or cognitive elements than private. The aesthetic stance, in contrast, accords selective attention to predominantly more of the penumbra of private feelings, attitudes, sensations, and ideas than to the public aspects. (383)

So, yes, Rosenblatt focuses on reading and on both information and analysis as well as on the appreciation of or emotional response to the text. Reader-response, then, did pay significant attention to reading, offering a deep exploration into reading behavior of a specific kind. Her perspective was unique in the true sense of that word.

This view is supported in the doctoral work of Elizabeth B. Hutton, director of the Howe Writing Center at the University of Miami of Ohio. Hutton, like Harkin, sees the composition/literature split as an explanation for why Rosenblatt's theory was not more widely accepted, noting the importance of the latter's understanding of cultural context in literacy as a key feature. This perspective suggests that reader-response has special relevance for the current understanding of transfer in literacy development:

> It is English studies' long-standing disciplinary habit of disaggregating the work of the writing classroom from the work of literary and cultural study that I see as the fundamental problem that Rosenblatt's work helps to reframe and begin to resolve . . .
>
> Rosenblatt's "aesthetic" and "efferent" stances, once viewed through the lens of her seminal philosophical commitments, offer a newly integrative explanatory model for the dynamics by which learners not only make meaning from texts, but also reinvest and repurpose ("transfer") their literacy knowledge, and not only across new contexts and tasks, but also across the dimensions of text-based literacy itself (reading and writing) . . .

> Rosenblatt's transactional theory presents literacy as an expansively cultural practice, a paradigm that encourages learners to draw more purposive, self-reflective, and critical connections between their reading and writing, and that helps learners to realize and leverage the ways that culturally supported literacy practices can themselves work to transform cultures in their turn. (Hutton 2018, viii, ix)

This analysis shows how useful Rosenblatt's theory could have been, had it not been blocked off from writing studies because it was thought to focus on reading literature and was thus excluded from use in writing classes.

Finally, as just one further example of Rosenblatt's particular angle on things, in a recent reprint (2018) of an overview of the entire reader-response theory, she offers this observation about the way reading needs to be integrated with writing as well as with the broader context of critical literacy, as provided in my model:

> Hence, the teaching of reading and writing at any developmental level should have as its first concern the creation of environments and activities in which students are motivated and encouraged to draw on their own resources to make "live" meanings. With this as the fundamental criterion, emphasis falls on strengthening the basic processes that we have seen to be shared by reading and writing. The teaching of one can then reinforce linguistic habits and semantic approaches useful in the other. Such teaching, concerned with the ability of the individual to generate meaning, will permit constructive cross-fertilization of the reading and writing (and speech) processes. (2018, 470)

Rosenblatt (1993, 383) makes a key point about the integration of speaking and listening with reading and writing, consistent with the view of critical literacy under discussion here: "Pragmatist transactionalism had led me to envision speaking and listening, writing and reading as interrelated aspects of the individual's transactions with the environment." From this point, she goes on to say that the processes are not mirror images of one another but that they share both similarities and differences. Rosenblatt acknowledges that readers need to be critical of the underlying framework of both a literary work and their own biases and preferences, including the sociocultural factors I have proposed in the model of critical literacy but that do not need to be analyzed critically in the terms used in my model. Reader-response theory, then, addresses some important aspects of reading but is limited in its impact because of the focus on responding mainly to literary works and because it fell out of favor as writing studies developed—as Harkin claims in her review of the larger context, a view shared by Hutton.

## Freire's Critical Literacy: Another Divergent View of Reading

Critical literacy studies offers yet another, radically different angle on reading, providing further evidence that scholars in different areas were paying attention to it. The critical literacy approach has been aptly discussed and reviewed by two highly respected scholars in the field of literacy research, University of British Columbia education professor Robert J. Tierney and University of California at Berkeley education professor P. David Pearson (2021). Their book offers detailed discussions of all the major movements in literacy research over the past century and a half. Their insights into the complexities of the work in critical literacy studies offer a useful guide to the work in this area. They include the work of Brazilian educator Paulo Freire, who worked on the importance of literacy in addressing poverty and political power. Critical theory grew out of the work of Freire and others; it has been woven into more recent efforts to improve diversity, equity, and inclusion. It is also part of the approach to education taken by feminists and others.

Tierney and Pearson (2021, 144) provide the broad context in which critical literacy theory arises: "Critical theory foregrounded the political nature of literacy at the same time as it advanced formative participatory research and development . . . in the interest of social improvements on behalf of communities . . . In order to establish systems that support an ecology of egalitarianism and openness and allow for ongoing organic change, the ends need to allow for diversity rather than uniformity and be aligned with considerations of the local and for community engagement." Thus, this view of literacy sees it specifically as a tool of political power or a way of limiting people's power by limiting their access to education for the development of literacy skills.

At the same time, Tierney and Pearson point out weaknesses in this way of thinking about literacy: "While a critical literacy lens has added immeasurably to our appreciation and understanding of power dynamics—especially the systems at play—it has not always done so in ways that are participatory and respectful of local situations . . . Concern over a one-size-fits-all approach to analyzing and proposing power has been critiqued by various groups concerned with places of intersection—especially those of race, gender and class. It has also been criticized in terms of its reach across borders to other cultures, with the understanding that this needs to be tempered and complicated" (145, 147). Other current views address these concerns, as noted in the recent *Handbook of Critical Literacies*, a collection of fifty chapters from diverse perspectives by scholars from all over the world (Pandya et al. 2021). As the editors note, the book is truly a group project; its 100-page bibliography points to the vast array of work in this area.

A more detailed look at critical literacy reveals that it is close to the view taken in the *Handbook*. Its key concepts have little to do with reading and analyzing literature but do take up the social justice concerns literacy can help address. The main ideas are captured in an education encyclopedia article by widely published American University literacy scholar and education professor Vivian Maria Vasquez (2017, n.p.):

> From a critical literacy perspective the world is seen as a socially constructed text that can be read. The earlier students are introduced to this idea, the sooner they are able to understand what it means to be researchers of language, image, spaces, and objects, exploring such issues as what counts as language, whose language counts, and who decides as well as explor[ing] ways texts can be revised, rewritten, or reconstructed to shift or reframe the message(s) conveyed. As such, texts are never neutral. What this means is that all texts are created from a particular perspective with the intention of conveying particular messages. As such these texts work to position readers in certain ways. We therefore need to question the perspective of others.
>
> Just as texts are never neutral, the ways we read text are also never neutral. Each time we read, write, or create, we draw from our past experiences and understanding about how the world works. We therefore should also analyze our own readings of text and unpack the position(s) from which we engage in literacy work.
>
> Critical literacy involves making sense of the sociopolitical systems through which we live our lives and questioning these systems. This means our work in critical literacy needs to focus on social issues, such as race, class, gender, or disability and the ways in which we use language to shape our understanding of these issues . . .
>
> Critical literacy practices can be transformative and contribute to change inequitable ways of being and problematic social practices.

This lengthy description gives a good sense of the critical literacy perspective, and it is accurate to say that worldwide, many, many scholars are working on reading and literacy from this vantage point. This claim is reflected in both the *Handbook of Critical Literacies* and Vasquez's article.

Three important questions come immediately to mind. First, as the leading theorist, what does Freire say specifically about reading and writing? Second, has critical literacy appeared in writing studies; if so, how? Finally, does critical literacy appear in first-year writing or other classrooms; if so, why are students still unable to judge material for factors like bias? Turning first to Freire, his widely known *Pedagogy of the Oppressed* (originally published in 1970 and revised and updated in a twentieth anniversary edition that appeared in 1993) makes clear how literacy can help people take control of their lives, work, and government. In it, he discusses the "banking concept" of education: "Education thus becomes an act of depositing, in which the students are the depositories and the teacher is the depositor. Instead of communicating, the teacher issues communiques and makes deposits which the students patiently receive, memorize, and repeat . . . In the banking concept of education, knowledge is a gift bestowed by those who consider themselves knowledgeable upon those who they consider to know nothing" (1993, 53). This kind of education is oppressive, as the teacher has all the power and the students have none.

By contrast, Freire (1993, 64) argues for "problem-posing education," which takes a different approach: "Banking education (for obvious reasons) attempts, by mythicizing reality, to conceal certain facts which explain the way human beings exist in the world; problem-posing education sets itself the task of demythologizing. Banking education resists dialogues; problem-posing education regards dialogue as indispensable to the act of cognition which unveils reality. Banking education treats students as objects of assistance; problem-posing education makes them critical thinkers." Freire is well-known for his opposition to the "banking" approach to education; it is a key focus of the *Pedagogy of the Oppressed*. Years after its original appearance in 1970, at a major conference on reading in São Paulo, Brazil, in 1981, he gave a speech that focused on reading specifically.

This speech is a source of Freire's (1983, 5) famous distinction between reading the word and reading the world: "Reading is not exhausted merely by decoding the written word or written language, but rather anticipated by and extending into knowledge of the world. Reading the world precedes reading the word, and the subsequent reading of the word cannot dispense with continually reading the world. Language and reality are dynamically intertwined. The understanding attained by critical reading of a text implies perceiving the relationship between text and context." What follows is a semi-autobiographical description of his childhood, including learning about the world and then learning to read and write. Given this background, it is easy to understand why Freire says reading the world precedes reading the word. He explains:

> First, I would like to affirm that I always saw teaching adults to read and write as a political act, an act of knowledge and therefore as a creative act . . . Learning to read and write [is not] merely . . . learning words, syllables, or letters, a process of teaching in which the teacher *fills* the supposedly *empty* heads of learners with his or her words . . .
> 
> Reading the world always precedes reading the word and reading the word implies continually reading the world. As I suggested earlier, this movement from the world to the word and from the word to the world is always present; even the spoken word flows from our reading of the world. In a way, however, we can go further, and say that reading the world is not preceded merely by reading the world, but by a certain form of *writing* it or *re-writing* it, that is, of transforming it by means of conscious practical work. For me, this dynamic movement is central to the literacy process. (10, original emphases)

In concluding the speech, Freire notes that reading is always subject to individual interpretation and always occurs in a political context. There are many points of connection between this original statement of critical literacy theory and the model developed in this book. Most notably, the sociocultural context in which literacy occurs must be a key point of focus. Freire clearly rejects the "banking" approach to education of all kinds, seeing reading and writing as integral to how people live and work in the world. At another point in the speech, he says that literacy can transform the way people see poverty and injustice as a move toward "practical work" that might lead to positive outcomes. Despite Freire's political and critical focus, there is little to suggest that he advocates direct attention to the evaluation of materials being read in either the world or the word.

The other two questions raised above remain, then. First, how has Freire's approach been integrated in writing studies as a field? Two scholars, over time, give some sense of what has happened to Freire's ideas, bearing in mind that Freire was much more attractive to writing studies in general than was Rosenblatt. He was, after all, not a literature scholar; moreover, his political and social concerns were well suited to the place where writing studies has always been as a field. First, widely respected College of the Holy Cross rhetorician Patricia Bizzell (1992) published an important book titled *Academic Discourse and Critical Consciousness*. She devotes a full chapter to the work of

Freire and others who share his approach. An array of different arguments can be made for and against teaching students to work with Standard English, according to Bizzell. Ultimately, though, like the peasants on whom Freire was focused, she thinks it is appropriate to teach students to use this form of the language as a way of empowering them to address social justice issues:

> I want to argue not just that mastery of academic discourse will not make critical consciousness impossible, but rather that it will foster it. Mastery of academic discourse lets students participate in the community primarily responsible in our society for generating knowledge. Whether they work inside or outside the academic community as adults, this training will enable them to reflect on experience and work for change with some power. Therefore, politically committed instruction in academic discourse can do more for the cause of social justice than simply keeping hands off the students' "own" language. Teachers can make a difference in the effects of current trends in composition instruction. (150)

This view of the role of language in power shows that for Bizzell, critical literacy played a key role in writing studies. But since her 1992 publication, attitudes toward language and power have shifted in many ways, especially since the pandemic and the many social inequalities it revealed. Moreover, unlike Freire and others, she pays little attention to critical reading, speaking, and listening.

A second scholar who has reflected on the impact of the critical literacy approach, including the work of Bizzell and others, is University of Cincinnati rhetorician Russel K. Durst (2009), who considers how critical literacy has played out in the field. He shows that writing teachers have a variety of roles as a result of Freire's influence: imposing limits and expanding them for both students and colleagues. As part of a changing "social turn" in writing studies, Durst (2009, 1666) says the political aspects of teaching writing have come to the fore, with implications for reading and literacy: "Rather than focusing primarily on developing writing abilities, the curriculum increasingly calls upon instructors to develop in students—through reading, writing, critical thinking, and discussion—a certain sensibility . . . the student writer is taught a commitment to community service, an awareness of inequities, a critical stance toward authority, and a questioning nature regarding established ways of thinking . . . Teachers also wrestle with marginal status in current studies of composition." These are just some of the ways Freire's critical literacy has played out from the perspective of a scholar who has extensively explored the history of the field. And Durst, of course, is not the only historian to discuss these issues.

More recent publications by Ohio State University historian of literacy Harvey J. Graff reflect the ongoing discussion in terms of the role of reading and critical literacy in writing studies as a field. Graff (2022) published a detailed discussion of these issues in his wide-ranging and authoritative book *Searching for Literacy*. A full chapter is devoted to reading as it has been treated in writing studies, and it is highly critical. He quotes his own statement of his well-known concept of the "literacy myth": "As I summarized in 2010, 'The Literacy Myth refers to the belief, articulated in educational, civic, religious, and other settings, contemporary and historical, that the acquisition of literacy is a necessary precursor to and inevitably results in economic development, democratic practice, cognitive enhancement, and upward social mobility'" (Graff 2022, 281). The chapter reviews the way reading has generally been seen as less important, less complex, less useful than writing in writing studies, even by well-respected scholars and people he considers friends and colleagues, such as Deborah Brandt.

Graff makes a broad case for paying much more attention to reading than has been the case over the course of the development of the field. As one of the leading scholars offering historical analysis, he is in an exceptionally good position to make this case. He begins with Freire, hence his relevance to the present chapter. Graff traces the general approach to reading in education, where it gets a great deal of attention in elementary schools but after that is generally set aside, except insofar as some students need additional help to improve their ability. But Graff says this approach is erroneous: "I do not exaggerate when I state unequivocally that *reading is the missing link in understanding, teaching, and practicing writing* . . . This declaration is analogous to my conviction that *orality is the missing link in understanding literacy*. Any perceived contradictions are necessary ones. They are rooted in the limits of our received wisdom and our repetition of assumptions that I seek to challenge" (2022, 145, original emphases). Graff sees the central role of reading in writing, and he also sees orality playing a key role in literacy. His view is reflected in the model I am proposing, as it integrates reading, writing, speaking, and listening in critical literacy. Furthermore, he claims that in the digital realm, reading and writing pass by one another, with some scholars suggesting that all things digital destroy reading while others see trouble with writing, but no one is talking to anyone else on either side.

The lack of interaction with scholars on both sides, Graff says, reflects the widely shared but incorrect view that writing is more important than reading. This view is common, but since there's little empirical evidence to support it, it is a serious misconception. In addition, writing is generally not well taught and certainly has many negative associations. Graff (2022, 146) points to Deborah Brandt's award-winning *Literacy in American Lives* (2001) to support this claim. I can vouch for Graff's accuracy from my own experience: if I say by way of introducing myself that I have been a writing teacher, the person I am talking to will almost always say "English was my worst class." In visual art, Graff points out that writing is often positively pictured whereas reading seldom appears, with signatures as a key issue reflected in paintings and the subject of discussions of putting one's "John Hancock" on a document.

From this critique of the value of writing over reading, Graff goes on to show how this view is reflected in the work of a number of literacy scholars, including Brandt. He is surprisingly stern in criticizing Brandt and others who take this perspective that writing is more important than reading: "The future of literacy studies, and of literacy, lies in the reconnection of reading and writing and their movement together. This is one form of translation across media and modes of understanding and expression that is central to both images and practices of literacy" (2022, 152). Graff here is making the same case I am trying to present, in favor of much more attention to reading even, or perhaps especially, in the digital environment.

He goes on to point out that reading does get some attention in visual art and, albeit negatively, in the form of predictions of reading's demise or of the declines in reading time or motivation. At the same time, books are still being published, bought, sold, read, and retained. And technology offers positive support for more communal or social reading as well as audio opportunities through audiobooks. So, the unwarranted discounting of reading still pervades the field: "Reading remains the missing link in the place of writing in literacy studies. However ironic, paradoxical, or contradictory, this absence to some degree or another marks composition studies, ethnographies, popular culture studies, New Literacy Studies, multimodal studies, and vocational projects" (172). In making a strong, positive case for more attention to reading, Graff writes:

> A renewed understanding and appreciation of reading must move between typical studies of the availability of print or other reading material and ideologies in support of certain kinds of reading and censure of others, on the one hand, and actual practices, valuations, and influences of reading, on the other. All kinds of reading of all kinds of materials must be recognized and valued. No less important, the interrelationships among reading and writing must be appreciated. The traditions of dichotomizing, opposing,

and devaluing one in favor of the other need to be criticized and revised. Just as "the reader" and "the author" have not died, neither reading nor writing can be understood or practiced without a role for the other. (156)

In this thorough tracing and critique of how reading has been treated in writing studies, starting with the positive impact of Freire and others, Graff shows how the critical literacy theory has played out, largely in the inconsistency of scholars' views.

Graff's history helps explain why reading has fallen by the wayside, despite Freire advocating for much more attention to it. The pattern is similar to the demise of reader-response theory. And this repeated inconsistency provides a small piece of the explanation for why students are still not able to read source materials online in ways that allow them to evaluate for authority, accuracy, bias, and other factors. If critical reading as defined here were getting the kind of thorough attention Graff and I are advocating, many more students would have the skills needed. Various scholars *have* been paying attention to reading, albeit somewhat intermittently and from different perspectives. Both reader-response theory and the critical literacy view offer important insights on reading from different vantage points. What is missing is the kind of comprehensive and current, flexible view my model proposes as well as focused, evidence-based approaches that can help students develop critical abilities to serve them in school and beyond. These approaches will be offered in chapter 7.

## *Other Angles on Reading*

One of the first professional papers I published was "The Connection of Writing to Reading: A Gloss on the Gospel of Mina Shaughnessy." It appeared in *College English* (Horning 1978) shortly after the publication of Shaughnessy's (1977) important book on the novice writers she was seeing as a by-product of open-admissions policies at the City University of New York. As I saw it then and still see it now, Shaughnessy missed the need to help students be better readers in order to become better writers. My reader of drafts this book, Norbert Elliot, has pointed out that the placement testing and other kinds of assessment that were going on at the time separated reading entirely from writing; teachers were likewise in different departments or parts of institutions. The many examples of student work in Shaughnessy's book suggest that open-admissions students lacked much experience with both reading academic texts and formal writing, resulting in writing that showed a lack of sense of what academic English looked and sounded like and in their inability to write the kinds of papers expected in college. I explored the importance of reading in more detail in *Teaching Writing as a Second Language* (Horning 1987). The observations I made then still hold today: students with limited reading experience have a hard time with academic writing because for them, it is largely a foreign language that can only be learned through reading. Results from recent assessments by the Programme for International Student Assessment (PISA) (reported in Horning 2021b) support these claims, showing that fifteen-year-olds in many Northern Hemisphere countries who read extensively are better readers and better writers.

Shaughnessy used data drawn from an analysis of basic writers' papers to support her claims, resulting in crucial insights into students' efforts to learn about written language. She pointed out that the errors students made in their writing showed that they were constructing rules and testing them; in this way, she tied her novices' efforts to more general strategies for language learning found among children learning their first language, as well as among children and adults learning a second language. Learners construct hypotheses about the rules for the language they are learning and then test them through use and feedback from other speakers. Novice writers in Shaughnessy's classroom showed similar patterns, suggesting that they had constructed rules for written language, subject to teacher correction or peer feedback. But the only source of input for the rules of written language is written language, so the lack of reading was a key problem, largely unaddressed. What those novice readers and writers needed was not only extensive reading but also explicit instruction in vocabulary, comprehension, and critical evaluation of texts to serve as input data on what written language looks and sounds like.

But the focus of most instruction in postsecondary reading—such as it is and where it still exists—takes the form of remediation, regardless of whether the targeted students are novice writers, English language learners (ELLs), or students admitted under a special program. At admission, standardized test scores (with all their weaknesses and problems, discussed in chapter 1) or writing samples used for placement point to poor reading ability. These students are often placed in a developmental reading class and do get specific, focused help with essential comprehension skills, vocabulary development, and critical tools they will need to be able to read textbooks and other materials in college courses. I've taught this kind of course and have seen students make huge progress as readers, going on to succeed even in reading-intensive courses like history and psychology. These are the lucky students who are identified and advised or required to get help with reading that can lead to success. The rest of the students are not so lucky; they don't read as well as they could and should, they don't get focused help with their reading in either a corequisite or an integrated reading/writing class, and they may be part of the 50 percent of students who will not complete a degree. Some of these students are fortunate to be placed into courses that integrate explicit critical reading instruction with writing, such as Peter Adams's (2020a) Accelerated Learning Program (ALP), discussed in chapter 2. Adams's evidence shows what a difference direct instruction in reading can make.

As I pointed out in chapter 1, no matter how reading is tested or assessed, it's clear that half or more of current postsecondary students lack the skills to succeed in college courses and beyond, as engaged members of our democracy. When that claim, backed by the evidence presented earlier, is put together with United States Department of Education statistics (2021) that show that roughly half of those who start any type of postsecondary work don't finish a degree within three or six years (depending on whether they are attending a two-year or a four-year institution), a relationship is at least a reasonable possibility, even keeping in mind the commonplace that correlation is *not* causation.

Just the possibility of a connection argues for more consistent attention to critical reading, even allowing for the fact that there are many reasons why students do not complete a degree. A second point is that students who are placed in developmental courses in English (and math) do not always need those courses. Their follow-up track records are poor, and they are more likely to drop out altogether (Oliveri, Mislevy, and Elliot 2020), or they may succeed despite these barriers, as US government educational policy analyst Xianglei Chen's (2016) study of two- and four-year student performance shows. Developmental courses often do not bear credit to fulfill degree requirements, costing students time and money. These issues were discussed in detail in chapter 2.

Furthermore, the classes on which these data are based are often not specifically *reading* courses; they might be English or integrated reading/writing courses or some other kind of class that may or may not provide explicit instruction on reading. In contrast, community college scholar and Manchester Community College faculty member Patrick Sullivan (2017, 359–364) discusses data showing a strong positive result from developmental courses in both English and math, albeit admitting that the findings on the impact of these courses is mixed. Two-year college scholars Arthur M.

Cohen, Florence B. Brawer, and Carrie B. Kisker (2014) come to the same conclusion—that developmental courses offer mixed results—in their comprehensive volume on community colleges. While these differing views persist, a much better approach that can serve all students would be to integrate reading instruction in not only first-year writing courses but in all courses, certainly in the first two undergraduate years. Good evidence, to be discussed in chapter 7, indicates that such an approach could make a real difference in how many students "cross the finish line" to graduation, developing the critical reading ability needed for their academic, personal, and professional lives.

Here again, though, it is important to note that reading *was* very much present in the field as a focus of discussion and concern. Indeed, a number of scholars were raising the reading issue and addressing it in a pragmatic way, as demonstrated by George Otte and Rebecca Williams Mlynarczyk (2010, 105–110) in their overview of the history of basic writing and especially in their commentary on one of the leading books that attempted to address students' reading needs, *Facts, Artifacts, and Counterfacts* by David Bartholomae and Anthony Petrosky (1986). This more theoretical book, along with a textbook by the same team, *Ways of Reading* (2008, 2020), directly addresses reading issues. The approaches to reading in key textbooks are discussed in detail in chapter 6. According to Otte and Mlynarczyk (2010, 108), *Facts* was specifically developed to guide the teaching of basic writing classes and intended to integrate reading and writing instruction. But there was also a strong call for more attention to reading, chiefly in a key article by Lynn Quitman Troyka (1987), who had been a leader in the field as a faculty member at Queensborough Community College and also as editor of the *Journal of Basic Writing* for a number of years.

When Troyka raised her voice about the importance of reading for basic writers, she made key points still relevant today. In her chapter, specifically commissioned for *A Sourcebook for Basic Writing Teachers* collection edited by University of Arizona rhetorician Theresa Enos (Troyka 1987), she argued strongly and specifically for much more attention to reading after reporting on a study of a national sample of basic writers' work. Troyka collected 109 papers from basic writers at two- and four-year institutions around the country, examining them for the writers' age and gender as well as for their skill level, as judged by their teachers and by an independent set of holistic readers. The findings lead Troyka to two key points. First, basic writers are a highly diverse group and thus need to be carefully described in presentations on and publications of research; generalizing about basic writers is thus probably inappropriate, given the range of variation in both demographics and abilities (9). Troyka's second point, highly pertinent for this book, is that basic writers, however defined, clearly need much more help with reading:

> Too long have most discussions of writing ignored reading. Too infrequently in our journals do we see essays that speak of reading as a complement to writing. Too often do we talk of "writing across the curriculum" when all college courses use complex textbooks that demand high skill in reading.
> Writing includes all language: speaking, listening, and reading. The student samples in this paper demonstrate that basic writers need to immerse themselves in language in all its forms. Unless people are at ease when speaking, unless they can rely on their minds' ears for disciplined listening, they cannot use important human resources when they write. Most important, in my view, is reading: Unless basic writers read widely, they will never learn to make reading from their writing. (12–13)

Troyka's findings and insights support many of the claims I have been making here, including the use of a language arts model for the role of reading in first-year writing as well as in the college curriculum more generally. But these points, raised in the 1980s, seem to have fallen by the wayside in the more than thirty years since her piece was published.

Troyka was writing from her own perspective as a faculty member at Queensborough Community College, one of seven two-year institutions that are part of the City University of New York. Community colleges are an important venue for reading instruction over time because they are often, but not always, open-admissions/open access institutions, accepting all who have a high school diploma or its equivalent; their policies have led me to the abbreviation TYCOA (two-year colleges and open access institutions) to capture their approach. These schools may have more than their share of students who might benefit from developmental coursework in writing, reading, and/or math. TYCOAs have been offering reading instruction for much of the time they have been in existence, which is more than fifty years.

There are essentially two reasons to pay attention to TYCOAs in looking at the history of reading instruction in relation to first-year writing. First, as Cohen and colleagues (scholars at the nonprofit Center for the Study of Community Colleges in Los Angeles) say in their detailed study of community colleges, these institutions are generally the ones "bearing the brunt of students' ill-preparedness" for postsecondary education (Cohen, Brawer, and Kisker 2014, ix), particularly in literacy skills. Second, though it is not possible to say exactly how much first-year writing is taught at TYCOAs compared to four-year schools, it is certainly correct to say that many students start their postsecondary work in these institutions; therefore, to gain a full picture of whether and how reading appears in first-year writing, it is essential to look at what is happening in community college classes as well as in four-year institutions.

In TYCOAs generally, not all students are placed in or advised to take developmental courses, but many are: "In a nationally representative sample of students who started at two-year public colleges in 2013–14, 60 percent took one or more remedial courses within three years. They took an average of 2.9 courses. That compares with 32 percent of four-year college students who took an average of two courses" (Community College Research Center 2022). While these numbers might be different following the pandemic, the data give some sense that community college students are more likely to need developmental work than those at four-year schools. These data points do not separate out whether the supplemental classes are in reading specifically or in English (including reading or not) or math. As is true elsewhere, it is difficult to find good data focused exclusively on reading. Moreover, the overall situation may be shifting in any number of ways in a post-pandemic world. A pre-pandemic study of integrated reading/writing courses by the Community College Research Center using programs from Virginia and North Carolina, however, showed a clear advantage in terms of student retention and degree completion resulting from the use of an integrated reading/writing course approach (Bickerstaff and Raufman 2017).

More recently, a 2019 report by the MDRC, a nonprofit social policy organization (mdrc.org) working together with the Community College Research Center, captures the changing situation in developmental education, based on its survey of the 2015–2016 school year: "The study data come from a survey disseminated to a nationally representative, random sample of 1,055 broad-access two-year and four-year colleges, universities, and postsecondary systems; and interviews with 127 college faculty, staff, administrators, and system leaders from 83 different two-year and four-year colleges, college systems, and state-level higher education governing bodies" (Rutschow et al. 2019, 4). This succinct summary of key issues does not focus exclusively on reading, as is true of many other studies and reports in this discussion, but it does give a clear picture of the situation that existed when the data were gathered:

> Research has suggested that far more students are referred to developmental education courses than necessary, and that developmental education

presents a monumental barrier to students' success. For instance, national reports have shown that up to 70 percent of entering college students are advised to take developmental courses before entering college-level classes. Additionally, research has shown that colleges' reliance on standardized tests to assess students' college readiness has resulted in many more students being placed into developmental education courses than is necessary—and that alternative information, such as high school performance, may more accurately predict college success. Furthermore, research indicates that the predominant mechanisms for delivering developmental education—multi-level, prerequisite developmental courses that can take multiple semesters or even years to complete—hinder students' progress, and large proportions of students fail to make it through these courses. As a result, practitioners and researchers have been experimenting with multiple ways to revise developmental education, with many practices showing promise for improving students' success. (1)

The MDRC, which works in cooperation with the federal government, has been looking at changes in developmental approaches in light of these findings; with respect to reading and writing, it has found several key differences in approaches some schools have put in place.

First, while most colleges and universities still use standardized tests for admission and placement, more are using high school grades and other indicators of students' ability levels at entry. Most places, especially community colleges, have multiple prerequisite courses or course sequences, usually offering no college credit. Fewer than half, even of community colleges, are experimenting with alternative approaches to developmental instruction—including more support services, integrated reading/writing courses, supplemental instruction, or compressed courses. Finally, developmental courses are much less common at four-year than at two-year schools (Rutschow et al. 2019, 4–10). Again, it is essential to keep in mind two features of these points and the other studies reported here: almost all are of pre-pandemic situations that will surely be different as the country recovers from the effects of shutdowns, online courses, and so forth. Second, the reports generally do not offer data specifically about reading courses or integrated reading/writing approaches, and few studies give specific data on reading problems among ELLs.

A different resource in this area is the *Handbook of College Reading and Study Strategy Research*, a compilation of work in the area of developmental courses and other kinds of programs for students with specific needs in reading.

The book appeared in a third edition in 2018, which suggests that it serves as a useful, albeit somewhat dated, resource on research in this area. At the same time, it does not include any of the work of Peter Adams—a key teacher and researcher on integrated reading and writing—or of scholars like Lynn Quitman Troyka, Patrick Sullivan, Joanne Baird Giordano, and Holly Hassel, though it does offer passing mention of Gregory R. Glau's "stretch" program at Arizona State University (Armstrong, Williams, and Stahl 2018, 146). The book offers chapters devoted to key areas of reading ability, such as vocabulary and comprehension. Of special interest to the current discussion is the chapter on reading and writing. Despite its exclusion of Adams's ALP, the chapter includes discussion of similar programs at the University of Pittsburgh, San Francisco State University, and Chabot College, a community college near San Francisco (143–167).

Based on their review of a small set of programs, Sonya L. Armstrong and colleagues focus on three kinds of knowledge essential to building a successful integrated reading/writing program. First is theoretical knowledge, or knowledge about theories of the connections between reading and writing based on the work of Timothy Shanahan and other reading scholars—such as the shared-cognition model, the sociocognitive model, and the combined use or tool view. A second kind of knowledge is content knowledge, including background in writing studies, developmental writing, and developmental reading, as well as subject-area knowledge if courses are based on substantive topics. A third necessary knowledge area is curriculum and pedagogy, or how to develop and deliver courses for students. Faculty also need to be able to use technology, especially because so much instruction has been moved to remote platforms and management systems as a result of the pandemic. And, of course, plans are needed for assessment and evaluation. The authors end with a plea for focused research to form the basis of programs for these kinds of courses. The model I am developing throughout this book addresses many of these points.

### *The Bay Area Writing Project/National Writing Project and the Common Core: K–12 Integration with Postsecondary Writing*

Eight years after the Dartmouth meeting, the now well-known and respected National Writing Project (NWP) began in San Francisco. A review of the NWP website finds this quick description in addition to the following history of its development from its origins as the Bay Area Writing Project:

> Unique in breadth and scale, the NWP is a network of sites anchored at colleges and universities and serving teachers across disciplines and at all levels, early childhood through university. We provide professional development, develop resources, generate research, and act on knowledge to improve the teaching of writing and learning in schools and communities. (National Writing Project 2022)
>
> [History] NWP began in 1974 in the Graduate School of Education at the University of California, Berkeley, where James Gray and his colleagues established a university-based program for K–16 teachers called the Bay Area Writing Project (BAWP) . . .
>
> In partnership with Bay Area school districts, BAWP created a range of professional development services for teachers and schools interested in improving the teaching of writing and the use of writing as a learning tool across the curriculum. The structure of this first writing project site's programs formed the basis of NWP's "teachers-teaching-teachers" model of professional development.
>
> Today, with its core grant from the U.S. Department of Education, supplemented by local, state, and private funds, the NWP comprises nearly 200 sites in all 50 states, the District of Columbia, Puerto Rico, and the U.S. Virgin Islands. (History of NWP 2022)

But a look at resources on reading currently on the site shows that most of the work is about ten years old; almost all of the books and articles address K–12 reading issues in some form. A search in Google Scholar similarly does not show the NWP paying any focused attention to critical reading.

The NWP, however, is still very much a functioning organization across the US, and it played an important sponsoring role in the development of a collaborative document titled the *Framework for Success in Postsecondary Writing* (2011). That document, created by the NWP together with the National Council of Teachers of English (NCTE) and the Council of Writing Program Administrators (CWPA), sets out the skills and "habits of mind" students need to build expertise in writing for college and beyond (2011). Among the skills are two that address critical reading: "Rhetorical knowledge—the ability to analyze and act on understandings of audiences, purposes, and contexts in creating and comprehending texts; Critical thinking—the ability to analyze a situation or text and make thoughtful decisions based on that analysis, through writing, reading, and research" (Council of Writing Program Administrators et al. 2011, 1). Building on this document, a later edited collection included chapters by University of Connecticut rhetorician and reading scholar Ellen C. Carillo and me about the need for more focused work on reading (Carillo and Horning 2021b; Horning 2017). We both saw the need for the *Framework* document to focus more explicitly on reading. Two key points here, though. First, the NWP did contribute to this document, which pays some attention to reading, albeit not explicitly so. Second, this document shows that three leading organizations in the field were paying at least passing attention to the reading situation of first-year writers, however indirect.

An additional venue in which reading receives some attention is a different approach to integration of K–12 education and postsecondary teaching and learning through the Common Core State Standards (CCSS) project, discussed in chapter 2. So, it isn't fair to say no one was or is paying any attention to reading. It also isn't fair to say that first-year college writing teachers can blame the high schools or K–12 education in general for students' inability to read critically and effectively. Both the NWP and the CCSS have paid attention to and tried to address students' reading. But these efforts have been largely indirect, as in the case of the NWP's contribution to the *Framework* document, or not as effective as they might have been, as the result of controversies of various kinds in the case of the CCSS. Similar observations of inconsistencies appear in an extended historical survey conducted for the Center for the Study of Writing at the University of California at Berkeley by history of education scholar Geraldine Joncich Clifford (1987). Clifford shows that over time, US public education has gone back and forth on the issue of integrating reading and writing instruction. The Dartmouth meeting, the efforts of the NWP and CCSS, and other programs and approaches all reflect the absence of consistent attention to reading, whether integrated with writing or not.

### *Programs Focused on Reading: Hooked on Books and Great Books*

Around the same time as the original Dartmouth Seminar in 1966, several other programs arose to focus on reading in response to an assortment of task forces, study groups, and national reports. In his history of the field, State University of New York at Albany education scholar Arthur N. Applebee (1974) mentions the *Hooked on Books* program developed by Daniel N. Fader at the University of Michigan (Fader and Shaevitz 1966). Originally, the program was designed for students at the Maxey Boys' Training School in Whitmore Lake, near Ann Arbor. Maxey was a juvenile detention facility for boys who were in trouble with the law. The object of the program was to offer a wide range of materials for the teenage boys to read that had high interest and relevance for them. Its success—which, according to both Applebee (1974, 228) and Fader himself (Fader and McNeil 1966), spread to many other states—demonstrates that interest motivates reading in ways no requirement or reward can. This program, along with the Great Books idea, demonstrates in a different way that attention was being paid to reading for teens and young adults beyond college writing classrooms, but it was not attention to the kind of sophisticated critical reading needed by everyone, then and now.

While not a college reading/writing program, *Hooked on Books* does illustrate several pertinent points about reading and literacy instruction in the educational landscape writ large. Fader's books suggest that high-interest materials could attract teens, especially boys, to reading. In his work at the Maxey School, Fader focused not just on extensive reading, although that was a big part of the program, but on developing limited, critical reading skills through work on such texts as *Diary of Anne Frank* and *West Side Story*. Some of the sample lesson plans ask critical questions about Anne Frank that develop students' ability to reach beyond plot summary, such as "Why does Anne's diary symbolize 'the triumph of the human spirit'?" and "In the Introduction, Eleanor Roosevelt said, 'War's greatest evil is the degradation of the human spirit.' In your own words, tell what you think this statement means" (Fader and McNeil 1966, 129). Various kinds of tests of literacy of the boys in the program—including measures of vocabulary, verbal proficiency, and so forth (215–226)—along with teachers' subjective evaluations, show substantial growth in students' literacy. Although Applebee (1974, 241) claimed that the evidence of the program's success with a group of challenging students was "weak" and could be largely accounted for by teacher enthusiasm, it demonstrates that there was focused interest in and successful work on reading for students often thought of as "reluctant" readers.

A more mixed outcome, in college writing classes and elsewhere in university programs, could be claimed for the Great Books program. In his doctoral dissertation at Loyola University Chicago, Tim Lacy (2006) traces the history of the Great Books idea, started in the 1920s and 1930s at Columbia and at the University of Chicago. It's important to keep in mind that the Great Books lists and sets of books published by Encyclopedia Britannica did not ensure that students or anyone else involved was actually reading the books or even that they could do so; it's also easy to see the concept as a spin-off from the uniform lists issued earlier by Harvard University. Lacy notes that the Great

Books idea became popular around the turn of the twentieth century (49) as a by-product of people working less, resulting in greater availability of leisure time in which to read. Related trends were the expansion of libraries, fostered to some degree by the Carnegie funding of buildings and collection development, which I have discussed elsewhere, along with a general but widespread interest in self-improvement that also gave rise to the Chautauqua program nationwide (Horning 2018, 94–96). Lacy (2006, 53–56) points to increasing levels of schooling and literacy ability as other factors. Libraries also offered lists for readers who wanted to guidance on what to read, but it was the universities that adopted the Great Books idea most substantively, albeit briefly: the University of Chicago, Harvard, Berkeley, and in due course, other universities (59–69).

Building on Lacy's and other dissertation studies, journalist Alex Beam (2008) presented a fairly comprehensive history of the Great Books idea and the college programs that drew on or integrated it. Although the idea had been around for some time, as Lacy (2006, 1) pointed out, the real push came with the publication of sets of volumes launched by Britannica in 1952. Long before, the idea had been presented and adopted at the University of Chicago; at Columbia University; at a small private school, St. John's College, at its two campuses in Annapolis, Maryland, and Santa Fe, New Mexico (St. John's Reading List 2022); and in the Core Curriculum offered at Boston University (Core Curriculum n.d.). There were two parts to the program: the college part and the part that served as the basis for adult education courses, library discussions, and book groups (Lacy 2006, 19).

Robert Hutchins, who became president of the University of Chicago, was a prime supporter, along with Mortimer J. Adler, a friend and fellow scholar and teacher. The program was briefly wildly popular in adult education classes (Beam 2008, 62), as well as at Chicago and subsequently at Columbia and elsewhere. But by the time the Britannica sets appeared, the idea was already diminishing in most places—except at St. John's College (where it persists as of this writing), to which Beam devotes a full chapter (165–180), and in antecedent forms in general education or "core curriculum" approaches, as mentioned earlier. While these forms persist in reading groups and weekend seminars according to Beam, who attended some of the seminars (181–190), they have largely lost out to other kinds of pastimes and the internet. Beam points out, however, that the idea of common readings persists in other forms, such as Oprah's Book Club and the Great Courses audio and video recordings and similar activities, only some of which are focused on reading per se. And the political division in the country at large limits the possibilities for open discussion of differing points of view. So, the concept and its offshoots survive in a few ways, but one piece of its legacy does focus directly on reading per se: the popular *How to Read a Book*.

More than twenty years before the Dartmouth Seminar, in 1940, Adler published his *How to Read a Book*. It was reprinted years later in a revised and updated edition with Charles Van Doren (Adler and Van Doren 1972). The book was addressed to a general audience but contained specific rules for reading the Great Books list. The book built on the Great Books idea and list. The list was meant to capture the great ideas of Western civilization and culture, and Adler's book gave instructions for how to read the various works. There are numerous problems with both the list and Adler's reading guidance, though, chiefly concerning the fact that the list (in its many and varied forms) lacks attention to newer authors, to authors from diverse backgrounds, and to an array of different points of view. Without attending them, it is hard to assess how much critical reading is taught in any of these programs. However, Adler's book is a great resource, and he does point directly to the essentials of critical reading.

Adler advises multiple stages of reading, but the core is "analytical reading," which begins with a thorough understanding of the content of a book and the structure of the argument presented. He then focuses on the importance of recognizing the difference between when the author is offering information and when what appears is personal opinion. Then comes this list: "Show wherein the author is uninformed. Show wherein the author is misinformed. Show wherein the author is illogical. Show wherein the author's analysis or account is incomplete" (Adler and Van Doren 1972, 164). Adler goes on to say that readers should be asking two key questions: is the information presented true, and if it is, so what (165)? Beyond these questions, he acknowledges that most people won't read every book or even many books using this kind of critical evaluation, but stronger readers will attempt to get close to this level of critical reading in at least some of the books they read. Iowa State University history of rhetoric scholar David R. Russell (1991, 190–198) points out that the Hutchins/Adler approach included what today is called a "writing to learn" strategy. Readers did some writing (albeit not a lot) to facilitate their ability to summarize, analyze, and synthesize reading from the Great Books.

The Great Books program played a direct role in some courses and influenced curricula at the college level, while Fader's program focused on younger students, as it was developed for use in a high school for troubled boys. Fader was working in the background in the same period in which the Dartmouth Seminar occurred (late 1960s and early 1970s), and his program was one element in the larger landscape of reading in the early years of the second period in the history of writing studies. Neither Hooked on Books nor the Great Books program had a huge impact on college reading and writing. For Great Books, the Great Depression and World War II limited the spread of the program directly to other institutions; in the postwar period, the influx of returning soldiers had vastly different needs and backgrounds than did the University of Chicago students who first encountered Hutchins's Great Books (Beam 2008, 42–59). These programs do show that there was interest in and concern about reading, accompanied by specific approaches to, support for, and activity around developing reading skills among the population in general and among students in particular—albeit not necessarily in postsecondary English classes.

## *Writing Studies Today and the Absence of Reading*

My goal in this chapter has been to discuss developments in the field of writing studies that bear on reading, from the Dartmouth Seminar to the present day, as well as various other programs that address reading issues. It should be clear that interest in and work on postsecondary reading per se is limited in terms of producing useful data derived from controlled research studies of representative samples of students. Work on reading in K–12 education is conducted by the Institute of Education Sciences (IES), the research branch of the United States Department of Education, but it does not examine postsecondary reading issues. A second notable exception is the ongoing work of the Stanford History Education Group, discussed in detail in chapter 1. The Stanford studies generally include middle, high school, and postsecondary students. Overall, though, postsecondary teaching and learning of critical reading gets attention here and there, now and then, willy-nilly. Moreover, limited empirical research exists on either the state of college students' reading abilities or on what approaches make sense and might make a difference to address their needs, with the notable exception of the third edition of Rona F. Flippo and Thomas W. Bean's *Handbook of College Reading and Study Strategy Research* (2018), which compiles pertinent studies.

It is essential to read this work carefully, as some of it draws inferences from standardized tests that may offer results that over- or under-represent concepts or populations; it also draws from ongoing projects with specific groups that cannot be generalized because of sample sizes or other research-related issues. The issue of fairness in testing of all kinds is an essential consideration, as is made clear in a detailed exploration of the concept of fairness and its implications as well as its history by University of Massachusetts assessment scholars Stephen G. Sireci and Jennifer Randall (2022). A further cautionary point is that many of the studies in the *Handbook* are focused on reading per se, not on how reading is handled in first-year writing classes. As I have noted throughout this book, reading is a deeply contextualized activity, and generalizations or inferences across groups of students at different places in their educational journeys are difficult to make. A look at the current situation with respect to reading in first-year writing offers three issues that warrant careful consideration.

First, a study of work on reading appearing at the main conferences in writing studies and in the field's major professional journals shows that these venues pay little attention to reading. Second, a study of a small sample of graduate programs in writing studies that are preparing faculty to teach writing shows that they provide virtually no training and preparation for teaching reading, consistent with Carillo's findings (2015) that most faculty feel unprepared to teach reading. Finally, the Reading Squad, as I have come to think of the small network of professionals working on reading at two-year and four-year schools, is extremely small; we have found minimal support for our efforts despite apparent interest in and concern for reading based on attendance at reading-focused sessions at the CCCC, submissions to special journal issues, and calls for papers for recent books.

## READING AT THE CONFERENCES

In this section, I am building on my earlier study that appeared in Ellen C. Carillo's collection on the work of Robert Scholes (Horning 2021b), as well as earlier work of my own and others. The following are a few condensed updates to the work reported in 2021. I have searched the conference programs of the major conference in writing studies (i.e., CCCC) and the tables of contents of the five major journals in the field: *College Composition and Communication, College English, Research in the Teaching of English, Teaching English in the Two-Year College,* and *WPA: Writing Program Administration.* The more recent data are through the period of the pandemic when CCCC was twice held virtually; that format surely had some impact on the number of sessions and range of possible topics.

To pick up more or less where the previous study ended (with 2018), I went back (from the time of writing in late 2021) three years for the conference and the same for the journals, so this includes 2019, 2020, and 2021. I used the search terms *reading* and *literacy*. The approach is admittedly generic, but the results are clear-cut. When I searched the conference program, current terminology immediately became an important issue. Reading, in the critical reading sense of this book, appears here and there, often in sessions in which I presented. But literacy is used many different ways, often in a phrase with another word and not always defined—academic, critical, digital, information literacy—and the program text was not particularly helpful. Using *literacy* as the search term thus may give misleading results. Also, there is overlap in the way the sessions are titled and categorized, so I tried to avoid double counting. However, the overall point remains the same: the numbers of sessions that addressed critical reading and literacy are tiny, even if some are double counted. Reading and literacy are not absent, that is, not ignored; it is simply that the attention to these areas is minimal relative to the program as a whole. Also, keep in mind that 2019 was the last year of a traditional CCCC meeting prior to the pandemic; it was face-to-face without restrictions, masks, or efforts to make the conference hybrid in some way. Both 2020 and 2021 were entirely virtual, surely impacting the total number of sessions and other matters. Table 5.1 captures the results. The percentage for 2019 does not include the posters or Special Interest Group sessions, but even with those added, the attention to reading, it should be clear, is minimal.

**TABLE 5.1. CCCC sessions with presentations on reading or literacy**

| Year | "Reading" | "Literacy" | Total R or L | Total Sessions | Percent R/L |
|---|---|---|---|---|---|
| 2019 | 6 | 8 | 14 | 614 | 2 |
| 2020 | 15 | 26 | 41 | 643 | 6 |
| 2021 | 7 | 15 | 22 | 289 | 6 |

In 2020, the meeting was entirely virtual, assembled with the challenges of the pandemic and on relatively short notice. The original plan was to be in-person in Milwaukee that year, so the number of sessions was a little larger than usual (643). Again, the posters (three) and Special Interest Group (SIG) sessions (two) were not included in this count. Here again, there is not a complete absence of attention to reading or literacy, but that attention is minimal.

In 2021, CCCC was planned in advance as a virtual meeting, and it was much smaller than the in-person meetings typically are, with a mix of live online sessions and pre-recorded sessions. Here again, there was one poster presentation, one workshop focused specifically on reading in first-year composition, and a SIG that was held outside of the convention time window.

I did also study the Council of Writing Program Administrators' meeting, which was held in person in 2019 in Baltimore, Maryland, and then cancelled for 2020 and 2021. In 2019, there were only two sessions where reading was mentioned and three with literacy in the title, all focused on information literacy.

## READING IN THE JOURNALS

It's easy to think that even though reading gets little attention at the conferences, where space on the program has always been very competitive and recently has been even more so due to the need for the meetings to be virtual during the pandemic. But the five major journals in the field have continued to publish through these years at consistent levels, that is, similar numbers of issues with similar numbers of articles per issue. Again, picking up from my previous study (2021b), I reviewed three years (2019, 2020, and 2021) of the five major professional journals in the field. The first four—*College Composition and Communication* (*CCC*), *College English* (*CE*), *Teaching English in the Two-Year College* (*TETYC*), and *Research in the Teaching of English* (*RTE*)—are regular NCTE publications. The fifth of the journals, *WPA: Writing Program Administration*, is the publication of the Council of Writing Program Administrators, which is independent of the NCTE. Here again, the *WPA* can be dealt with easily, since a review of its three issues per year for 2019, 2020, and 2021 shows that no articles mentioned reading or literacy in their titles (table 5.2).

TABLE 5.2. Journal articles 2019–2021 with reading or literacy in the title

| Journal | "Reading" | "Literacy" | Total R or L | Total Articles | Percent R/L |
|---|---|---|---|---|---|
| CCC | 0 | 2 | 2 | 44 | 5 |
| CE | 2 | 9 | 11 | 59 | 19 |
| TETYC | 5 | 0 | 5 | 43 | 12 |
| RTE | 2 | 10 | 12 | 39 | 31 |

Note: The *RTE* publishes research on K–16 English language arts education, but very little of it pertains to first-year writing.

In the case of the *RTE*, its focus is on K–16 research—that is, including research conducted at the college level—but it pays no specific attention to college-level writing or first-year composition. The picture in the journals, then, is clear, even allowing for this approach being broad, as it only takes a very rough count using two key words. Still, very small percentages of the articles in all the major journals in the field put together appear to address reading or literacy. While other journals do attend to reading more directly, such as *READER* and the International Literacy Association's *Journal of Adolescent and Adult Literacy* and *Reading Research Quarterly*, they are not the primary journals in the field of writing studies.

## Preparing Writing Teachers to Help with Reading

My earlier study (2021b) included a review of a sample of about a third of all the PhD programs in writing studies in the US, looking for required or recommended coursework in reading theory or pedagogy. I used the CCCC Doctoral Consortium website to access a list of all the programs and randomly chose every third program to check. I looked at the program's website or catalog to study the requirements and courses. I found that no program required PhD candidates in writing studies to take any coursework in reading, either within the program or in a related department (such as psychology) or the School of Education. Some programs had space for electives but no list of recommended courses pointing to reading. Some programs had courses with "literacy" in the title, but they were typically courses in the history of literacy, not in critical reading. I hope to do a follow-up study soon that will be a comprehensive review of every program on the CCCC Doctoral Consortium list. However, I expect the outcome to be the same.

It should be clear that doctoral programs are not preparing teachers of writing to help students become efficient and effective critical readers of texts of all kinds. According to Carillo (2015), most practicing teachers are aware of this lack of preparation to work with students on reading; they consistently report not knowing enough to address reading issues in teaching their classes. A close look at writing faculty members' reflections on their writing, as reported by Bowling Green University rhetorician Christine E. Tulley (2018), likewise shows virtually no attention to reading in their professional work. Her interviews with fifteen well-known writing studies faculty members do not mention reading in any substantive way, so even when faculty are asked directly about reading in their teaching or in their own work, they are paying little or no attention to it.

## Who Will Help Students Become Better Readers?

What happens when writing studies faculty get into postsecondary classrooms and confront students' reading difficulties? I can't speak for all other faculty, but I can recount my own experience confronting this issue. I was teaching the first term of a first-year two-course writing sequence. I had become so frustrated with students' reading problems that I had taken to requiring students in all my classes—writing, linguistics, or whatever—to read two complete books and to write about them in enough detail so I could be certain they had actually read them. They also needed to address the critical criteria of authority, accuracy, currency, relevance, appropriateness, and bias. I did not intend to discuss the books directly in class in most cases, but students often brought them into class discussion, which thrilled me. My idea was that they simply needed much more practice in reading extended nonfiction prose.

In the first-year class, I assigned *The Shallows* (Carr 2020) and did use it as a springboard for class discussion and some writing. The first chapter discussion was a little slow, but it was only week 2 or 3 of the term. Class discussion of the second chapter was flat. Students reported that they found the writing, which I thought was lively and accessible, very challenging. I sent them off to reread the chapter and asked that they mark three words on each page that they did not understand, on the theory that perhaps the vocabulary was a barrier. At the next class, they told me the words they had marked. I put them on the board and was astonished. One student would call out a word, and several others would say they had also marked it. Words like *garret* and *metaphysical* I could see as problems, but when they noted words like *mainstream*, *heretic*, and *apparatus*, I was stunned. I wondered, silently, how they had reached college without knowing words of this kind.

Thereafter, I worked with them more closely on vocabulary, brought in lessons on word roots and meanings, helped them learn to use a printed dictionary appropriately rather than leaning on a quick check of dictionary.com on their phones, and did other kinds of exercises to address their needs. But I'm a linguist with expertise in reading, so turning to lexicographic pedagogies came naturally to me as a way to engage students; there are, of course, other ways to help students with these needs. Students' reading troubles persist when faculty lack the preparation to teach them the critical literacy skills they need for success in college and beyond. This situation is clear in the conferences and journals, in the coursework for writing studies PhDs, and in the small community of writing studies scholars and teachers who are paying attention to reading.

## Looking Back and Looking Ahead

This chapter's foray into the history of writing studies as a field in the last fifty-plus years shows the way reading has been lost and found. It isn't fair to say that reading has been ignored, since there has been *some* attention to it here and there. While reading wasn't central to the discussion at Dartmouth in 1966, the scholars there and thereafter were certainly thinking about students reading literature. The arguments made famous by Erika Lindemann and Gary Tate about literature and composition consider reading in a de facto way because those on the literature side were, after all, in favor of students reading literature, notably including Rosenblatt and other reader-response theorists. The critical literacy scholars following Freire were also strong advocates for reading in a social and political context, but neither of these groups of scholars had a sustained impact on writing studies.

The work of the National Writing Project and the Common Core, at different times, also addressed reading; it is particularly noteworthy (though a source of much of the pushback against it) that the Common Core directly addressed the need to teach students to read nonfiction and informational texts of many kinds. In other areas discussed here, such as the Great Books program, a direct effort was made to support and encourage reading. So, it isn't the case that no one was doing anything about reading. However, looking at the last few years of the major conferences and journals, even with challenges resulting from the pandemic, it's clear that a focus on working directly to improve students' critical reading has been extremely limited. The result is that little evidence-based pedagogy based on sound principles exists that instructors might use to help students become effective and efficient critical readers. In chapter 7, an array of such pedagogy will help faculty in writing studies and beyond work confidently on students' abilities. Before moving to these useful approaches, one last piece of a wide view of the field comes from a look at its textbooks, the subject of chapter 6.

PART 3

# Making the Case for Critical Literacy

*What Writing Studies Can/Should/Must Do for Students Now*

More so now than ever, in the face of uncertain shifts in teaching, students, higher education, and everything else, practicing faculty want to know what to do on Monday. How, in the current environment, can we best help students become effective and efficient critically literate participants in school and beyond in their personal and professional lives? How can we prepare students to become fully functional citizens in our society and our government? What tools and techniques are available to assist in this work? Some answers to these questions are discussed in the last two chapters of this book. Chapter 6 examines textbooks and other tools for teaching reading and writing. In many ways, textbooks and online resources reflect the status of the field, a point made by history of science scholar Thomas S. Kuhn (1966) in his careful exploration of the nature of scientific revolutions. By reviewing some of the key textbooks in the field over time, the view of reading at various points comes into sharper focus. Finally, in chapter 7, a more complete model of critical literacy is offered for discussion and review; it provides the basis for a proposed set of classroom strategies for teaching critical literacy in first-year writing and beyond. Figure 6.0 presents a preview of the full model.

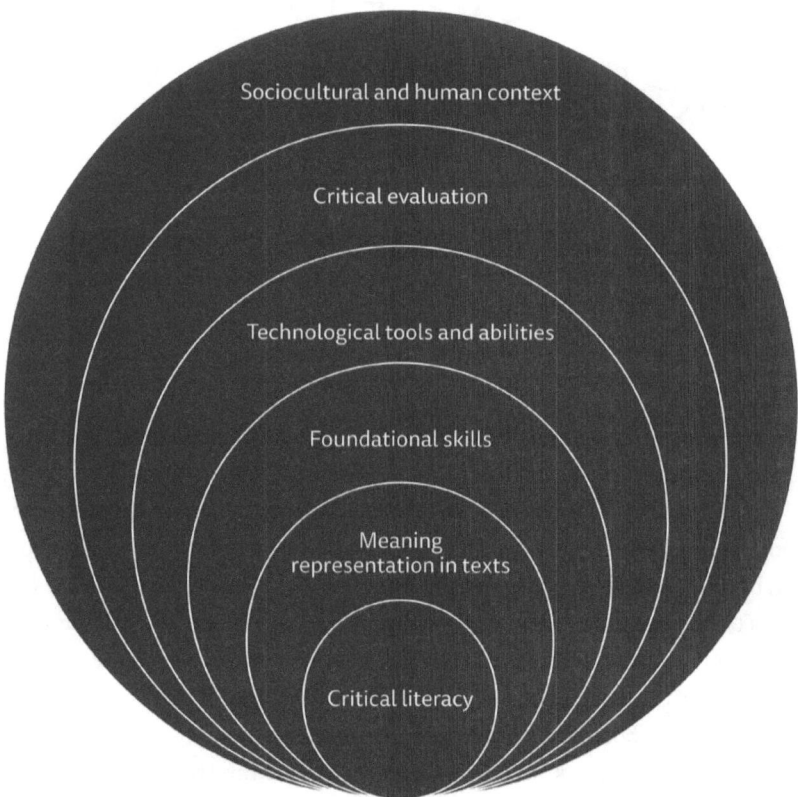

**FIGURE 6.0.** The complete model revisited

# 6
## Textbooks, Digital Tools, and Reading

I am an amateur science buff, probably because if I had received better instruction in math and science throughout my schooling, I would have been well suited to a career in science, given my personality and preference for hands-on activities. When I had my first introduction to linguistics as a field in conjunction with my graduate teaching assistantship in English as a Second Language (ESL), I really took to it. Subsequent linguistics courses introduced me to *The Structure of Scientific Revolutions* (Kuhn 1996) as applied to the development of linguistics as a field of study, and it made sense to me. Thomas S. Kuhn's analytical framework attracted a great deal of attention among scientists and elsewhere, including among those in writing studies (cf. Maxine Hairston's [1982] often-cited article). While the overall analytic scheme is not directly relevant here, one point Kuhn makes is pertinent to the present chapter, concerning the role of textbooks in a field.

Kuhn makes clear that textbooks generally capture the state of "normal science" at the time they are written, and they must be rewritten after a revolution takes place. Calling textbooks "pedagogic vehicles for the perpetuation of normal science," Kuhn (1996) insists that they "have to be rewritten in whole or part whenever the language, problem-structure, or standards of normal science change" (137). Moreover, Kuhn goes on to say that the sense of historical perspective that scientists or others might gain from textbooks reflects a lack of awareness of the full history of the discipline: "Unless he has personally experienced a revolution in his own lifetime, the historical sense either of the working scientist or of the lay reader of textbook literature extends only to the outcome of the most recent revolutions in the field" (137). It might be fair, then, to say that textbooks provide a kind of snapshot of where a field is at the time of their publication, that is, "normal science" in Kuhn's terms. This view is essentially the same one Lynn Z. Bloom (1999) takes in her study of the essay canon discussed below, which entails a detailed review of a sampling of first-year composition readers published between 1946 and 1996.

If we accept Kuhn's point (keeping in mind that many aspects of his views were and still are matters of controversy), then there's good reason to look at the history of textbooks in writing studies to see how reading has been treated as "normal science," that is, the general, prevailing status quo. By looking at one text from the early days of the field (Genung 1902), several from the field over time, and four more contemporary approaches with varying degrees of success and popularity (Bartholomae and Petrosky 2008; Parfitt 2016; Harkin 1999; Eastman et al. 1965; Goldthwaite et al. 2020a), the treatment of reading at various points of "normal science" is easy to see. To begin, a look back to a late edition of a very early textbook by prolific rhetorician John F. Genung offers one such snapshot from its publication in 1902. Then as now, Genung's rhetoric texts appeared in multiple editions, some with examples and some without; but then and now, publishers did not issue multiple editions in the absence of demand. An early edition of Genung's book appeared in 1886 (discussed in Horning 2018), with essentially the same content on reading still appearing in the 1902 edition. The book thus gives a sense of the "normal science" about reading at the time, little changed from earlier to later editions.

Before taking up Genung's book as a starting point, the context in which he was writing and teaching is important to keep in mind. A set of federal government statistics provides a good look at students of all kinds based on census data beginning in 1880 (Snyder 1993). This compilation of data shows that the number of colleges and universities was much smaller than it is now. The number of students attending was likewise much smaller, and the students represented a much more elite population. One key to college admission and success was knowledge of Greek, as coursework required Greek and sometimes Latin as well. The population of students who might have used any of Genung's books, then, was a small, elite, and already well-educated group, almost surely mostly white; even at that, they still had difficulty with various parts of the Harvard entrance exams, as carefully explored by writing studies history scholar John C. Brereton (2012). At the same time, some students had trouble with the writing exam; it was not much of a test of their reading ability, as Brereton shows from the test questions that ask for little critical reading or analysis (32–33). So, it is easy to see why Genung's discussion of reading was limited, to say the least, although he does pay attention to reading in a specific and focused way that warrants exploration.

At the outset, it is important to note about this early textbook and all the others in this discussion that they assume that students have the foundational skills sketched in my model: they can grasp the main ideas and details of a text and so forth. However, as reflected in the results on various measures reported in chapter 1, perhaps half or more of current students may lack even those foundational skills. One result of the neglect of students' need for help with foundational skills is their inability to apply critical criteria to all kinds of materials they work with in school assignments. The needs in both areas require attention from writing studies, from librarians helping students with research projects, and from faculty in every discipline. Because good evidence-based research supports teaching techniques to address these needs, to be discussed in chapter 7, every faculty member can work to help students become more efficient and effective critical readers. The textbooks offer a mixed bag of approaches to these needs.

In the newer (1902) edition of Genung's popular book, he devotes 9 pages (of the almost 400 pages in the book) explicitly to "Habits of Reading" as a tool for invention in writing. As in the earlier versions, Genung points to four kinds of reading students might do, starting with disciplinary reading. Disciplinary reading is in-depth and thorough, and it possibly requires more than one pass; it is intended to be done sparingly, for masterpieces. Genung says this kind of reading should be done in preparation for "literary tasks" (239). A second kind of reading is rapid, meant for conducting a general survey for the purpose of getting information from texts. Reading by topics is a third kind of reading; it entails reading a book by parts to get "cardinal points" (241) through the table of contents, a list of chapter topics, the preface, and so forth. Students are advised to take notes in this third kind of reading using a commonplace book or scrapbook. Finally, a fourth approach is broad and deep reading beyond immediate needs to provide a clear context for material that has been found and will be used in writing, as well as serving as preparation for later projects. A survey of the rest of the book shows no other discussion of reading. While these types of reading at least give students guidance to vary their reading for different purposes and make clear that reading plays an important role in writing, Genung offers little help for struggling readers, those who have limited experience with a range of types of texts, or those who cannot manage complex vocabulary. He also does not prepare readers specifically for analysis or synthesis. No instructor manual accompanies Genung's book or others of the time that I am aware of; such manuals might have given faculty guidance on how to help students develop these kinds of skills.

These points are hardly surprising given that most of the elite students using Genung's books probably had little trouble with reading. The picture, it should be clear, is mixed: well-educated students might not need much help, but Genung does provide some guidance, albeit not guidance on critical reading as discussed in this book. Here again, as in the previous chapters, it is important to note that reading is not completely ignored. In fact, a section in Genung's book provides students with advice on how to read in support of invention in writing. And perhaps it is unfair to criticize Genung based on current standards, expectations, and needs rather than on those of his time. At the same time, it's easy to see both that this discussion offers a rather minimal set of guidelines for reading and that these few pages show how reading was presented in writing classes at the time, a statement of the "normal science" of teaching writing. Finally, Genung's books appeared years before Edmund B. Huey's (1908) groundbreaking research on the psychology of reading that would provoke a "revolution" (in Kuhn's terms) in the understanding of the nature of the reading process.

This last point suggests that textbooks on writing might have approached reading somewhat differently following the appearance of Huey's work in 1908. But the examples of early "Textbooks for a New Discipline," compiled by Brereton (1995), suggest that Huey's work had little impact on the way reading was presented and used in textbooks for writing courses. The samples Brereton presents begin with one published before English A was instituted at Harvard University in 1875, include Genung's first edition of *Practical Elements* in 1885 and an assortment of others, ending with six readers of various kinds and other texts on writing per se such as Strunk's *Elements of Style* from 1918 or 1919. What the readers (i.e., collections of essays and articles of various kinds) in Brereton's compilation suggest, though, is that students were to read the included pieces as models to be followed in their own writing.

The use of models was a very old idea that had been in field since English A and persisted as part of the general approach to first-year writing in composition and literature courses, discussed in chapter 5. Students like me in the late 1960s read literature in freshman English, along with literary criticism, and then wrote critical papers using the criticism we read as a model for what to do and how to do it. Catherine Hobbs from the University of Oklahoma and James Berlin at Purdue University (271–272) observe that the impact of research in cognitive psychology drove a shift to a process view of writing and a resulting shift to teaching students about drafting, revising, and using feedback through peer review, among other strategies. This shift happened alongside the changes proposed following the Dartmouth meeting in 1966.

A number of other theories and approaches followed, coalescing in the 1970s and 1980s into three main paradigms, according to Hobbs and Berlin (2001, 280–289): cognitive rhetoric, as seen in the work of Linda Flower, John Hayes, Sondra Perl, and Nancy Sommers, among others; expressivist views, found in the work of Donald Murray, Peter Elbow, and Ken Macrorie; and social constructionist approaches that appeared in the work of Lisa Ede, Andrea Lunsford, Kenneth Bruffee, and Charles Bazerman. Since then, concerns about literacy, broadly defined, have competed with linguistic issues, with the growing demand over time for social justice everywhere in education and society at large, and with the huge shift—especially recently—to the use of an array of technology for reading and writing, all of which have had an impact on the field and resulted in changes to textbooks. However, while changes in readers like the *Norton Reader* reflect diverse voices and differing approaches to writing, there is surprisingly relatively little change in the very limited attention given to reading in writing studies. A great deal of attention is given to reading in education, psychology, and other disciplines, just not in writing studies. As elsewhere, it is not that there's *no* attention to reading in writing studies, but it is limited, somewhat random, and not focused on the kinds of critical literacy skills students need in and beyond school and as full participants in a democracy.

From educational psychology, where there has been more of a focus on reading/literacy, comes an array of different paradigms or approaches recently integrated specifically with writing and speaking. These paradigms have been reviewed by University of Maryland educational psychologists Patricia A. Alexander and Emily Fox (2018) in a historical survey chapter in *Theoretical Models and Processes of Literacy*, a landmark periodic compilation of reading and literacy theory and practice across all educational levels. Their historical review begins with the founding of what is now the International Literacy Association in 1956; its name change points to a useful view of reading as one of the language arts areas along with writing and speaking, so that *literacy* becomes a more appropriate term (2018). While their discussion focuses to some degree on early reading, their generic overview of eras of research reveals the key paradigms over time. Their earliest paradigm starts with behaviorism, drawing on the work of B. F. Skinner, as a prevailing view in the 1950s and early 1960s, then quickly moves to a more holistic and psycholinguistically based view through the work of scholars like Noam Chomsky, Kenneth and Yetta Goodman, and Frank Smith. Thereafter, linguists and cognitive psychologists offer empirical and theoretical proposals that push reading paradigms toward information processing—emphasizing the role of prior knowledge, novice-expert differences, and text processing along with prediction as key principles.

These views gave way in the late 1990s to sociocultural views of reading, considering the importance of context in how readers interact with texts. Schools, seen as sociocultural institutions, play an important role in teaching and learning; their influence might be positive or negative, especially when under-represented populations are included. By the late 1990s and early 2000s, students' active engagement in reading was clearly central, given the beginnings of the shift away from traditional printed text and toward online digital and visual arrays in addition to alphabetic texts of all kinds. The importance of readers being able to evaluate texts for accuracy and bias increased in the face of more online materials. Technological developments also allowed for a better understanding of reading problems through MRIs and other kinds of brain imaging. The importance of testing also played a role in how reading came to be viewed, as students took more standardized tests of reading performance for better or worse, including those focused on the principles of the Common Core State Standards. Changing demographics led to more interest in non-native speakers and those with backgrounds in different dialects who may need to transfer reading skills from one language or modality to another.

Finally, personal and individualized approaches to reading are now coming to the fore, in part as a result of the impact of the internet on all kinds of reading. The widespread use of email, texts, and chats, coupled with the expanding use of sites like YouTube and Instagram, creates challenges that will increase with more different ways to create and share information and ideas, so personalization will have to address both quantity and quality of the information being written and read. It's easy to see how a number of these paradigms and trends are still very much with us in the current environment, both in terms of learning to read and in postsecondary literacy, but they don't show up directly in the textbooks in the field. The review of current books begins with the two most significant readers in wide use as this book is being written (*Ways of Reading* and *The Norton Reader*). They best reflect the "normal science" of writing textbooks and the way reading is currently presented by leaders in the field.

A later look at an assortment of other texts and the computer programs that claim to help with reading will show the limited attention given to reading in the field.

## The Leaders: Ways of Reading *and the* Norton Reader

### WAYS OF READING

If textbooks really provide a general sense of the current paradigm or "normal science" or the status of things, then a possibly more effective way to get a sense of that paradigm entails looking at two of the current leading texts used in first-year writing that address reading directly: Bedford's *Ways of Reading* (WoR; Bartholomae, Petrosky, and Waite 2020) and Norton's *Norton Reader* (NR; Eastman et al. 1965). Both companies publish many books for first-year writing, including some mentioned earlier in this book—such as Peter Adams's *The Hub* (2020b), also a Bedford product. Each has a particular view of reading and goals in helping students become better readers to a greater or lesser extent, which are usually presented in the introduction and are sometimes clear from the apparatus the book provides.

Both of these books were included in University of Connecticut rhetorician Lynn Z. Bloom's (1999) sample of readers using the multiple editions strategy for choosing which books to include in her study of the "essay canon." Her discussion reveals that while a number of essays appear repeatedly in these books, there is relatively little about reading per se in either of them. Moreover, she points out in a later article, drawing on the same body of research, that all the anthologies at the time of her survey (published in 1999) are heavily biased toward middle-class norms and middle-class English, despite the inclusion of a few essays from middle-class aspirants and others outside these norms (Bloom 2007).

Beginning with *WoR*, then, it is clear that it is one of the reigning top choices for writing classes, with a twelfth edition in 2020. Publishers do not continue to issue new editions unless sales warrant them, so even without exact sales figures, it is safe to assume that *WoR* is a popular and widely used book. The title points to the focus on reading in the seventeen-page introduction by University of Pittsburgh scholars David Bartholomae and Anthony Petrosky, who co-edited the book, with more recent editions in collaboration with University of Nebraska English professor Stacey Waite. In this introduction, the editors explain that they offer an open and flexible view of reading as an activity that goes well beyond grasping main ideas and details, seeing it as an active process of meaning construction by readers. Bloom (1999, 413) points out in her study of readers that WoR is different from others in its "focus on long and complicated texts." Students can draw on their own experience in combination with other readings to respond to what appears in a text. The editors write that "active readings, in other words, put a premium on individual acts of attention and composition" (Bartholomae, Petrosky, and Waite 2020, 7). They freely admit that the readings in the book are challenging; for this reason; they advocate multiple readings and provide, in the apparatus, guidance to students for second readings of the included selections.

The book's editors offer further specific advice on how students should deal with the difficult texts in WoR. The work involves "Reading with and against the Grain," by which they mean students should work first to understand the main ideas of a text but then also work to read critically with a series of questions in mind, seeking to "understand where this work comes from, whose interests it serves, how and where it is kept together by will rather than desire, and what it might have to do with you" (Bartholomae, Petrosky, and Waite 2020, 9). Thus, reading entails multiple steps and an array of options for understanding and use. Writing is a necessary complement to reading, especially with difficult material: "Active readers, we've said, remake what they have read to serve their own ends, putting things together, figuring out how ideas and examples relate, explaining as best they can material that is difficult or problematic, translating concepts . . . into their own terms . . . You have the chance to become an expert reader, a reader with a project in hand, one who has already done some reading, who has watched others at work, and who has begun to develop a method of analysis and a set of key terms" (12–13).

In a second and subsequent readings, students should try to see what a text says and what it does (14), which is hardly new advice (this approach, cited in many textbooks, was evidently first suggested by Kenneth A. Bruffee [1982, 23–24] in *A Short Course in Writing*, a textbook that went to a fourth edition in 2007 and is now out of print). That is, to see the content and rhetorical structure of a text, students should both be able to summarize key ideas (what it says) and see how writers develop their arguments using examples, comparisons, descriptions, and other rhetorical strategies (what it does). These steps provide students with starting points in reading so they can use any of the three types of assignments for writing presented in each chapter: they can respond, they can discuss one reading in relation to another, or they can follow an assignment sequence that involves multiple pieces from the book as a base for writing on an issue or a topic.

In her careful examination of *WoR* as a manifestation of the way reading was treated in writing studies in the 1980s and 1990s, University of Connecticut reading and writing scholar Ellen C. Carillo (2015) points out that the book is distinct from other textbooks because of the features I have described here. But its success seems to arise mainly from the attitude toward reading and writing that the book conveys, according to Carillo's queries to Bartholomae and to Bedford on its sales status. That is, the approach in *WoR* challenges students to work with difficult and extended texts in ways that go beyond just getting main ideas and details, even though some—including English language learners—might need help with those foundational skills, including vocabulary. The book, Carillo says, "directly and consistently challenges theories and pedagogies of reading that reduce reading to a mechanical, simplistic, over-determined practice" (100). Bedford used this sense of intellectual engagement as a marketing approach but does not point specifically to the reading techniques the book offers, such as they are. *WoR* does address reading directly, offering students a wide array of extended and substantive texts, which is a step in the right direction.

It is important to note, then, that *WoR* is a major text in first-year writing that takes on reading directly and explicitly. This look at the book's introduction shows that the editors recognize the essential role reading plays in students' writing process. The editors do give passing attention to reading "against the grain," with critical questions students might have in mind while reading. This is a good starting point for helping students build the critical abilities needed for college and careers. But it is also not nearly enough, for several reasons. First, it deals with printed texts in paper form. While many of them are longer than typical textbook excerpts or reprints, which is surely a good thing, students will need to be able to read full-length journal articles and books, investigative reports, white papers, research studies, and other kinds of materials—on paper and online. The essays themselves were biased in terms of white middle-class language and expectations in earlier editions, according to Bloom (2007, 71–75), but the array of authors and topics has been diversified in the latest edition.

Second, *WoR* does not address the different challenges of reading digital materials, although students may access the book in a digital format. Reading websites and other kinds of materials designed for the screen is substantively different from reading printed text, as American University reading scholar Naomi Baron (2021) has argued, using an assortment of research studies that demonstrate the distinctions between the two formats. Students do and will need strong foundational skills for both traditional and online reading in an increasingly digital environment. Moreover, students will need especially strong critical skills to evaluate sources online, since materials found by Google search are less likely to be fact-checked and edited. In particular, the few questions that *WoR* gives students for critical analysis are not as robust as they might be for a thorough critical analysis of any kind of reading; in addition, they do not give students specific tools for evaluating materials for authority, accuracy, currency, relevance, and bias.

In addition to the introduction in the latest and, presumably, earlier editions of *WoR*, a separate volume titled *Resources for Teaching Ways of Reading* was published to accompany the seventh edition (Bartholomae and Petrosky 2005). The *Resources* volume offers much basic guidance about teaching from the book, including a sample syllabus by Bartholomae (11–21). There are specific approaches for a good number of the readings and a set of papers from then current and former graduate students enrolled in a practicum course while teaching from the book about their use of it. While the collection is interesting for its array of pedagogical approaches, it is notable for the absence of explicit discussion of teaching students to read efficiently and critically; the updated version may address reading issues, but I did not have access to it at the time of writing. Bartholomae and Petrosky are, in sum, strong fans of reading the chapters twice, providing guide questions for second readings for all selections. However, the book does not substantively and directly address critical reading strategies.

### NORTON READER

The other leading reader that warrants discussion here is the *Norton Reader*. Its first edition (Eastman et al. 1965) contained a brief preface but no introduction. Unsurprisingly, the preface in the original edition says little about reading. The limited guidance on reading that does appear is remarkably close to the aforementioned "says/does" approach, advising students to write about either the content (i.e., what it says) of a reading assigned to them or the form (i.e., what it does) and then using the piece as a model to follow (xviii). Presumably, the headnotes and such with each chapter or section encourage readers to pay attention to both form and content. The current edition (the fifteenth; Goldthwaite et al. 2020b), however, has a section on reading strategies in the preface to the book, which is available for Kindle as well as in traditional printed form. In about fifteen pages, *NR* takes up "Reading the *Norton Reader*." Readers are advised to read rhetorically (i.e., consider audience, author, topic and context, purpose, genre, and strategies used by the writer, that is, rhetorical modes like description and narration). Strategies provided for "critical reading" include previewing, annotating, analyzing, summarizing, keeping a reading journal, using the study questions provided, rereading and sharing with others, and creating a personal glossary—presumably for vocabulary development. There is nothing in this prefatory material that encourages evaluation of readings for key critical elements.

In addition to the book itself, the most current edition has an accompanying *Guide for Teachers* (hereafter Guide), mentioned in the preface and shared with me by W. W. Norton staff (Goldthwaite et al. 2020a). I was particularly interested in seeing this Guide, since the book's preface promises that it has new material to help teachers improve student reading. Three sections in the Guide address reading most directly, although some effort is devoted to work on reading in the apparatus that accompanies each reading. In the first few pages of the Guide, teachers are reminded that many students, including those with diverse backgrounds or who might be nontraditional students, might already have substantial critical thinking skills derived from their life experience. The two main suggestions (6–8) are for the teacher to read parts of the text aloud or have students do so and to point to models of academic essays that appear in the collection. The reading aloud can help students hear what formal academic prose sounds like (cf. the model of critical literacy as presented here, including listening and speaking in combination with reading and writing) and can also show when students struggle with vocabulary or meaning. Pointing to models is useful because many of the pieces included are *not* formal academic essays, and doing so can help students see those that constitute formal writing as a distinct genre. The academic essay is, after all, no one's native language, so seeing and especially hearing this type of material can be helpful.

In a separate section of the Guide (Goldthwaite et al. 2020a, 9–15), the editors offer advice for teachers in community colleges and those teaching in programs like Peter Adams's Accelerated Learning Program, discussed in chapter 2 of this book. Here, the suggestions for teaching are more focused on what might be called "guided reading," with careful attention to main ideas and details or examples. After such reading, teachers are encouraged to have students write a summary as a whole-group activity. In a third section that presents a "30-minute thing to do" (57), the editors suggest that teachers guide students in analyzing the readings. They describe having students divide a sheet of paper in half vertically, writing summaries by section on the left half and thoughts or emotions elicited by the text on the right half. In none of this discussion is there any effort to help students evaluate the readings critically. *NR*'s teacher's guide, then, pays some attention to reading but not to critical reading.

Finally, one important additional source on *NR* is Gordon A. Sabine's (1993) memoir about its original creation based on discussion between the Norton editorial staff and faculty at the University of Michigan. Sabine, who spent his career in East Lansing (at Michigan State University) rather than Ann Arbor, and was a professor of communication and a journalist. According to his preface, the memoir was written in response to the appearance of the eighth edition of *NR*, partly out of friendship with lead editor Arthur Eastman (1993, xi–xii) and as an acknowledgment of the work over the years. Sabine takes up some pertinent points in two chapters: *NR* was aimed at a cross-section of readers, from two-year college and open access university (TYCOA) students to public and private four-year schools like the University of Michigan and Stanford University. Each reading had a headnote explaining the context and giving background about the author, along with explanatory footnotes providing information readers would be unlikely to know, such as factual information about people and places. The "How to Use This Book" that Sabine discusses in connection with the eighth edition that was the basis of his memoir does not appear in the current edition (41). In *NR*, then, there is less focused attention to reading than in *WoR*, but there is some, again not focused on critical elements.

One other analysis takes up both *WoR* and *NR* along with several other, similar anthologies: the work of Lynn Bloom (1999) in her study of the "essay canon" in an important article of that title, along with a few other reports from her research. While Bloom does not examine the current editions of either book or any contemporary readers in current wide use, she offers insightful perspective on textbooks generally and on readers specifically as evidence of the current shape of writing studies and its approaches to reading; her perspective thus remains relevant to understanding how the field sees reading. About *NR*, she notes its dominance in the field at the time of her research: "Four of the five most influential [texts] are Readers with a liberal arts orientation; *Patterns of Exposition* alone among these emphasizes modes of discourse. The leader is the *Norton Reader*, where 25 of the 174 canonical authors first appeared. The ubiquity of the *Norton Reader* and the propensity of other editors to copy its selections make it the industry point of reference" (412).

So, *NR* was important to the field (that is, representative of the current paradigm, then and now, using Kuhn's term), and Bloom (1999, 421) claims, based on her personal experience as Eastman's student, that he was "concerned with careful and precise reading, not only the letter of the text, but the spirit—of the author, of the age, of the nature of the work, its music, its silence." Despite this concern, the *NR* pays only limited attention to reading. If these two texts are taken as indicators of the status of reading in writing studies, they show that reading does receive some attention, but it is minimal in length and depth; moreover, even current iterations offered in ebook format do not address the increasing status of digital reading of different kinds of materials in addition to essays. Students will need to be much more adept at reading all kinds of materials on all kinds of platforms to be effective and efficient critical readers in their personal and professional lives. They and all of us will need to be especially critical readers in the face of widespread misinformation, disinformation, "fake news," and other issues in the current information landscape.

## Other Textbooks and Technological Approaches to Reading

As noted throughout this book, the field of writing studies hasn't completely ignored reading, but the attention it has received has been minimal, scattershot, and only occasionally based on substantive research—qualitative or quantitative. The same observation could be made about the situation regarding textbooks like Genung's, *WoR*, and *NR*. All of the textbooks mentioned in this chapter assume that students can get meaning from print (possibly not a correct assumption as shown in Foorman et al. 2016); it is the skills beyond the first and second circles of my model that are at issue for a majority. So, it is important to see how other textbooks have offered help with reading and been fairly successful. A Bedford/Macmillan product that fits this description is Matthew Parfitt's *Writing in Response* (2016). (Full disclosure: This book came to my attention through a collaboration with Parfitt on a CCCC regional conference held virtually in the summer of 2021. I have not used the book in teaching.) It is a "short rhetoric," according to Parfitt's introduction for instructors (v), with three opening chapters that focus on reading. In addition, in the research paper section, Parfitt offers useful guidance on critical evaluation of source materials and builds on the reading guidance provided in the opening chapters in the discussion of how to read sources in the context of a research project.

Because eight readings of articles or book chapters are included, it is easy for Parfitt (2016) to give students specific tasks to help them develop an array of reading skills and strategies useful for writing. As he says, "Reading and note-taking—of a particularly careful and thoughtful kind—play so essential a role in the process of college writing that it makes sense to devote a good deal of time and attention to them" (3). The introduction discusses academic discourse and why detailed reading, evaluation, and rational thought are part of the critical reading, writing, and thinking expected and developed in college courses. The opening chapter, "Reading with a Purpose," takes up the importance of reading generally while attending to rhetorical context, purpose, and genre in the kinds of texts students will face in their coursework. This chapter, along with the others in the book, ends with a detailed checklist feature that highlights these key points.

The second and third chapters, "Active Reading" and "Further Strategies for Active Reading," respectively, give specific activities for students to do while reading. Parfitt (2016) offers references to other approaches to reading, such as the dialectical notebook, the "believing/doubting game" (well-known from the work of Peter Elbow [Elbow and Belanoff 1989, 32]), and a "says/does" analysis as approaches students can use to help themselves stay focused when reading. His use of student examples, coupled with suggestions for working with technology as well as careful attention to vocabulary development, provide students with key guidance on ways to improve their reading. While Parfitt points to these chapters as resources specifically on reading, he offers more guidance later in the book as well.

In part 2 on developing an essay, for instance, one section called "Thinking Like a Reader" (147–148) includes the important psycholinguistic insight that helping readers see the organizational structure of a text is essential to the efficacy of writing. And the final part on research writing provides a clear list of points for evaluating websites and other materials (318) that includes authority, accuracy, currency, and other issues. In this part, Parfitt reminds students of the strategies from the opening chapters but also includes advice close to that presented by Genung in *Practical Rhetoric* (1902). Reading widely and "reading for gist" (Parfitt 2016, 320) are what Genung was recommending long ago. But Parfitt's book stands as a contemporary example of a book that does take up critical reading in a very direct way, albeit with advice widely available elsewhere.

A slightly older book that focused on reading, drawing on reader-response and other critical theory sources, is *Acts of Reading* by Patricia Harkin (1999). Harkin told me (personal Zoom conversation, January 30, 2023) that she had studied with reader-response theorist Wolfgang Iser early in her career.

Those theories, discussed in more detail in chapter 5 of this book, had clear usefulness in the classroom, and Harkin created a reader to accomplish that. The book has an easy, friendly tone—offering a broad array of readings that includes poems, stories, and nonfiction from a wide range of authors, along with a sophisticated explanation of what happens when people read. Drawing on both rhetorical concepts like unity, coherence, and significance as conventions and concepts like tropes and intertextuality, *Acts of Reading* provides students with a useful set of strategies for reading materials of all kinds. In presenting research papers as a way readers share their views or "how readers talk with one another about texts" (Harkin 1999, 655), Harkin told me that one of the major challenges in preparing the book was finding good examples to illustrate the reading issues presented (personal Zoom communication, January 30, 2023). She achieves this outcome effectively by presenting a long excerpt of the play *Oleanna*, followed by reviews by John Lahr and Elaine Showalter and other less formal responses to the play (Harkin 1999, 695–711); she then provides prompts for students to write their own responses to *Oleanna* using different sets of conventions for reviews, letters to friends, and other formats. Other sections of the book offer similar flexible discussions and effective prompts for writing. Although the book was not widely used and Prentice-Hall declined to produce a second edition, according to Harkin, this textbook, like Parfitt's, is one of the few that offer a much-needed full and focused treatment of reading.

A different approach to reading appears in University of Connecticut reading scholar and English professor Ellen C. Carillo's two books that are meant for students reading in a digital environment: *A Writer's Guide to Mindful Reading* (Carillo 2017b) (hereafter *Mindful*) and the *MLA Guide to Digital Literacy* (Carillo 2022) (hereafter *Digital*). In *Mindful*'s first part, Carillo offers an array of different strategies and approaches for reading different kinds of texts, presents a set of readings about reading, and then offers readings on technology—all with apparatus designed to guide students' reading and writing. Readers are reminded of the strategies presented in the first part of the book and are then given an assortment of writing tasks for analysis and response. What distinguishes *Mindful* from the other texts discussed here is that Carillo addresses reading directly in about fifty pages at the start of the book, then invites students to reflect on their choices of reading strategies as they deal with the readings in the second part. At the end of each chapter of readings is a "Reflecting on Your Reading Strategies and Annotations" section to keep the focus on "mindful reading." Carillo (2017b, xii) offers this definition: "Mindful reading acts as a framework that is intended to remind you of the importance of becoming an active reader who makes careful and deliberate decisions about the reading strategies you might use."

In her discussion of strategies, Carillo (2017b) begins with annotation and highlighting, pointing out that both can be done on paper or digitally using mechanisms online. Annotating entails adding notes to a text, whereas highlighting merely calls attention to key parts. But the bigger goal in all reading is to be aware of the purpose and then to choose from an array of different strategies those most useful for a particular text. The strategies include previewing, skimming, employing says/does, engaging in rhetorical reading (including purpose, audience, claims and evidence, ethos, logos, and pathos), reading aloud to paraphrase, mapping (notes on content in some visual form), believing/doubting, reading like a writer, and using specific evaluation techniques for online sources. In a later chapter, Carillo discusses ways to make reading "visible," including keeping a reading journal to record different kinds of reading strategies used for different reading tasks. Students are advised to also try creating a difficulty inventory to attempt to clarify why a reading task is hard. A third option is a passage-based paper in which the reader chooses a small excerpt as the basis for a written response.

A final approach is "Source Synthesis" (Carillo 2017, 30), in which Carillo offers guidance on how to bring multiple sources together on an issue or a topic. Further chapters take up academic essays and the use of sources, including assorted reminders of the reading strategies presented in the first part of the book. Part two offers readings with apparatus that direct students to deploy the strategies from part one as they read the wide range of selections, which vary in length and degree of challenge for college students: Plato's "Allegory of the Cave" and more contemporary pieces like "The Rise of Crowdsourcing" and "Forget Shorter Showers" are a sampling of the range of material included. According to publisher Mike Palmquist of the WAC Clearinghouse, *Mindful* has had over 100,000 visitors since its publication in 2017 and almost as many downloads of the entire book or some portion of it (personal communication, November 8, 2021).

The fact that the book has been downloaded so many times is good evidence of interest and likely use by students, but it does not constitute direct proof that this approach improves students' critical reading. For that, Carillo is engaged in an ongoing study of the impact of *Mindful*. With a grant from the Council of Writing Program Administrators, she is following a small but diverse group of students from three different institutions as they use this approach in their reading. The IRB-reviewed, exempt study includes a survey and an interview component for student volunteers drawn from classes in which the *Mindful* text has been adopted. She reports (Ellen C. Carillo, personal communication, June 7, 2022) that the study will take significant time and that no community college students chose to participate in the interview process. Thus, the data rely on self-reporting by two of the three groups, but they nevertheless represent a direct exploration of students' understanding and use of the approach. Preliminary findings make a strong case for teaching students explicitly to use skimming as an approach to reading, particularly since it is a strategy they already report using extensively; teachers can help students become more efficient users of skimming but also help them see when deeper reading is needed (Carillo forthcoming). Since, as nearly as I have been able to determine, there are no other data of this kind (or of any other kind, other than the studies reported in chapter 1), Carillo's forthcoming study represents a useful and detailed look at how students respond to the recommendations from a book that attempts to improve their reading.

In contrast to *Mindful*, *Digital* (Carillo 2022) offers a focus specifically on *digital* sources and the reading of them. It includes a number of the same strategies for reading as are found in *Mindful*, but *Digital* takes them up in the context of dealing with all types of online materials. Unlike *Mindful*, which is free through the WAC Clearinghouse, *Digital* must be purchased; but like *Mindful*, it can be accessed in either paper or digital form (on Kindle). *Digital* is much shorter than *Mindful* but is also addressed to college students. After defining digital literacy, using the American Library Association's definition of it as "the ability to use information and communication technologies to find, evaluate, create, and communicate information, requiring both cognitive and technical skills" (quoted in Carillo 2022, 1), the book focuses on the whole environment in which digital reading occurs. Carillo begins by taking up the use of algorithms and bots, among other strategies that control what readers see. Online searching approaches come next, including the nature of different types of sources.

At the end of each chapter or section are brief exercises inviting students to see how various items appear on their own screens. Carillo (2022) goes on to discuss primary and secondary sources, an issue most students know little about as they begin to use digital sources. Once students have sources in hand, Carillo advises on rhetorical reading, a twenty-five-word summary, and other strategies similar to those in *Mindful*. Lateral reading (checking sources by stepping away from them to evaluate credibility, a proven critical reading approach) and other types of critical reading give students an assortment of useful techniques for evaluating materials they find online. Each chapter's "Try It" exercises provide experience using the recommended strategies. Many of the techniques and approaches have no research evidence to support them, as noted earlier, but are commonsense strategies or ones Carillo and many other teachers have used effectively in the classroom.

Unlike most of the other publications discussed here, both *Mindful* and *Digital* have extensive and direct guidance for students on strategies to improve their reading; it's particularly important that *Digital* focuses on the online environment where so much reading now takes place. Naomi Baron's (2021) research (discussed below) shows that students and the rest of us are not very good at doing critical reading online. While *Digital* has not sold as well as *Mindful* (allowing that *Mindful* is a free download; *Digital* sold almost 1,000 copies in its first year, according to personal communication from Carillo, November 9, 2021), the Modern Language Association has published a second edition, with plans to make the first edition and its handbook available on the MLA website.

While Parfitt, Harkin, and Carillo all address reading directly, offering specific techniques for students, another approach appears in the volume *Writing Spaces*, which was published in a fourth edition in 2022 (Driscoll et al. 2022). The open access textbook, the oldest of its kind in the field, is available as both a print version and a free version from the web. It is available online for anyone to download and in all editions has probably been downloaded more than 3 million times, according to Parlor Press publisher David Blakesley (personal communication, November 1, 2021). The fourth edition offers a chapter focused on reading that Ellen Carillo and I prepared together (Carillo and Horning 2022), and one other chapter discusses synthesis in some detail, offering a template for students to analyze their reading of several sources on a topic with an eye toward synthesizing them in their own written work (Seeley, Xu, and Chen 2022).

The volume has no introduction or apparatus for students, though it does offer suggestions for teaching at the end of each chapter that include discussion questions. Otherwise, it offers no focused advice or help for teachers to address students' reading problems or to improve their reading. Dana Lynn Driscoll agreed that there is an urgent need for much more attention to reading (telephone interview, November 10, 2021). For this reason, the co-editors of *Writing Spaces* plan to have two new chapters in the upcoming edition (volume 5) that focus on digital reading, one on "social annotation" and another on reading online, including "fake news" and related issues. In addition, a chapter that deals with genre will also touch on reading matters.

Driscoll mentioned other points in our conversation that shed additional light on reading in the current writing studies teaching environment. She is a professor of English who also directs the Jones White Writing Center at Indiana University of Pennsylvania (IUP), a medium-size public university northeast of Pittsburgh. In her work in the writing center, she sees students' reading troubles from the point of view of both faculty and students. Faculty members often send students to the writing center with what they see as writing problems that are a result of students' difficulties with reading. Students may have trouble reading and understanding the assignments or difficulty understanding the readings on which they are based. These reading difficulties lead to other kinds of problems that limit students' chances for success in college; they are often of long standing, as government research shows a need to focus on foundational skills from the beginning of K–12 education, as discussed earlier (Foorman et al. 2016). Further, Driscoll finds that one of the key challenges for faculty contributors to *Writing Spaces* is that they do not always understand the needs of the student audience, and they write for a scholarly academic audience. Thus, despite the extensive style guide that details issues of tone, audience, and language, many authors need to make revisions toward a student-centered readership in their submitted chapters.

For some students (at IUP and elsewhere), there is help with reading by virtue of placement into developmental courses, although these courses can be inappropriate and sometimes do more harm than good, as shown in a careful study of consequences by writing placement and assessment experts and discussed in chapter 2 (Poe, Nastal, and Elliot 2019). In any case, most students (again, locally on Driscoll's campus and nationwide) need more help than they get from most textbooks or their teachers, even though some books such as *Writing Spaces* provide limited guidance directly (like the chapter I contributed with Carillo) and indirectly (like Mara Grayson's chapter on "racial literacy" [2022, 166-183], which offers some reading direction, as do other chapters in the current edition of *Writing Spaces*). Most faculty do not think they should have to teach students reading techniques, as they have no training and no time to do so, a view confirmed by Carillo's research (2015). Finally, Driscoll pointed out that while writing across the curriculum has made some progress on her campus and elsewhere, there is no comparable work on reading, such as a formal reading across the curriculum approach where focused instruction on reading might be a component of every class (telephone conversation,

November 10, 2021). Here again, as elsewhere, some attention is given to reading, but it is limited. Students' need for focused and extensive critical reading instruction is not being addressed by these few efforts.

## Technological Help with Reading

Beyond textbooks online or off, a digital option that attempts to work with students on reading—albeit indirectly—is PowerNotes (PN), along with two similar open-source products: Hypothes.is and Perusall. All of these options offer resources for annotating readings of all kinds for research purposes. PN is specifically focused on helping students with some aspects of the reading process through multiple steps, according to its website:

> First, when a researcher identifies and highlights a useful passage, PowerNotes prompts the researcher to categorize that passage within the researcher's thesis, argument, or framework. Categorization is a critical mental step that begins to anchor the passage and its meaning for the researcher.
>
> Second, immediately after categorizing a passage, PowerNotes prompts the researcher to annotate. This step causes the researcher to start synthesizing and internalizing the passage.
>
> Third, when the researcher has categorized and annotated the passage, PowerNotes automatically moves the passage and annotations into an outline while gathering and organizing the source URL, date and time visited, and other metadata so the researcher always has a research trail and attribution information. This takes the administrative burden of recording this information off the researcher so they can continue reading uninterrupted. (PowerNotes 2021b)

It should be clear that this program is focused on some key aspects of critical reading such as categorization and annotation, useful in the research process. What is less clear is whether PN prompts readers to evaluate source materials and, if so, how it does that.

PN, however, does offer some key advantages over other, similar programs like Hypothes.is and Perusall (PowerNotes 2021a). One advantage, according to a PN blog comparing the various programs, is that PN puts a reader's annotations on note cards that are not immediately displayed on the text site, so readers can engage with the text on their own rather than rely on what others have marked and said about it as they read the material in preparing for class discussion or writing. This approach provides an important advantage for teachers who can see how well individual readers have understood the text from the note cards but still allows readers to share their comments and understanding with one another. A second advantage of PN is the record of citation information so that when writing, the source reference is clear; it also separates the source material with citation from the writers' notes and responses to avoid inadvertent plagiarism, a common problem among student writers (PowerNotes 2021b).

This discussion is admittedly biased. I have known PN's former director of business development, Jimmy Fleming, for many years, first as a textbook salesperson for Bedford/St. Martin's and more recently in his role at PN. He told me that the basic form of PN is free to users, though the company offers a premium version that is somewhat more flexible and easier to use. Based on email exchanges with Fleming, I tried out PN to see how it works, using it to read an article from my library's database to copy quotes and annotate. Once I figured out how to make the article and PN talk to each other by downloading a browser extension and then putting the tool on the screen while reading the article, it was remarkably easy to use and easy to see how it could be useful in both reading and writing. The citation information is saved in the record along with the notes and whatever quotes the reader copies from the source onto note cards. It's also easy to see how readers can create topics, that is, categorize notes or quotes in terms of sections of a paper or a report within the project. So, like many other resources, PN is a good start, but it does not prompt readers to engage in source evaluation of any kind. That aspect of critical reading must come from the readers themselves if they have been taught to do it.

Two other online annotation programs, Hypothes.is and Perusall, are free, open-source programs. Hypothes.is states its mission explicitly on its website: "Hypothes.is is a new effort to implement an old idea: A conversation layer over the entire web that works everywhere, without needing implementation by any underlying site. Our team creates open source software, pushes for standards, and fosters community. Using annotation, we enable sentence-level note taking or critique on top of classroom reading, news, blogs, scientific articles, books, terms of service, ballot initiatives, legislation and more. Everything we build is guided by our principles. In particular that it be free, open, neutral, and lasting to name a few" (Hypothes.is 2022). From what I can tell on the website, the program offers annotation tools for any kind of online material but not the categorization feature or readers' option to keep notes out of view offered by PN.

Perusall has an essentially similar mission. Like Hypothes.is, it is free unless instructors require it as part of an assigned text for a class. It integrates easily with Blackboard and Canvas and probably with the other widely used learning management systems. Its website offers an array of studies on its use and effectiveness in improving student reading (Perusall 2022b).

> We aim to change the nature of reading—from the traditional solitary experience to an engaging and collective one. We aim to change education—so all students do the reading, come to class prepared, and are motivated to do so because they care about the content. And we aim to advance behavioral science and AI research in the service of improving education—using our work at Harvard University and Perusall Labs to improve the Perusall platform and to help students, educators, researchers, and society at large.
>
> Our story
>
> We began Perusall following a major four-year research project at Harvard University; we created the platform to serve students in our classes, and then in 2015 built the business to bring our research to students and instructors everywhere. Perusall is now a profitable business serving 1,000,000 students at 3,000 educational institutions in 85 countries. We grow mostly by word of mouth when instructors share their experiences teaching using Perusall with friends and colleagues. (Perusall 2022a)

All of these programs are surely steps that will help move students toward the full range of critical literacy abilities presented in my model, to be discussed in chapter 7. The software recognizes that so much of the reading students (and the rest of us) do today is on a screen. When readers want to take excerpts from sources, preserving the source information and keeping it separate from readers' notes is very important. Still at issue is the teaching and learning of critical evaluation of all material; here, Parfitt's and Carillo's work offer exemplary approaches that help students become effective and efficient critical readers. These kinds of approaches urgently need to be tested and replicated, with much more attention for all students; early research studies listed on Perusall's (2022a) website are encouraging, especially given the growing use of the tool.

### *Textbooks, Technology, Paradigm Shift, and the Need for Critical Reading*

Textbooks, then—from the beginning of the field of writing studies and more recently—digital guides, and digital tools for reading all offer small steps toward helping students develop critical literacy skills. But taken together with the "normal science" representations of reading in the two leading readers of the day, they all fall notably short, often for multiple reasons. As

Georgetown University English professor and rhetorician James F. Slevin (2001) made clear more than two decades ago in his discussion of critical reading and writing, a thorough and contextual view of reading offers key advantages urgently needed now; he was writing presciently about this issue at the turn of the twenty-first century: "The view of reading and writing I am suggesting expands, indeed radically alters, the rhetorical schema with which we would be working. It introduces not implied but actual authors and readers as figures constituted by period, class, gender, race, and age. It sets discourse within the economy of textual production, within the institutions that enable and constrain it, that shape it and misshape it. And this view examines the way the text's language—by both what it says and what it does not bother to say—reproduces unjust social hierarchies" (140).

Slevin suggests a "radical" shift in the way we approach critical reading and writing, that is, a revolution in Kuhn's terms, moving from the snapshot of normal science that appears in the textbooks and tools reviewed here. He was well ahead of his time, noting that such a shift could allow much greater focus on "unjust social hierarchies" from diverse perspectives than is currently available. The approach Slevin advocates is addressed in part by scholars like University of Michigan rhetorician Anne Ruggles Gere and colleagues (2021), arguing for "critical language awareness [CLA]," a view of critical literacy that incorporates CLA but goes beyond it. Readers must not only be aware of social injustice but also must be able to discern other issues of authority, accuracy, currency, and so forth. Putting this view into full practice in the classroom is suggested by Middlebury College linguist Shawna Shapiro (2022). She shows how useful a CLA approach can be, although her specific strategies to help students with reading are already well accepted, such as having them keep a reading log.

In a way, these more recent views do pick up and integrate the critical literacy approach of Freire and others. They understand literacy as a force for linguistic and social justice. Many other scholars share this way of thinking. Michigan State University distinguished African American studies professor Geneva Smitherman (1977) has been calling for linguistic justice (albeit not using exactly that term) since she published her first book on Black English. Following the appearance of *Talkin and Testifyin: The Language of Black America* (1977), Smitherman went on to publish a number of other books on language and power, including *Talkin That Talk* (Smitherman 2000) and a memoir that takes up these same issues, *My Soul Look Back in Wonder* (Smitherman 2022).

A similar view of the importance of the change Slevin proposes is seen in recent analysis of the status of disinformation in the contemporary information landscape. This view makes clear why textbooks are important in helping improve students' critical literacy and why it matters that writing studies as embodied in current textbooks is not doing enough to address this need. Richard Stengel, a former editor at *Time* and US under-secretary of state (2013–2016), has written that improved media literacy is essential to counteract the effects of disinformation. Disinformation is widely spread on the internet, and only humans who have been taught about it can offset its effects. He rigorously defines disinformation as "the deliberate creation and distribution of information that is false and deceptive in order to mislead an audience . . . Disinformation doesn't have to be 100 percent false to be disinformation. In fact, the most effective forms of disinformation are a mixture of information that is both false and true" (Stengel 2019, 290).

The ability to judge disinformation requires media literacy skills. Stengel (2019) argues that legislation to control it is also needed, along with better privacy protections, more transparency by big companies, and effective news rating systems in addition to thorough teaching. While media organizations should become more transparent in making clear how they are getting their information, "Students need to be taught how news organizations work, and how to identify the provenance of information. Making journalism a staple of secondary education would go a long way toward solving the 'fake news' problem" (301). Stengel proposes that online news articles provide transcripts and source information, including footnotes and bibliographies as appropriate. While readers might not look at all the source materials, their inclusion would make news reports more trustworthy and transparent. Clickbait and advertising are other areas that need attention, but ultimately, dealing with disinformation, misinformation, and other flawed information is up to us; textbooks and good teaching that focus on critical literacy are the most effective ways to "diminish the power of disinformation" (307). Continually revised textbooks must keep up as the paradigm continues to shift.

As both Slevin and Stengel make clear, writing studies should lead the way, and it has not done so other than the few exceptions discussed in this chapter. Further, the books that focus directly on improving students' reading abilities (like those by Parfitt and Carillo) have not been adopted in great numbers, as have the leading readers (*WoR* and *NR*) discussed earlier. The computer programs that do help with a few aspects of critical reading don't do enough to support critical analysis. Other current analyses of the contemporary reading situation make an even stronger case for more direct and focused attention on critical reading skills for students in writing studies and across the curriculum. As just one example, Naomi Baron, American University linguist and author of several books and many articles on reading in a digital environment, has recently made this case, with extensive evidence.

In Baron's (2021) *How We Read Now*, not only does she present a detailed review of research on the current state of reading, but the book's foreword—written by Maryanne Wolf (2021, xi), another leading researcher—makes the case for more attention to critical reading. The book is broken into four parts, each of which is devoted to an aspect of the contemporary reading landscape, including traditional print and the array of digital options, audio and video. This approach is noteworthy in light of the language arts framework used in this book, since it recognizes the increasing integration of listening and speaking with reading and writing. The book's first part addresses traditional reading of texts on paper, noting that research shows that not all the conventional strategies recommended to students work effectively; the ones that do help are those that require active engagement with the text. So, highlighting and underlining are not especially useful, but quizzes (in the text itself or mindfully self-imposed) and summaries that probe main ideas and details can be useful if done carefully. These print-based approaches can also be useful when dealing with texts in media other than traditional print, as discussed in the rest of her book.

Baron (2021) is especially good at synthesizing current research on reading in different media, and her skill is on full display in the second part of the book, where she presents the research on digital reading. Here, most but not all studies show that reading digital materials is generally less effective than reading traditional print. For support, Baron relies on the work of the Stanford History Education researchers discussed in chapter 1 of the present book. Results of standardized testing of students, allowing for the flaws and biases of such testing discussed earlier, make clear that they do not perform as well on digital texts and tests as they do on paper (114–115). Still, digital reading is happening; its affordance of access to multiple texts and quick movements among them will warrant much further study. Meanwhile, print-based skills, such as drawing on prior knowledge and summarizing, will be useful as both teachers and students work to develop skill in the search, synthesis, and appraisal of varied resources online.

Maintaining the reading of literature of all kinds as well as informational reading is going to remain important, as is the ability to sustain attention for full-length texts like books. Baron concludes her review of research on reading multiple texts this way: "Online reading potentially encourages less complex and reflective thinking than reading in print, for both single and multiple document reading" (121). Still, she predicts a future in which much reading will include both print and digital reading, the same "biliteracy" approach supported by UCLA literacy scholar Maryanne Wolf (2018) based on her own research. Baron's (2021) final point in this section is that this view is important to "digital reading for civic good" (150) because it encourages fact-checking and other antidotes to so-called fake news so that readers will be "better equipped . . . to vote knowledgably and to participate in civic discourse" (151).

In the book's third part, Baron (2021) examines audiobooks and other audio "reading." This part is possibly my favorite, since I am a huge audiobook fan. Audiobooks have a number of advantages insofar as they slow down reading and ensure that every word comes to readers/listeners, something that is not true of print reading. Taken together with video, these alternative media do present some key challenges in that they are much more transient than printed text. For this reason, watchers/listeners must pay full attention, resisting the temptation to multitask (195). Taking handwritten notes is also critical with audio and video texts, which for now lack the technology to allow note taking within the body of the material—although such notes are now possible for alphabetic texts with programs like PowerNotes, discussed earlier. A few online video/audio annotation tools are available, with more sure to come (cf. Vialogues, a free program [196]). So, strategies and technology are available for listening and watching, even though many studies show that reading is less effective in these forms.

Finally, in the book's last part, Baron provides her view of what is likely to happen next in the reading environment, with strategies for effective reading and learning as the technology continues to develop. Awareness of the purposes for reading and conscious choices of strategy (as suggested by Carillo's mindful reading) will always be important, since they allow for appropriate choices of level of engagement and speed. Reading carefully rather than superficially skimming, avoiding distraction, and making use of different "containers" (i.e., print, digital, audio, and video) can improve reading outcomes. Finally, Baron concedes that not enough is being done to develop students' critical thinking abilities (219–223), though reading will always be a part of this set of skills. She encourages readers to advocate strongly for more and better reading instruction across the educational spectrum with her reading "plate," following food writer Michael Pollan's eating advice: "Read more. Focus when you do. Medium matters" (230).

This detailed summary of Baron's book offers a thorough snapshot of what is happening with reading. The conclusion that parents and other readers should advocate for more and better reading instruction in schools and colleges is consistent with the advice of Stengel and Slevin. It also says a great deal about the current paradigm for reading. Baron draws extensively on current reading research to support a multi-pronged approach to understanding how reading is affected by technology in various ways. The paradigm may be shifting as more texts are available in different media. As she says, the outcome is probably not going to be either/or but more like both/and, allowing an increasingly diverse set of readers (as projected by Washington think tanks, cf. Teixeira, Frey, and Griffin 2015) to maximize all forms and formats to extract meaning from different kinds of texts, with skill in thorough critical analysis for authority, accuracy, currency, relevance, and bias. Writing studies is not but can and should be at the leading edge of this effort.

## *Textbooks as Snapshots of "Normal Science"*

While Kuhn had his critics, his view of textbooks as reflections of a field's status quo provides a base for looking at what has happened to reading in writing studies. As with other aspects of the field discussed in this book, in textbook publishing, some attention has been given to reading—although, as elsewhere, there has been little of the consistent attention that would help students become strong critical readers. From the earliest popular texts like Genung's, there is often at least a section or sometimes an entire volume that discusses reading. More recent books pay increased attention to reading directly or indirectly, with the most popular ones like *WoR* and *NR* providing models that are followed by others. Individual authors like Matthew Parfitt and Ellen Carillo have attempted to ensure that students and teachers work on reading as they develop their writing skills. Moreover, new tech tools such as PowerNotes and Perusall open up more options for engaged reading in the digital environment. As Baron and other theorists note, though, much more attention to critical reading is still in order. Chapter 7 addresses this need with evidence-based approaches that can make a difference in writing classrooms and elsewhere.

# 7
## What to Do on Monday

*Steps to Address Students' Reading Needs*

Working professional educators know this phenomenon well: you go to a conference or a workshop and go back to work thoroughly energized and prepared to use what you have learned from your experience to change and, if possible, enhance your work with students. You have handouts or images you've saved electronically to point you in the right direction. But over time, the flush of new ideas from the workshop fades, and even with some residual small changes, you are back to doing what you have always done despite your heightened awareness of problems and solutions. In a post-pandemic environment, it is easy to understand why this outcome occurs, since many frontline teachers—both K–12 and postsecondary—are just trying to keep moving students forward in the face of the challenges of intermittent remote instruction and various difficulties on both sides of the desk. So yes, it will be hard to implement many of the changes needed now.

This review of the history of the field of writing studies reveals the inconsistent way critical literacy has been treated. Attention to reading has waxed and waned over time, whether the start of the field is placed at the first offerings of English A at Harvard University in 1885 or with the varied discussions at the Dartmouth meeting in 1966. This history shows our inability to create a consistent approach to critical reading, based on different kinds of evidence. The

https://doi.org/10.7330/9781646426270.c007

earlier chapters of this book, moreover, reveal the widespread need for much more attention to critical literacy for students. Recent studies of standardized test scores (flawed though the tests may be), data from students' own writing like the Citation Project findings, and assorted other types of measures make clear the need for a focus on critical literacy. Moreover, in the face of so much misinformation and disinformation during the pandemic, along with other changes in our lives such as the widespread use of social media to explore all kinds of topics, the importance of critical reading cannot be overemphasized. Steps for reaching the goal of consistent, evidence-based attention to critical reading are presented here.

While the need for more and better critical reading among students has long been present and is increasing, research shows (Carillo 2015) that most college faculty do not have any preparation for teaching critical reading; this claim is true of writing teachers and the rest of the faculty as well. So, step one needs to be to prepare current college faculty to work on reading in every class. Pace University literacy scholar Meaghan Brewer's study of graduate students' conceptions of literacy suggests that they come to graduate school with ideas that will change substantially as a by-product of their training. However, Brewer's (2020) work shows that these future teachers need to consider and will often improve their understanding of literacy if they receive good guidance through their coursework and research.

Further help can come from faculty development, possibly through centers for teaching excellence and from the relatively small group who have expertise in postsecondary reading pedagogy (Patrick Sullivan, Howard Tinberg, Ellen C. Carillo) and perhaps those who are working in the science of reading (Naomi Baron, Mark Seidenberg, Maryanne Wolf, Daniel Willingham). As noted, graduate programs in writing studies urgently need to provide preparation for reading integration in their curricula for future faculty; beyond this preparatory starting point, everyone can draw profitably from colleagues in the education field as well as those in any college or university library. Library faculty who are members of the Association of College and Research Libraries are doing their own work on these matters, and every librarian has skills and strategies to help faculty address students' reading needs more effectively (Head 2021). One option might be to create a series of tutorials that could be posted online for viewing by faculty as needed, perhaps offered by the Consortium of Doctoral Programs or the Conference on College Composition and Communication (CCCC) itself.

A second step is to ensure that all faculty have a basic knowledge of the psycholinguistics of reading. The key features of reading as a psycholinguistic process are discussed here in a condensed form, with references to an array of accessible resources for further study. Then, as a third step, the language arts model that has been discussed intermittently throughout this book comes around in its full form to the present moment; the model is intended to be a flexible snapshot of how information is sent through speaking and writing and received through listening and reading. Flexible though it is, the model provides the base for a fourth step: a series of recommendations for Monday morning drawn from several types of evidence—empirical studies; meta-analyses of empirical and other studies; research that looks above, below, and beyond those peer-reviewed studies; expert recommendations and statements (like the CCCC position statements); and finally, teacher knowledge based on classroom experience. Not only teachers of first-year writing but the entire faculty must take up these recommendations to prepare students for the rest of their lives as students, workers, and citizens.

### *Starting Close, Then Reaching Out*

Research I reported in 2021 (Horning 2021b), which was a follow-up to my earlier work and that of several other scholars, shows clearly that PhD programs in writing studies consistently fail to prepare college writing teachers to help students with reading. There are no required courses in reading; almost no recommended courses in the lists of electives, if any, and no option to take courses in education or psychology, based on my sample of a third of the current writing studies PhD programs. While some faculty may feel prepared to help students with critical reading or think they are doing so, half or more reported to Ellen C. Carillo (2015) that they did not feel able to work directly on reading. So, job one, as Carillo and other scholars have been saying for a long time, is to add this kind of training to every PhD program in writing studies—perhaps through online tutorials, seminars, or workshops, as suggested earlier. Failure to do this work neglects the needs of students discussed in the opening chapters of this book.

One example of how such an approach might work is offered by the Modern Language Association (MLA), which is the major professional organization for faculty in English and foreign languages. The MLA recently received a substantial grant from the Andrew W. Mellon Foundation to better prepare graduate students and early-career faculty to teach reading and writing at "access-oriented institutions"—that is, community colleges and regional public institutions that are accessible to a wider population of students, according to Howard Tinberg (personal Zoom communication, February 22, 2022), who has worked with the MLA to direct this program despite his retirement from Bristol Community College in Connecticut. MLA's approach is to offer stipend-supported week-long summer institutes in reading and writing pedagogy for these younger, practicing faculty and those soon to join the ranks. The institutes are based at different campuses around the country.

Tinberg told me that the focus of the program is first-year composition because it is widely offered and usually required. The institutes introduce deep-reading approaches of various kinds, such as annotation, writing to read, and other strategies to make reading a visible focus in writing courses. Because the program is offered by the MLA, it naturally concentrates on reading and writing as humanities, with discussions and participant projects centered on choosing and using texts appropriate to the context on a particular campus. Attention is paid to an array of reading issues, such as the need to make mindful choices of reading technique, the differences in reading on pages versus reading on screens, and how reading techniques might differ for alphabetic as opposed to visual texts of various kinds. Tinberg (personal Zoom communication, February 22, 2022) noted that the institutes might vary from place to place, depending on the needs of the sponsoring institutions. As this book was being written, the MLA had not conducted follow-up evaluation, but Tinberg reported that the projects participants have completed—presented as posters at the MLA conference—are very well done and suggest that young faculty leave the institutes better equipped to integrate reading into their writing courses.

Beyond the training of future faculty, the same need is extant and equally important for faculty working in classrooms today. In the post-pandemic environment, with so many demands on faculty and students alike, much more attention to critical reading should still be at the top of the list of priorities in college classrooms. Among the key lessons of the pandemic, indeed, is the ways misinformation and disinformation have contributed to the overall response to widespread Covid across the country. Our education system, especially colleges and universities, must teach people to read critically so they can evaluate information and make appropriate decisions. The specific approaches discussed later in this chapter are a start in this direction, but proper training for future faculty and in-service training for current faculty must be part of a full-court press on reading. Organizations such as the POD Network (podnetwork.org) and the Lilly International Teaching Cooperative (lillyconferences.com) can support ongoing work on reading across all disciplines, as can centers for teaching now functioning on many campuses. A few certificate programs are specifically designed for those teaching postsecondary reading, but they are very few in number and largely intended for those teaching in community colleges (San Francisco State University and the University of Cincinnati are two examples). In response to the decline in focused developmental reading and study strategy courses reported in 2023 (Appatova and Horning 2023), these organizations, certificate programs, and meetings offer professional development for working faculty who can and should adopt a stronger focus on critical reading.

I have argued elsewhere that the field itself could reform its key documents in ways that would address reading more thoroughly and directly. In a full volume on the *Framework for Success in Postsecondary Writing* (Council of Writing Program Administrators, National Council of Teachers of English, and the National Writing Project 2017), Ellen Carillo and I suggested ways of expanding the *Framework* document. Such revisions would improve the focus on reading for all faculty in postsecondary environments of all kinds. While this particular change has not yet happened, the publication of the *CCCC Position Statement on the Role of Reading in College Writing Classrooms* (Conference on College Composition and Communication 2021) is a step in the right direction, discussed in more detail below.

Critical reading can also usefully be thought of as a team sport, a point I like to make in in-service workshops and presentations around the country. The point here is that the work of critical reading is not the sole responsibility of the writing program. On the one hand, it is probably fair to say that writing faculty have the best access to the student body at large, since writing courses are required at almost all colleges and universities. On the other hand, however, every student in every course should be learning to read critically, whatever that means for the discipline under study. In a typical English/composition 101 course, there may be no reason to teach students to read formal empirical research reports, even with a research paper component. But in psychology or biology, students need to understand the IMRaD pattern (Introduction, Methods, Results, and Discussion) so they can go beyond the article abstract to be able to understand and evaluate the findings of a study. Moreover, new research suggests that approaches like explanatory writing, distinct from argumentative or strict empirical formats, might reduce the current atmosphere of polarization and open up broader perspectives; this finding comes from the work of University of Michigan linguist and rhetorician Laura L. Aull and University of Pennsylvania writing scholar Valerie Ross (Aull and Ross 2020). Everyone needs to be on the reading team at every level, working to make students effective and efficient critical readers of all kinds of texts while in school and, later, as professionals and citizens.

A key group that should be part of all these efforts is the library faculty. As noted elsewhere in this book, librarians are in a unique position on every campus because they are a potential point of contact with students when they are actively engaged in research for course assignments. While on many campuses they offer single-session library orientations and sometimes library research courses that are credit-bearing electives, they are a frequently overlooked resource for work on the information literacy aspect of critical reading. For example, at Oakland University, a public research-intensive university in Michigan where I taught for most of my career, there is now a course on library research called LIB 2500, Introduction to Library Research and Technology in the Information Age. This four-credit course teaches students about the organization of information, access, evaluation, and ethics, among other matters. It satisfies two General Education requirements that apply to all students and is offered entirely online. These approaches from the library move students toward much stronger critical literacy skills and are a further step in the right direction.

Because librarians have had a long-standing concern with students' critical reading skills or more commonly, the lack of them, they have made their own broader efforts to address students' needs. Specifically, the Association of College and Research Libraries (2016), the professional section of the American Library Association for postsecondary librarians, has created its own information literacy framework document, describing essential skills for students. It also has assorted books, journals, and research based on the Framework document, supporting classroom approaches to improve students' information literacy abilities (see, for example, D'Angelo et al. 2016). In addition, the research of Project Information Literacy under the direction of Harvard librarian Alison Head, discussed in chapter 1, indicates that information literacy should be a focal point in every course at every institution.

In my experience, when I have asked librarians to meet with my upper-level undergraduate and graduate students prior to the students undertaking research projects in linguistics, they have responded enthusiastically when given the chance to present helpful, discipline-based research strategies to students. They have also offered individual research consultations to students as a follow-up to the in-class talks, and students consistently report that they are extremely helpful. These faculty are available on most campuses, and they are a vastly under-used and essential resource for faculty in every discipline. The librarians are only one helpful resource for both students and faculty; the goal should be to make critical reading a focal point in all undergraduate education.

## Understanding What Happens in Reading

My own fascination with reading might come from the fact that my older sister taught me to read when I was around age four, chiefly to stop me from pestering her to read to me, as mentioned earlier in this book. Neither of us can recall how she did it, but I do remember that we had a small blackboard on an easel that she surely used, and both of us recall having at least one *Alice and Jerry* book on hand, the provenance of which is a mystery to us. My guess is that she used the book because it had my name in print. My guess is also that I was simply ready to read, so teaching me might have been easy. While my sister still outdoes me as a fast and voracious reader, my recent addiction to audiobooks has greatly increased my book consumption. I have always loved reading, still do, and surely always will. That love has led to a lifetime of reading, studying the process, doing research on it, and seeking every possible way to foster the teaching and learning especially of critical reading, as in this book.

The essential principles involved in reading have been studied for a long time and are well understood from a psycholinguistic perspective. Following is a brief foray into the principles involved. A good handful of highly accessible books can supplement these basics for readers who want a deeper understanding (Baron 2021; Dehaene 2009; Huey 1908; Wolf 2018); an awareness of the role of cultural differences might also be useful, as captured in the model that has been developing throughout this book (Bruggink et al. 2022; Nash 2021). Reading is generally fast, meaning-driven, and not strictly or even largely visual. Exploring these key features can help both faculty and students understand what is happening when effective and efficient critical reading is occurring.

The speed of reading comes as a surprise to many people. Reasonably capable adult readers read about 400 words a minute on average, according to French cognitive scientist Stanislas Dehaene (2009, 17). Speeds vary, of course, with the type of material and the purpose of reading. For most readers, reading theoretical physics is going to take much longer than the latest thriller or beach book. Reasons for this difference range from more challenging or specialized vocabulary to greater levels of syntactic density, among other matters. For many readers, the last *Harry Potter* book, at 800–900 pages, was worth staying up all night to read but was devoured at a much higher words-per-minute speed than would be the case with denser material.

Readers' prior knowledge and motivation also play a huge role in reading of every kind. Slowing down can be detrimental to efficient reading; if readers move so slowly through a text that they can't recall the beginning of a sentence when they get to its end, that's no good.

It's also not good if readers slow down that much because reading can be simply defined as the psycholinguistic process of getting meaning from print. So, students who run their eyes over the lines of print in a textbook chapter but have no idea what they have read when done have not really read the chapter, by this definition. If readers don't get meaning, they have not read the text. Reading is a psycholinguistic process insofar as it entails the interaction of what readers already know (about both the topic and the language of the text) with the visual display on the page or screen before them. The reason a thriller reads more quickly than theoretical physics has a lot to do with the prior knowledge required to get meaning. The drive to get meaning is fairly strong in ordinary reading, so much so that readers will often wait for a writer to provide meaning from context for an unfamiliar word, even when it is essential to the narrative.

Consider this example, and, assuming there is a word you don't know, try to keep track of the point at which you decide what the word means:

"What is it?"

"A krait," he said.

"A <u>krait</u>! Oh, my God! Where'd it bite you? How long ago?"

. . .

"I haven't been bitten," he whispered. "Not yet. It's on my stomach. Lying there asleep."

. . .

"Then out of the corner of my eye I saw this little krait sliding over my pyjamas. Small, about ten inches."

. . .

As a matter of fact it wasn't a surprising thing for a krait to do. They hang around people's houses and they go for the warm places . . . The bite is quite deadly except sometimes when you catch it at once and they kill a fair number of people each year in Bengal.

. . .

I . . . fetched a small sharp knife from the kitchen . . . I was going to be ready to cut the bitten place and try to suck the venom out . . .

5 pages later

"It is not safe," he continued, "because a snake is cold-blooded and anesthetic does not work so well or so quick with such animals." (Dahl 2006, 260–265)

In workshops, my participants agree that they would not go in search of the dictionary to find the meaning of *krait* but instead would use the clues given by the author—including its ability to bite and to slide, that it has length as its main feature, and that it is poisonous—to decide it is a snake. This decision is confirmed, but not until five pages later. Meaning drives reading; good readers will use context clues as seen here to get meaning, usually successfully.

New technology supports reading as a meaning-getting process. In electronic texts, it is easy to call up a dictionary to get the meaning of an unfamiliar word quickly and easily. Even in textbooks, authors and publishers provide glossaries either in the back of a print book or at the ends of chapters, and they are readily accessible online as a resource for readers. And various note-taking programs now help readers focus and get meaning from print that they can then distill into notes for further use in their own writing or for whatever purposes they might have (see, for example, PowerNotes or Hypothes.is, discussed in chapter 6). Reading online also allows access not only to dictionaries but to all sorts of other information that might improve or expand readers' understanding of a text.

As the meaning-getting process of reading moves forward, readers rely less on the visual display before their eyes and much more on their prior knowledge, so much so that in a famous article, psycholinguist and reading researcher Paul A. Kolers (1967) claimed "Reading Is Only Incidentally Visual." More recently, eye-tracking data confirm Kolers's claim (Ginestet et al. 2021). Readers do not look at or see or need to see most of the text to get meaning from print. Despite the sense of reading continuous text, normal readers actually only sample a small portion of the words and get full meaning. Students will recognize one manifestation of this phenomenon. They hand in papers they claim they have proofread carefully, yet when their work is returned, many obvious errors will have been marked by an instructor: words missing or incorrect, word endings omitted, and so forth—problems that spell-check will not find and that students miss because they do not look at or see much of what is on the page. The more they go over the text, the less they see since, as the text becomes more familiar, they actually look at even less.

Even armed with these key psycholinguistic features of reading, faculty need to teach students more about their reading environment, which is much more complex now because so much reading is done online and not necessarily with traditional alphabetic text. From this perspective, more has been written recently about the way information is presented in all digital forms. Studies and reports show that readers must be savvy about what they see on screens of all kinds. Two issues in this regard seem especially noteworthy now: the way information is controlled by major companies, political groups, or others, with biases across the political spectrum, and how the internet makes it possible for racism to flourish in the online environment. University of Michigan American studies and digital studies scholar John Cheney-Lippold (2017) has written about the role of data online.

He explains: "Algorithms are everywhere, organizing the near limitless data that exists in our world. Derived from our every search, like, click, and purchase, algorithms determine the news we get, the ads we see, the information accessible to us and even who our friends are. These complex configurations not only form knowledge and social relationships in the digital and physical world, but also determine who we are and who we can be, both on and offline. Algorithms create and recreate us, using our data to assign and reassign our gender, race, sexuality, and citizenship status" (description online). The result, Cheney-Lippold says, is that "a simple web search from even the most unsophisticated of smart phones generates a lengthy record of new data. This includes your initial search term, the location of your phone, the time and day when you searched, what terms you searched for before/after, your phone's operating system, your phone's IP address, and even what apps you installed on your phone. Add onto this list everything else you do with that phone, everything else you do on your computer, and everything else that might be recorded about your life by surveilling agents" (4). This kind of surveillance and control over the nature of the information we produce and see online has a particularly negative impact insofar as it can foster racism.

The research of Safiya Umoja Noble, director of the UCLA Center for Critical Internet Inquiry and author of *Algorithms of Oppression* (2018), makes clear the climate of racism that appears across the internet. Her research shows how racial bias, particularly against women of color, shows up in search results. Noble, who is also a MacArthur Fellows award recipient, draws on her background in library and information science to demonstrate the importance of critical literacy for students and everyone else. She argues that we all need a better understanding of how algorithms used by search engines like Google function to convey racist ideas. Much greater digital literacy is essential to understand how search engines work in this way. This kind of background would allow people of color and especially women to develop "alternative search engines that are less disturbing and that reflect and prioritize a wider range of informational needs and perspectives" (26) to address the widespread misrepresentation in search engines. Since the goal of most search engines is to get attention and yield profits, there is, she says, much "need for significant degrees of digital literacy for the public" (106). The urgent need for students to be equipped with critical reading skills should be clear from the work of these scholars, among others.

The work of librarians plays a key role here again, as discussed by University of California at Merced faculty librarian Donald A. Barclay (2018). Barclay's experience includes teaching first-year writing in addition to information literacy classes, so he is familiar with how library instruction usually works in writing classes. His review of the history of fake news and other terms relevant to misinformation and disinformation shows that the current problems have been around longer than social media and other contemporary sources, although technology has clearly made it more difficult to sort fact from fiction. He presents a useful reminder of the array of logical fallacies readers often miss in the barrage of information online.

To address this problem, he presents a set of nine questions that readers should apply to all material to verify its factual status: author, publisher, content, sources, age, opinions of others about the content, primary or secondary source status, possible humorous intent, and variation from other sources. Because he cites no studies to support these questions, it seems clear that they are based on his teacher knowledge and classroom/library experience. They overlap with another series of issues mentioned elsewhere in this book: authority, accuracy, currency, relevance, appropriateness, and bias. The specific recommendations below draw on this kind of teacher expertise along with assorted other kinds of studies that provide evidence for what to do on Monday.

### *The Language Arts Model Revisited*

As I said in my first discussion of an integrated language arts model in this book, it took me a while to see the usefulness of this approach. Fortunately, my ever-persistent and collegial reader, Norbert Elliot, convinced me of the idea of a model as the basis for change in how reading should best be incorporated into first-year writing and all other undergraduate education. As this book has developed, the advantage of having a detailed but evolving, integrated model in mind has become increasingly clear. To some extent, this development has happened because I have focused my thinking more on digital resources: YouTube videos, Wikipedia, social media in all its forms, traditional texts accessed online, and so forth all make use of reading, writing, speaking, and listening together in some form and to a greater or lesser degree, depending on the source. For an audiobook addict like me, it's clear that traditional texts printed on paper are competing increasingly with audio, video, and other digital sources of information. Plus, it's not just the sources that are changing; devices are too, so that while smart phones can be a source of problematic addiction and other kinds of trouble, as detailed by *New York Times* technology specialist Kevin Roose (2021), they are also frequently the device of choice or possibly the default device for many students. They offer sounds, images, alphabetic texts, and recording capabilities with wide-ranging implications, both positive and negative. Thus, it is essential to consider listening, speaking, reading, and writing together as aspects of input and output when looking at critical literacy.

So here is the model yet again, in its most fully realized form for now (figure 7.1). It has changed several times over the course of this book, from the skeleton form presented in chapter 1 to the limited shape offered by the Dartmouth Conference in 1966 that was to be the definitive plan for the teaching of

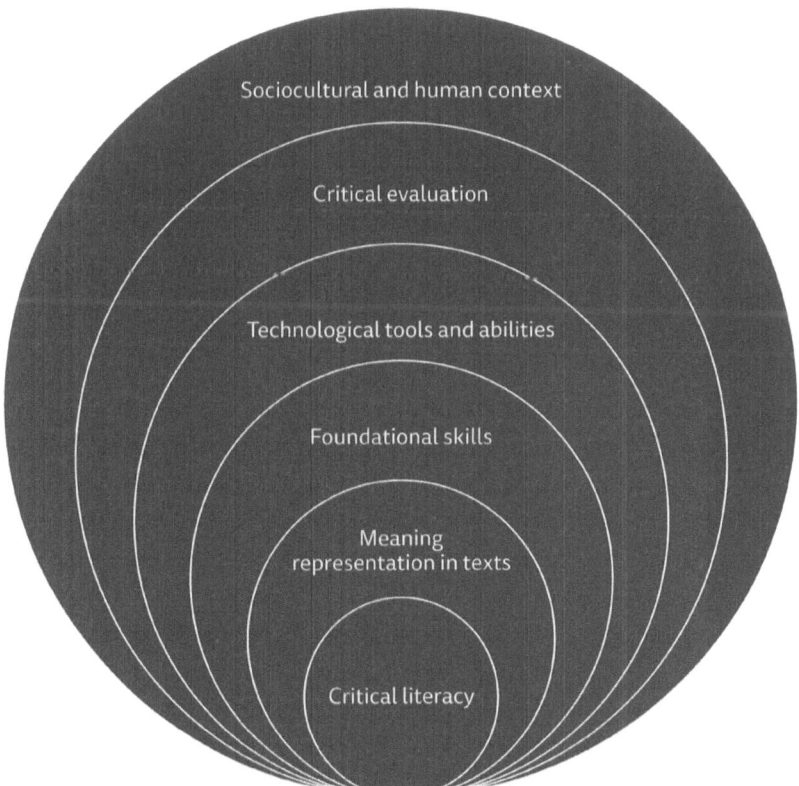

FIGURE 7.1. The complete model in final form

English both K–12 and postsecondary. This version of the model will continue to evolve as technology changes. There are four key points to make here. First, the model is only a visual representation of a complex set of abilities needed to deal with information in texts of all kinds in the current environment. Second, critical literacy is deliberately at the center and must continue to be the goal of all the instruction and guidance that writing teachers, disciplinary faculty, and librarians can provide. Third, the critical evaluative tools (e.g., authority, accuracy) on the perimeter must be thoroughly integrated into the work of teaching speaking, listening, reading, and writing.

The fourth point is more complex, addressing the people on all sides of the exchanges that happen through critical literacy. The population is shifting in a variety of ways as a result of global and local changes affecting us all, demonstrated clearly in research from the nonpartisan Center for American Progress (Teixeira, Frey, and Griffin 2015) as well as in studies of migration patterns by the United Nations (International Organization for Migration 2022). The pandemic is only the most recent reminder of the ways we are all interconnected. Student and faculty populations are diversifying in ways that must be considered with an eye toward linguistic and social justice. The model takes these ongoing changes into account by positioning the sociocultural and human context as the enveloping circle in the image.

Within this circle, as the further description of the model makes clear, such factors as the evolving shape of the native-born American population and the influence and impact of immigration are part of the picture. Recent research of Indiana University of Pennsylvania rhetorician Wenqi Cui (2019), building on Krista Ratcliffe's (2005) theory of rhetorical listening, reveals the impact of cross-cultural factors in critical literacy—further supporting this model of critical literacy that integrates speaking and listening with reading and writing. These human changes bring shifting views of language that bear on every aspect of every sort of text at the core of critical literacy. As Manchester Community College professor and widely respected writing studies scholar Patrick Sullivan (2014, 2021) has made clear, the work of Ratcliffe and others shows the importance of this integration.

One more point on the evolution of the model. In this book, the model has changed several times, as noted. One aspect of the ongoing changes in the reading landscape that is not captured by the model is that text reading and note-taking programs continue to improve even while you are reading this book. Possibly, you are reading this book on some kind of device and not on paper pages: a smart phone, a Kindle or other tablet, or a laptop/desktop computer. Any kind of digital device connected to the internet is going to allow you to look up words you don't know and to bookmark parts of the text you want to be able to find again later. It might let you take notes, analyzing and synthesizing for your own purposes. It might allow you to access a library database to see what else I've written on this subject or to check my credentials as an author. What else might be possible? It's difficult to know, but changes keep coming, so the model will need to continue to evolve with all these possibilities.

Figure 7.1, then, is the model of critical literacy, meant now to provide a basis for the evidence-based recommendations to follow. I offer this detailed model with the hope that others will discuss, debate, and improve it. Such revision is to be expected in work on the complicated nature of critical literacy; my former colleague Anne Becker, an Oakland University writing and journalism scholar, demonstrated this process years ago in her review of cognitive process models of writing and revision in our co-edited collection on revision (Becker 2006). Earlier in the book, I offered preliminary versions of this model, intended to reflect the view that writing studies began with a focus on fragments of literacy, including only those that seemed relevant at the time. The earlier versions of the model were meant as selective views of what critical literacy looked like at each historical moment, not as a critique of the field.

Now, however, a fuller understanding of critical literacy is essential to the work of writing studies and, for that matter, the work of higher education altogether. It is the responsibility of all faculty, especially writing studies faculty, to help students develop the highest possible levels of critical literacy. This responsibility falls to writing studies faculty specifically because our classes and related classes (writing across the curriculum and writing in the disciplines, for example) are typically the ones all students are required to take at almost every institution of higher education. While writing and reading are foundational in every field, the crux of my argument is that critical literacy—integrating reading with writing, speaking, and listening—must be our goal.

The model begins with the core of critical literacy as defined at the start of the book and with a focus on texts. The "stuff" of critical literacy is texts of all kinds. A text might be a printed book or article or a tweet or a blog or a TV series or a rap song: anything that represents a meaning can comprise a text, presented on a page or a screen, large or small, created and/or perceived using handwriting, printing, drawing, sound, color, movement, and so forth. To receive or produce meaning, people use their foundational skills, such as comprehension of main ideas and details, word meanings, sentence structure, text structure, style, point of view, and related matters. The recent research on transactional views of reading as well as studies by cognitive scientists of brain functions in reading support the idea of reading as integrating all four skills, readers' prior knowledge, and their sociocultural situation, according to Bronx Community College scholar and teacher Jonathan Scott (2022). Text creation and perception using these integrated foundational skills is mediated with technological tools like computers, smart phones, paper, writing implements, musical instruments, headphones, keyboards, and the like—using abilities such as writing, typing, drawing, speaking and listening, manipulating computer images, playing music, or combining color, sound, and movement to send or receive a message. This view is also supported by the National Council of Teachers of English (NCTE 2022) in its recent position statement on media education and literacy.

Critical evaluation must play a key role in this integrated approach to critical literacy. Materials, whether sent or especially received, require evaluation on several discrete dimensions. First, they should be examined for authority, considering the source of the material, its provenance, and its credentials. Accuracy can be assessed by comparing the source text to others, using especially known and trusted sources to see if the information is consistent with that reported elsewhere and is thus trustworthy. Currency is relatively easy to establish, since time frames for printing or posting are usually readily available. Depending on the type of text, the most recent might be best, or the most closely related in time to an event under discussion might be best. Much depends on the type of text for this kind of evaluation. Relevance is another category of evaluation that is often easy to assess. In simple web searching or using a library database, the search tool will sort according its own judgment of relevance. But a reader or listener can also judge the content's pertinence to the question, issue, or topic under discussion.

Appropriateness might be harder to evaluate, but the reader or listener again must consider the use of the text: the situation of readers simply trying to find information for their own interest is different from that of college students writing research papers or government officials preparing reports for leaders. Different situations call for different kinds of texts. Finally, the most challenging type of evaluation is for the bias inherent in every kind of text. Students can and should learn important tools, including recognizing the loaded language of persuasion along with logical fallacies often used in texts of all kinds, but some of this evaluation must come from study and use.

While readers or listeners should always have these criteria at top of mind, writers and speakers should prepare their texts with the same mind-set. The model is meant to show that bias is an area that requires much more attention than it is currently receiving.

One example of how this integrated model might work in the classroom comes from high school teacher Robert B. Crisp. He offers a strong argument for the use of film in teaching students to read critically, making good use of literature to convey the essential points just listed:

> For film to be effective as a teaching tool . . . give students a text and have them plan it out first, and then compare [it] to a film version. Or compare multiple film versions of a given scene to see how different directors envision the story. The important takeaway is that a film represents one director's vision, which is a very different thing from saying it represents "The Truth." By extension, then, every person—every student—is entitled to their own vision as well. Once students are able to internalize that their perspective is valid, they learn to trust it. Then they learn to develop it. Finally, when they go back to that print text, they have an entirely different experience. They "see" the world of the story. They can "hear" the characters' voices. And they begin to interact with the text in a whole new way. Why did that happen? Why couldn't this happen? They begin to evaluate, to analyze, and to consider options. And isn't that what we want? (Crisp 2021, 2)

In this kind of classroom work, students will read the original text, watch and listen to the film, and write their own versions of it. In addition, though, the use of a film in this way sets up multiple versions to be evaluated and analyzed by students, using the alphabetic text as a base. It is easy to see how this work in the classroom can prepare students to view all kinds of texts in this way, reflected in the model offered in figure 7.1.

Finally, the model is not intended to suggest a hierarchy, as this example should make clear, but rather to show that each aspect of critical literacy is shaped and enfolded by the next. So, the biggest circle is the overall context in which critical literacy occurs, the sociocultural and human landscape in which we produce and understand meanings in texts of all kinds. These variables are probably too great in number to list here, but a small sampling might include "activity, culture, language, and systems of knowing of everyday life and experience that shape cognitive frameworks, worldviews, literacy practices, and other ways of thinking" (Smagorinsky et al. 2020, 62)—coming from a range of geographical locations within and beyond our borders, as well as those differently endowed through neurodiversity and varying levels and kinds of ability.

Just one example from the broad array of perspectives the sociocultural circle might include offers a sense of how one set of variables may impact critical literacy. This useful vantage point on sociocultural matters is derived from the Canadian approach to Indigenous studies. Writing about digital literacy among Indigenous people, Jennifer Hardwick, who works in this field at Kwanten Polytechnic University in British Columbia, reports on a study of digital literacy with students at multiple levels at her university. Beyond teaching students how to find materials and use lateral reading and other forms of fact-checking on sources, Hardwick introduces the ethics of information literacy using the principles of OCAP (ownership, control, access, and possession), as established by the First Nations Information Governance Center in Canada in 2020. These principles help students understand and think critically about what information they have access to and why, as well as appropriate uses of materials of all kinds (Hardwick 2021, 89).

This example is only one of the many perspectives that warrant consideration in a detailed model of critical literacy. The full model (figure 7.1) is consistent with a number of the key features of the recent NCTE position statement *Media Education in English Language Arts* (2022), as noted earlier. Critical literacy is highly complex but requires all of these factors and others not named here. The model (figure 7.1) is meant to show that the core process of meaning exchange draws on foundational skills related chiefly to the language of the text, technological tools and abilities, and critical evaluation in the context of sociocultural and human factors that might include gender, race/ethnicity, and class—which always play an essential role.

UCLA reading scholar Maryanne Wolf (2018) makes clear why the model must be continually updated and why critical reading is important in first-year writing and beyond. She writes that reading entails complex intellectual skills that will be essential in students' future lives:

> These are the very intellectual skills and personal attributes that provide young adults with the most important foundation for being able to recognize and manage the unavoidable changes and complexities ahead of them. Their development in the college years prepares them for the far more challenging forms of intellectual tenacity required of them after graduation: whether it is to write well-argued reports, documents, and briefs in their future professional lives; to critically read and evaluate the worth of a referendum, a court decision, medical documents, wills, investigative journalism, or a political candidate's personal record; or even to differentiate truth from falsehood in the escalating issues around false news and reports. A

democratic society requires the careful development of these abilities in its citizens, both young and old. (94)

Wolf's view presents the range of texts students will likely need to deal with in the future, whether they are reading, writing, speaking, or listening to them. Moreover, she makes the key point about the importance of these skills for those in and beyond school who will in due course become participants in a democratic society. Specific steps for classroom teachers are thus essential; the ones that follow are evidence-based and should be of use in every postsecondary classroom.

## Recommendations for What to Do on Monday

When I do workshops, at the end I try to get my audience members to commit to specific approaches they will take into their classes and use to improve students' critical literacy abilities. I tell them that I have attended far too many workshops and talks that offered great ideas that get buried on my desk with the handouts from the session. Of course, I want to think that faculty *will* use what I have given them, but I still feel it is important to ask them to say aloud the strategies they plan to use. Given the needs of students discussed earlier in this book and the uneven track record of writing studies as a discipline in its work on students' reading ability, there is reason to be skeptical. Here, then, is a series of recommendations for classroom practice, chosen based on very specific criteria. All of the following recommendations are derived from evidence of various kinds, including controlled empirical studies, less formal research analyses, experts' advice, teacher knowledge and classroom experience, and so forth. Relying on evidence is essential to ensure that these approaches will work in all sorts of postsecondary classrooms.

The importance of using evidence-based approaches cannot be overstated. The federal government believes that relying on evidence is so important that the United States Congress passed a law requiring the use of evidence-based practices in many areas (Pub. L. 115–435, enacted in 2019). A family member who works on housing issues in Washington, DC, assures me that this law specifically shapes the daily work of the government because it is part of the Administrative Procedures Act that has been in place for more than seventy years. The act states: "EVIDENCE.—Except as statutes otherwise provide, the proponent of a rule or order shall have the burden of proof. Any oral or documentary evidence may be received, but every agency shall as a matter of policy provide for the exclusion of irrelevant, immaterial, or unduly repetitious evidence and no sanction shall be imposed or rule or order be issued except upon consideration of the whole record or such portions thereof as may be cited by any party and as supported by and in accordance with the reliable, probative, and substantial evidence" (Administrative Procedures Act 1946). More recently, Congress convened a Commission on Evidence-Based Policy, which prepared a comprehensive report on the issue of using evidence to make federal government policy (Abraham et al. 2017). Its recommendations were turned into legislation that was signed into law in 2019 (Foundations for Evidence-Based Policymaking Act ["Evidence Act"], signed into law as Pub. L. 115–435). While extensive dialogue about scientific evidence occurred through the years of the pandemic, evidence of various kinds is still the key to choosing the best strategies for understanding and teaching critical reading in postsecondary classrooms.

There is one further cautionary point to keep in mind. In a meta-analysis, or study of studies, researchers Dolores Perin and Jodi Patrick Holschuh (2019) from Teachers College Columbia and Texas State University, respectively, looked at thirty-six studies of under-prepared students from across the country. Their report looks back over twenty years of research on literacy instruction of students whose abilities are not as strong as they should be at college entry, based on an assortment of measures. The findings show a need for rigorous research to confirm approaches that achieve positive outcomes for students, along with studies of which professional development approaches make a difference among faculty. Now, some studies point to such approaches that do help students develop their critical literacy abilities.

All of the recommendations that follow, whether focused on this particular group of under-prepared students or on all students, warrant further investigation. That further investigation, moreover, should include replication of studies, a case made clearly by Frostburg State University scholar John Raucci (2021). Raucci notes that many findings in writing studies research of all kinds are from years ago; much has changed in all aspects of higher education that make replication of earlier findings essential. This observation is especially true in reading, where, as I have shown, inconsistent attention has been the norm. Still, these recommendations do have evidence of some kind as their base.

I sought out strategies that derive from research or experience drawn mostly from work with nationally representative samples of students, so these recommendations are likely to work in any kind of postsecondary setting. I am presenting the most current findings because more and more information, texts, resources, and materials of all kinds come to readers in ever-varying digital forms. I am connecting the recommended strategies to the current fully developed model of the integrated language arts needed for critical literacy, presented in this book, as it is essential to focus on the growing array of digital materials that use printed alphabetic text, sounds, images, and movement to convey information. And I am including not only formal, empirical, peer-reviewed research but also the three other kinds of evidence mentioned earlier so that a wide array of research approaches form the basis of the recommendations. For all these reasons, I hope that every reader can take these recommendations directly into the classroom.

## MONDAY MORNING: RECOMMENDATIONS FROM EMPIRICAL EVIDENCE

Some of the most useful studies that point directly to the classroom come from the Stanford History Education Group (SHEG). SHEG has done a series of studies of students' critical reading online, where they get most of their information. These studies were discussed in some detail in chapter 1 of this book. The most recent study as of this writing (Breakstone et al. 2022) looks at a national sample of more than 3,000 high school students who were asked to evaluate a series of websites and other online materials for credibility. While the sample was not fully random and had other imperfections, it is still a large sample of students across the country who urgently need instruction in critical reading. In particular, Joel Breakstone and his colleagues list these skills: "choosing effective search terms, conducting reverse image searches, checking archived versions of webpages in the Internet Archive" (Breakstone et al. 2021, n.p.).

Earlier studies by the SHEG researchers point to specific approaches useful in the classroom, including teaching students to use fact-checkers' techniques of taking bearings and engaging in lateral reading to evaluate sources before using them in their own work. Taking bearings follows the kind of wayfinding used by experienced hikers, to get a sense of the area and set a compass for directional guidance (Wineburg and McGrew 2017). The internet has no compass per se, but getting a sense of what is available on the topic or issue to have some sense of direction is an important first step. Fact-checkers took bearings by looking around online to see what other information was available on the topic. Students should be taught how to take bearings on their research topics.

The second specific strategy discussed by the SHEG researchers that was used by the fact-checkers in their study is lateral reading. This approach entails going beyond looking at a website itself by, for example, checking its "about" page. Fact-checkers used lateral reading by leaving a site through opening new tabs to see what else has been said on the topic or issue. Sam Wineburg and Sarah McGrew (2017, 37) describe the approach this way:

> When reading laterally, one leaves a website and opens new tabs along a horizontal axis in order to use the resources of the Internet to learn more about a site and its claims. Lateral reading contrasts with vertical reading. Reading vertically, our eyes go up and down a screen to evaluate the features of a site. Does it look professional, free of typos and banner ads? Does it quote well-known sources? Are bias or faulty logic detectable? In contrast, lateral readers paid little attention to such features, leaping off a site after a few seconds and opening new tabs. They investigated a site by leaving it.

Teaching students to take bearings and to use lateral reading are specific steps teachers can take to show students how to do this kind of critical reading. Wineburg and McGrew (2017, 44–45) point out that these strategies move students beyond checklist approaches, such as the CRAAP (currency, relevance, authority, accuracy, and purpose) test discussed earlier in this book, because that test and others like it entail a focus on aspects of a website that do not always reveal its credibility. A more recent study shows how effectively this approach can work in classrooms, demonstrating with focused lessons that students who learned lateral reading techniques were significantly more successful at credibility evaluation (Wineburg et al. 2021); a cross-institutional research project based on this approach provides further support (Brodsky et al. 2021).

In an interview, SHEG director and Stanford University historian Joel Breakstone (telephone conversation, February 9, 2022) discussed the SHEG team's recent findings. He acknowledged that many faculty members, while aware of students' reading difficulties and willing to help, lack the background, training, and tools to provide helpful instruction. Teachers at all levels feel the press of trying to cover the curriculum in a specific course or grade level as a demand on their time; teaching critical reading is beyond their expertise, and they see it as drawing them away from required material. The concern is also acknowledged by foundations and other funders, such as the McCormick Foundation, a nonprofit organization in Chicago (https://www.mccormickfoundation.org/), which Breakstone said funded the original set of SHEG studies. The foundation wanted to assess the efficacy of some of the programs it was offering and asked the SHEG scholars to design studies to evaluate them.

In Breakstone and colleagues' study (2021), a nationally representative sample of almost 3,500 high school students was given a series of tasks to test their ability to evaluate materials on the internet. The tasks were similar to those in the studies reported in chapter 1: judging the credibility of a site, distinguishing an ad from fact-based news reporting, and so forth. The published report provides a breakdown of the students' backgrounds, showing that while all the students had difficulty with all of the tasks, there was some variation based on demographic characteristics. In summary, Breakstone and his colleagues write: Students struggled on all of the tasks. At least two thirds of the student responses were scored as Beginning for each of the six tasks. On four of the six tasks, more than 90 percent of students' responses were scored as Beginning. Of all the student responses to the six tasks, fewer than 3 percent received a Mastery score. (2021, n.p.)

The analysis of student performance showed that students who reported higher grades did better than those with lower grades, and those further along in school (that is, seniors compared to first-year students) also did better. In terms of socioeconomic status, using proxy measures, students' eligibility for free lunch predicted lower performance and maternal education predicted higher performance. But overall, the SHEG researchers note, "We have emphasized the need to leave a site to get an accurate read on it. Students would obviously benefit by mastering a host of other skills: choosing effective search terms, conducting reverse image searches, checking archived versions of webpages in the Internet Archive, and so on" (2021, n.p.). Thus, specific instruction is urgently needed.

In our conversation, Breakstone mentioned another especially useful strategy students can be taught to improve their ability to evaluate materials online, created by Mike Caulfield at the University of Washington School of Information and called SIFT. SIFT is an acronym for four steps: stop, investigate, find and trace. (Caulfield's approach is summarized in detail by Butler, Sargent, and Smith [2021]). This approach has been widely shared and used in high schools and colleges to improve students' digital literacy and thus offers a specific series of steps that can be taught in classes of all kinds at all levels. It also goes beyond the checklist approach of CRAAP, as it is not a list but a deliberate strategy for critical thinking with guidance on how to look carefully at a website.

The online reading tool called Perusall, discussed in detail in chapter 6, offers another tested resource to help students read more effectively. A detailed study by Allison S. Walker (2019) at High Point University used this online reading and annotation tool to test its impact on students' reading skills. The tool rewards students for detailed analysis of the text and annotations of assigned material; it also allows them to communicate within a class to share insights and exchange questions and comments prior to class discussion. Walker compared the performances of 125 second-year students in second-semester writing courses in the disciplines, with some using Perusall and some blocked from accessing the tool. Both groups (multiple sections of different classes) had the same assignments and varied in terms of whether they were in online or in-person class configurations. The students who used Perusall showed significantly better reading and writing performance than those who read assigned materials as online PDFs or chose to print the material and read it on paper. Thus, online reading can, if used with a closely monitored system of support, make an important difference to students' development of key reading skills.

A different array of studies summarized by UCLA reading scholar Maryanne Wolf points clearly to the advantages of reading on paper as opposed to reading on any kind of screen or device. While in some of the research shows conflicting results, most findings suggest that especially for longer materials like books, readers understand and remember more if they read on paper rather than on a screen (Wolf 2018, 78–82). A key point here is that materials published in the traditional format are much more likely to have been edited and reviewed for accuracy than are websites of dubious origin.

So, what to do in class? Here is a summary of strategies based on empirical studies:

- Teach taking bearings and lateral reading
- Explore use of the SIFT approach for research purposes
- Consider using Perusall or another online tool that focuses students' attention specifically on close reading and annotation
- Have students see for themselves the increased efficacy of reading longer works like books or full-length research reports on paper.

### MONDAY MORNING: RECOMMENDATIONS FROM OTHER KINDS OF STUDIES

Not all of the research that has been done on reading comes from large-scale empirical studies that some scholars consider the gold standard. Certainly, in science and medicine, that standard is probably appropriate. However, for the classroom, other kinds of studies and teachers' real-world experience are equally useful and warrant consideration. They can provide helpful guidance for Monday morning practitioners wanting to know what to do and how to do it. One example is a small study done by Beth Counihan (2021) at Queensborough Community College of the City University of New York. Though small, the study is useful because it was carefully done after IRB review and involved a group of fifty college students from diverse backgrounds at a two-year college and open access (TYCOA) institution. Counihan had students write summaries of newspaper articles and then run them through an Open Educational Resource reading tool called the Flesch-Kincaid Readability Statistics program (readable.com). The program provides a grade-level estimate for any text and is freely available online.

Students used the results to revise their writing; 85 percent were able to increase the grade level of their writing by two levels through revision. Counihan pointed out to me that Word, among other programs or software, can also provide readability statistics for free (Beth Counihan, personal communication, January 13, 2022). But Counihan also reports that the students looked carefully at readable.com and realized what it said about reading per se, that is, that it was superficial and did not pay attention to inferences and other important features of reading. But the students also found the program easy to use and a motivational tool to improve their writing (Counihan 2021). This study has several attractive features: it involved a diverse student population, used a free online tool readily available to all students, and provided writing students with important insights relevant to their reading as well as their writing. This sort of approach builds directly on the language arts model presented in this book.

Different research on the nature of online materials that focuses on algorithms discussed earlier in this chapter leads to additional teaching suggestions. Teachers should certainly look at the sources cited, but an in-class demonstration of how algorithms work could be an eye-opening experience. UCLA scholar Safiya Umoja Noble (2018) in particular has research to support her claims about racism and bias in search engines. She discusses how her own searches have revealed widespread biases in terms of race, gender assignment and gender identity, ethnicity, and other issues on the internet. While her argument ultimately is for a need for greater regulation of search tools, readers need to understand right now how the search process works and the various ways it is biased. Library faculty, as noted above, can also be helpful in guiding students to a more critical approach to searching.

Project Information Literacy (PIL) has also looked at algorithms, among other issues that confront students at the postsecondary level. A careful qualitative study done by Alison J. Head and the PIL researchers (Head, Fister, and MacMillan 2020) offers specific recommendations for helping students understand how algorithms work to shape what they get from the internet, among other needs for more and better critical reading. The study was a yearlong qualitative study involving focus group discussions among 103 undergraduate students and 37 faculty members at eight institutions across the country. The insights gained from these conversations led to four specific recommendations: (1) peer-to-peer contact will be best for learning, as students think faculty are insufficiently current and adept; (2) systematic instruction on algorithms and other aspects of the information landscape must be coherent and organized across educational levels and disciplines; (3) news organizations can be more transparent and explicit about their use of algorithms and readers'/viewers' options for limiting their impact; and (4) faculty can introduce "algorithmic justice" as a key part of the curriculum along with outreach to community members at large.

More recently, Head (2021) wrote an article in the Provocation Series on the PIL website that summarizes her own and others' research, including more than forty references to prior studies on college students' reading abilities and challenges. From these prior studies, Head offers four additional specific recommendations for faculty and librarians: (1) provide a tangible context for the readings students are assigned, possibly by reading part of a text aloud and explaining how the reading fits into the current work and offering critical guide questions as students do the assignment; (2) show students how reading is a key part of the search process by reading a piece collaboratively, actively exploring a series of critical questions, and preparing to evaluate the article through other sources and thus modeling the kind of research and critical reading students should be doing for their own projects; (3) make strategic decisions about what and how much reading to assign, since research shows that less reading with deeper engagement may lead to more effective reading and learning; and (4) help students read with empathy, to understand differing views and how they get attention in the current information landscape.

So, what to do in class? Here are strategies based on these kinds of studies:

- Present the readable.com readability tool and have students use it with their writing, perhaps after discussion of what the tool does and does

not say about reading; encourage reading and writing with empathy for both sources and readers.
- Bring in librarians anywhere and everywhere: as a resource for student research projects, as presenters in class at the start of a project, as consultants; have them demonstrate the role of active and critical reading in the search process.
- Ratchet up instruction on algorithms as discussed above and how to work with and around them, preferably with live demos that will surprise students and make a big impression. Librarians can help here too, as can peer-to-peer exchange.
- Provide context and rationale for reading assignments, along with specific strategies for active reading, while considering how much and what kind of reading to assign with an idea that perhaps "less is more."

## MONDAY MORNING: EXPERT RECOMMENDATIONS AND STATEMENTS

Another way of looking for guidance for Monday morning is to see what experts have said above and beyond specific research studies that lead to teaching strategies. Professional organizations have moved in this direction, either directly or indirectly, because the work on reading needs to happen both at the K–12 level and at colleges and universities of all kinds. For example, at the K–12 level, the American Federation of Teachers (AFT), the major professional organization for public school teachers, has recognized the need for greater emphasis on reading. In addition to front-line classroom work and even under the duress of the pandemic, in 2021, AFT members began a new initiative called "Reading Opens the World" (Weingarten 2021).

This initiative entails several key goals: giving kids free books, providing focused professional development for all staff, giving parents tools and strategies to enhance kids' literacy, and building partnerships of schools, parents, and communities in support of literacy activities. In cooperation with First Book, a national nonprofit organization that donates free books to children in need (firstbook.org), the AFT has given away millions of books to children. Teachers need considerable additional training to work with students who need help with reading, which the AFT is working to provide in the form of both an extant forty-hour course and a more flexible ten-hour online course to improve teachers' skills and strategies for working with such students. Various other events and options are planned as well (Weingarten 2021). A similar major initiative at the postsecondary level is vastly overdue and urgently needed everywhere.

At the postsecondary level, I was the instigator and co-chair of a task force of experts on reading issues, created by the Conference on College Composition and Communication (CCCC), the college section of the National Council of Teachers of English. There were eight of us from a variety of two-year and four-year public and private institutions nationwide, all with expertise in postsecondary reading. Our charge was to create a position statement for the organization on the importance of reading in the teaching of college writing. The statement was drafted and discussed among us at length, then submitted for two rounds of review by CCCC's Executive Committee. It was posted on the organization's website in March 2021 and can be found at https://cccc.ncte.org/cccc/the-role-of-reading. The position statement is meant to indicate the organization's view on the issue at hand; its website features a number of such position statements.

The key principles quoted here are followed by sets of specific classroom strategies: "Principle 1: Teach Reading Comprehension; Principle 2: Teach Reading Approaches That Move Beyond Basic Comprehension; Principle 3: Foster Mindful Reading to Encourage Students to Think Metacognitively about Their Reading in Preparation for a Variety of Reading in Different Contexts; Principle 4: Teach Students How to Read Texts Closely and Focus on Significant Details and Patterns" (Conference on College Composition and Communication 2021). Because CCCC is the major professional organization for teachers of college writing, it can fairly be described as the main authority in the field. In addition, other major professional organizations of experts do have recommendations for teachers. For instance, the Modern Language Association is the major professional organization for teachers of literature in English and other languages; MLA's recent work on reading was mentioned earlier in this chapter.

The major professional organization focused on teaching reading, mainly but not exclusively in K–12 schools, is the International Literacy Association. While much of the organization's work is focused on basic reading instruction, it also touches on postsecondary reading—particularly in one of its journals, *Reading Research Quarterly* (*RRQ*), and in conference sessions devoted to literacy at the college level. It is a huge organization of 300,000 teachers and scholars from 128 countries, according to its website (International Literacy Association 2022). It offers a focused definition of literacy: "Literacy is the ability to identify, understand, interpret, create, compute, and communicate using visual, audible, and digital materials across disciplines and in any context" (International Literacy Association 2022). In 2020, the association published a two-part special issue on the science of reading, a compilation of twenty-six articles from the leading scholars in the field (https://ila.onlinelibrary.wiley.com/journal/19362722/science-of-reading).

The two parts include summary/overview articles on many aspects of the teaching and learning of reading. Of these, two are particularly pertinent here. The first is a report by Steve Graham (2020) on the need for more collaboration between reading and writing scholars, since many studies show that improving students' abilities in one area improves their abilities in the other, as discussed earlier in this book. A second article in the special issue of *RRQ* points to the relevance of listening comprehension in the development of reading ability, both in learning to read and as students move through school. While it does not seem to point specifically to the usefulness of listening to postsecondary reading, the article suggests that listening can play an ongoing role in the development of reading ability (Cervetti et al. 2020). These two pieces, taken together, support much of the model of critical literacy I am proposing that integrates writing and listening with speaking and reading. Online material across a range of different types of resources requires critical literacy skills in all four areas. These articles don't point specifically to in-class teaching strategies but do provide support for the model of critical literacy proposed here and show that writing and listening play key roles.

Other professional organizations may be paying some attention to reading, but it isn't always easy to see this on their websites. A good positive example is the site of the American Association of Chemistry Teachers, an organization for postsecondary chemistry faculty. Among other things, it offers webinars and in 2021 had two on reading listed on its website. The first was a professional development discussion of the book *Readicide: How Schools Are Killing Reading and What You Can Do about It* by Kelly Gallagher (2009). The plan was to discuss the book and show how using a close reading strategy could help students improve their reading along with their understanding of chemistry concepts and applications. A second session was designed to show teachers how to create what is called a 5E reading lesson based on any current chemistry report (in a magazine or newspaper, for instance). The 5Es are engage, explore, explain, elaborate, evaluate—an easy list of principles clearly consistent with the aspects of critical reading discussed earlier (American Association of Chemistry Teachers 2020). A key point here is that by using this strategy with material students have already been assigned to read, faculty can achieve their own instructional goals while helping students become more effective and efficient critical readers.

The American Historical Association (AHA) is another organization that offers some direction regarding critical reading. In an online publication, the organization offers a guide to using new media to teach history at the college level developed by John McClymer (2005), an Assumption College American history professor. While it is not presented as a statement of the organization's position on teaching reading, the guide is clearly identified as an AHA publication and so presumably offers views the organization supports. McClymer generally suggests that students need guidance on close reading of materials they find online, but while faculty need to provide structure, they also need to allow students the flexibility to find the key points and issues in materials on their own. An important problem McClymer points out is that abundant material on many historical topics is available online, so faculty setting up appropriate selections or showing students how to select for themselves and for class purposes is essential. These suggestions provide generic advice for teaching that can be used in any subject area. From these two samples, it should be clear that as is true in earlier parts of the book, it's inaccurate to say that no attention is being paid to reading among the various academic disciplines. Attention is being paid, but it is limited, somewhat scattered, and not necessarily focused on the essential aspects of critical reading urgently needed by all students.

So, what to do in class? Here are strategies based on experts' views and recommendations:

- Integrate reading, writing, speaking, and listening whenever possible
- Teach basic reading comprehension and critical evaluation skills
- Help students understand options for different kinds of reading to make mindful choices given topic and purpose
- Demonstrate, encourage, require, and incentivize active, close reading techniques using 5E or similar approaches
- Get additional professional training (through online professional development, workshops, and coursework) on how to help students become better readers.

## MONDAY MORNING: RECOMMENDATIONS BASED ON TEACHER KNOWLEDGE/CLASSROOM EXPERIENCE

Not all evidence-based approaches come from empirical studies and other kinds of formal research. Reading is sufficiently complex that no single kind of research will do justice to the need for more attention to students' reading needs; it is surely better to think of a range of different kinds of evidence, as discussed here. Some of the evidence comes from front-line teachers in classrooms who have used different strategies they deemed necessary for their own students. Several examples point to the ways teacher knowledge can be used immediately, as appropriate, with different groups of students. As mentioned earlier, the MLA, to its credit, has paid considerable attention to reading—including, for instance, inviting a blog post on its *Style* site from Kingsborough Community College reading scholars Annie Del Principe and Rachel Ihara (2019).

They offer a series of recommendations for teachers, some of which can be taken straight to the classroom:

—Often, nonlinear or cursory reading is all that students are being asked to do.
—We often do the same things students do when we read.
—We faculty members mean different things when we talk about reading.
—There is not one right way to read or consume texts.
—We should take the time to learn how our students actually read and bring that knowledge into the classroom" (Del Principe and Ihara 2019). These scholars have used their classroom experiences to reach these insights; many faculty members will see them as consistent with their own work with students. Conversations with students can reveal their current approaches to reading, if they are comfortable sharing this information. Understanding what students are thinking and doing and why can allow open discussion of more and better choices. Ellen C. Carillo's work, discussed earlier, suggests that mindful choices about reading can make an important difference in students' performance.

A more direct strategy is offered by Virginia Tech educational psychology professor Peter Doolittle. His approach entails having students prepare twenty-five-word written summaries of reading assignments. I can vouch for this approach, which I saw Doolittle demonstrate at a Lilly Teaching Conference years ago and have been using ever since. The method is presented most clearly on Doolittle's (n.d.) website, along with instructions or criteria for grading. When I have used this approach on sections of a textbook reading, for example, students approach it as a kind of game to see if they can pack the key ideas of a text section into a coherent twenty-five-word statement; these summaries, if done by small groups in class (or breakout groups on Zoom), can be posted to a discussion board in Blackboard or a similar platform, resulting in the entire class having a substantive summary of a chapter.

The best part of these discussions is that students focus on the material's content and will argue about the meaning of the main ideas of their assigned section—exactly what most faculty want to happen in small-group discussion. The second-best feature of the twenty-five-word summary work is that it entails an integration of reading, writing, speaking, and listening if it is done as class discussion, since students must listen to one another as they speak about the reading and they must have read the material to write their summaries. To ensure that all students do both the reading and writing parts, each student can do a summary, then they can all share their work to create a single group summary. In workshops I have presented, faculty from across the disciplines see why this approach has many advantages and immediately claim that they will use it.

As an alternative, for those who are looking for the presentation of an entire course or sequence of assignments, other published sources can provide this kind of guidance. One carefully done example is in Arlene Fish Wilner's *Rethinking Reading in College* (2020), an NCTE publication that deserves more attention than it has received to date. Wilner takes up the nature of the reading process in detail, with clear explanations for non-specialists. She discusses the importance of teaching reading in writing classes and beyond. At the end of the book, she offers assignments and examples. A similar kind of assignment set appears in Patrick Sullivan's 2021 book, discussed earlier in this book, again based on years of classroom experience. Sometimes, seeing the full sequence of assignments for a complete course can make it easier to create a suitable approach for a particular set of students. These assignment sets are based on the evidence of teacher experience and expertise.

So, what to do in class? Here are strategies based on teacher expertise and classroom experience:

- Talk to students about their reading approaches and strategies
- Abandon the idea that there is only one approach to postsecondary critical reading so that mindful choices among varied strategies are possible depending on topic and purpose
- Use twenty-five-word summaries as a springboard for class discussion based on the language arts model for efficient reading and writing, speaking and listening.

I have organized this discussion by the type of evidence that supports specific strategies for teachers. It should be clear that the evidence points to a number of ways teachers can improve the way they think about critical reading, allowing them to shape their courses and assignments in ways that lead students to more effective and efficient critical reading. Faculty can also take direct steps in the classroom to help students understand what they are reading, why they are reading it, and how to make strategic choices about doing the reading; they can give students tools and techniques to use as they read course material and as they do their own research that integrates reading, writing, speaking, and listening. Postsecondary teachers should immediately engage in active collaboration with their library colleagues who have been working on information literacy for years; these colleagues have knowledge and skills with respect to algorithms, searches, lateral reading, hoax sites, credibility, and other issues that they will gladly share with students in class or through research consultations.

To date, writing studies has treated critical reading like a lost relative, only vaguely there beyond the active work of the field, a sort of "weddings and funerals" attendee at occasional meetings (like Dartmouth) or a few conference sessions but mostly neglected or set aside. In this review of the status of students' reading challenges, writing studies' inconsistent and incidental attention to reading over its history makes clear how faculty in the field and others in every discipline in higher education have failed to address this urgent need. Textbook publishers and those producing other kinds of instructional tools in both print and digital forms can and should pay much more attention to the critical reading students will need in college and beyond. These are approaches, drawn from an array of different kinds of evidence, that writing studies faculty and all others can adopt for themselves as well as in their classrooms and in collaboration with librarians to move critical literacy to the center of undergraduate education for everyone.

# References

Abraham, Katharine G. and Ron Haskins, co-chairs. 2017. "The Promise of Evidence-Based Policymaking." *Report of the Commission on Evidence-Based Policymaking.* Washington, DC: United States Commission on Evidence-Based Policymaking.

ACT. 2021. "Reading Test Description for the ACT." https://www.act.org/content/act/en/products-and-services/the-act/test-preparation/description-of-reading-test.html.

ACT. 2024. "ACT for Higher Education Professionals." https://www.act.org/content/act/en/products-and-services/the-act-postsecondary-professionals/scores.html.

Adams, Peter. 2020a. "Giving Hope to the American Dream: Implementing a Corequisite Model of Developmental Writing." *Composition Studies* 48 (2): 19–34.

Adams, Peter. 2020b. *The Hub: A Place for Reading and Writing.* Boston: Bedford/St. Martin's/Macmillan.

Adams, Peter. 2020c. "Pedagogical Evolution: How My Teaching Has Changed in Ten Years of the Accelerated Learning Program (ALP)." In *Sixteen Teachers Teaching: Two-Year College Perspectives*, edited by Patrick Sullivan, 247–278. Logan: Utah State University Press.

Adler, Mortimer J., and Charles Van Doren. 1972. *How to Read a Book.* New York: Simon and Schuster.

Administrative Procedure Act. 1946. Public Law 404, 79th Congress. 5 USC §552. https://www.justice.gov › legacy › act-pl79–404.

Alexander, Patricia A., and Emily Fox. 2018. "Reading Research and Practice over the Decades." In *Theoretical Models and Processes of Literacy*, edited by Donna E. Alvermann, Norman J. Unrau, Misty Sailors, and Robert B. Ruddell, 35–64. New York: Routledge. https://www.routledgehandbooks.com/doi/10.4324/9781315110592-3.

Allington, Richard L., and Peter H. Johnston. 2002. *Reading to Learn: Lessons from Exemplary Fourth-Grade Classrooms*. New York: Guilford.

Alvermann, Donna E. 2010. "The Teaching of Reading." In *Reading the Past, Writing the Future: A Century of American Literacy Education and the National Council of Teachers of English*, edited by Erika Lindemann, 55–90. Urbana, IL: National Council of Teachers of English.

American Association of Chemistry Teachers. 2020. *How to Create a 5E Reading Lesson Using ChemMatters*. Webinars | How to Create a 5E Reading Lesson Using ChemMatters | AACT. teachchemistry.org.

American Association of Community Colleges. 2023. *Fast Facts 2023*. https://www.aacc.nche.edu/research-trends/fast-facts/.

Appatova, Victoria, and Alice S. Horning. 2023. "Developing Critical Literacy: An Urgent Goal." *To Improve the Academy: A Journal of Educational Development* 42 (2): n.p. https://doi.org/10.3998/tia.2032.

Applebee, Arthur N. 1974. *Tradition and Reform in the Teaching of English: A History*. Urbana, IL: National Council of Teachers of English.

Applebee, Arthur N. 2013. "Common Core State Standards: The Promise and the Peril in a National Palimpsest." *English Journal* 103: 25–33.

Applebee, Arthur N., Judith A. Langer, and Marc A. Nachowitz. 2010. "NCTE and the Teaching of Literature." In *Reading the Past, Writing the Future: A Century of American Literacy Education and the National Council of Teachers of English*, edited by Erika Lindemann, 173–216. Urbana IL: National Council of Teachers of English.

Armstrong, Sonya L., Jeanine L. Williams, and Norman A. Stahl. 2018. "Reading and Writing." In *Handbook of College Reading and Study Strategy Research*, 3rd ed., edited by Rona F. Flippo and Thomas W. Bean, 143–167. New York: Routledge/Taylor and Francis.

Association of College and Research Libraries. 2016. *Framework for Information Literacy for Higher Education*. http://www.ala.org/acrl/standards/ilframework.

Aull, Laura L. 2020. *How Students Write: A Linguistic Analysis*. New York: Modern Language Association.

Aull, Laura L., and Valerie Ross. 2020. "From Cow Paths to Conversation: Rethinking the Argumentative Essay." *Pedagogy* 20 (1): 21–34. https://doi.org/10.1215/15314200-7878955.

Bahr, Peter R., Loris P. Fagioli, John Hetts, Craig Hayward, Terrence Willett, Daniel Lamoree, Mallory Newell, Ken Sorey, and Rachel B. Baker. 2017. *Improving Placement Accuracy in California's Community Colleges Using Multiple Measures of High School Achievement*. Community College Research Center Multiple Measures Project. New York: Teachers College Columbia University. https://rpgroup.org/Portals/0/Documents/Projects/MultipleMeasures/Publications/Bahr_et_al-2017-Improving_Placement_Accuracy_in_California.pdf.

Bailey, Thomas R., Shanna Smith Jaggars, and Davis Jenkins. 2015. *Redesigning America's Community Colleges: A Clearer Path to Student Success*. Cambridge, MA: Harvard

University Press. https://search-ebscohost-com.proxy.lib.umich.edu/login.aspx?direct=true&db=e000xna&AN=986726&site=ehost-live&scope=site.

Baker-Bell, April. 2013. "'I Never Really Knew the History behind African American Language': Critical Language Pedagogy in an Advanced Placement English Language Arts Class." *Equity and Excellence in Education* 46 (3): 355–370. https://doi.org/10.1080/10665684.2013.806848.

Baker-Bell, April. 2020a. "Dismantling Anti-Black Linguistic Racism in English Language Arts Classrooms: Toward an Anti-Racist Black Language Pedagogy." *Theory into Practice* 59 (1): 8–21. https://doi.org/10.1080/00405841.2019.1665415.

Baker-Bell, April. 2020b. *Linguistic Justice: Black Language, Literacy, Identity, and Pedagogy*. New York: NCTE-Routledge Research Series.

Barclay, Donald A. 2018. *Fake News, Propaganda, and Plain Old Lies: How to Find Trustworthy Information in the Digital Age*. Lanham, MD: Rowman and Littlefield.

Barnett, Elisabeth A., Elizabeth Kopko, Dan Cullinan, and Clive R. Belfield. 2020. "Who Should Take College-Level Courses? Impact Findings from an Evaluation of a Multiple Measures Assessment Strategy." Center for the Analysis of Postsecondary Readiness. https://postsecondaryreadiness.org/lessons-learned-multiple-measures-assessment/.

Baron, Naomi. 2021. *How We Read Now: Strategic Choices for Print, Screen, and Audio*. New York: Oxford University Press.

Bartholomae, David, and Anthony Petrosky, eds. 1986. *Facts, Artifacts, and Counterfacts: Theory and Method for a Reading and Writing Course*. Portsmouth, NH: Boynton/Cook.

Bartholomae, David, and Anthony Petrosky, eds. 2005. *Resources for Teaching Ways of Reading*, 7th ed. Boston: Bedford/St. Martin's.

Bartholomae, David, and Anthony Petrosky, eds. 2008. *Ways of Reading: An Anthology for Writers*. Boston: Bedford/St. Martin's.

Bartholomae, David, Anthony Petrosky, and Stacey Waite, eds. 2020. *Ways of Reading: An Anthology for Writers, 12th ed*. Boston: Bedford/St. Martin's.

Bazerman, Charles. 1980. "A Relationship between Reading and Writing: The Conversation Model." *College English* 41 (6): 656–661.

Beam, Alex. 2008. *A Great Idea at the Time: The Rise, Fall, and Curious Afterlife of the Great Books*. New York: Public Affairs/Perseus Books.

Becker, Anne. 2006. "A Review of Writing Model Research Based on Cognitive Processes." In *Revision: History, Theory, and Practice*, edited by Alice Horning and Anne Becker, 25–49. West Lafayette, IN: Parlor Press/WAC Clearinghouse.

Belic, Roko. 2020. *Trust Me: Are You Being Manipulated?* Newburgh, NY: New Day Films. https://www.newday.com/film/trust-me.

Benjamin, Ruha. 2019. *Race after Technology: Abolitionist Tools for the New Jim Code*. Cambridge, UK: Polity.

Berman, Amy I., Edward H. Haertel, and James W. Pellegrino. 2020. *Comparability of Large-Scale Educational Assessments: Issues and Recommendations*. Washington, DC: National Academy of Education.

Bickerstaff, Susan, Katie Beal, Julia Raufman, Erika B. Lewy, and Austin Slaughter. 2022. *Five Principles for Reforming Developmental Education: A Review of the Evidence*.

Center for the Analysis of Postsecondary Readiness, Community College Research Center. New York: Teachers College Columbia University. https://ccrc.tc.columbia.edu/publications/faculty-experiences-teaching-developmental-reading-writing.html.

Bickerstaff, Susan, and Julia Raufman. 2017. *From "Additive" to "Integrative": Experiences of Faculty Teaching Developmental Integrated Reading and Writing Courses*. CCRC Working Paper 96. New York: Community College Research Center/Teachers College Columbia University. https://ccrc.tc.columbia.edu/media/k2/attachments/capr-synthesis-report-final.pdf.

Bizzell, Patricia. 1992. *Academic Discourse and Critical Consciousness*. Pittsburgh, PA: University of Pittsburgh Press. http://ebookcentral.proquest.com/lib/oakland/detail.action?docID=2038090.

Blaauw-Hara, Mark, Carrie S. Tebeau, and Dominic Borowiak. 2020. "Is a Writing-about-Writing Approach Appropriate for Community College Developmental Writers in a Corequisite Class?" *Composition Studies* 48 (2): 54–73. http://search.ebscohost.com.huaryu.kl.oakland.edu/login.aspx?direct=true&db=a9h&AN=147242265&site=ehost-live&scope=site.

Blackwell-Starnes, Katt, and Janice R. Walker. 2017. "Reports from the LILAC Project: Designing a Translocal Study." In *Points of Departure: Rethinking Student Source Use and Writing Studies Research Methods*, edited by Tricia Serviss and Sandra Jamieson, 62–82. Logan: Utah State University Press.

Blau, Sheridan. 2017. "How the Teaching of Literature in College Writing Classes Might Rescue Reading as It Never Has Before." In *Deep Reading: Teaching Reading in the Writing Classroom*, edited by Patrick Sullivan, Howard Tinberg, and Sheridan Blau, 265–290. Urbana, IL: National Council of Teachers of English.

Bleich, David. 1975. *Readings and Feelings: An Introduction to Subjective Criticism*. Urbana, IL: National Council of Teachers of English.

Bleich, David. 1978. *Subjective Criticism*. Baltimore, MD: Johns Hopkins University Press.

Blewett, Kelly, Tiane Donahue, and Cynthia Monroe, eds. 2021. *The Expanding Universe of Writing Studies: Higher Education Writing Research*. New York: Peter Lang.

Bloom, Lynn Z. 1999. "The Essay Canon." *College English* 61 (4): 401–430.

Bloom, Lynn Z. 2007. "The Ineluctable Elitism of Essays and Why They Prevail in First-Year Composition Courses." *Open Words* 1 (2): 62–78.

Boehm, Shelby. 2020. "Rethinking Summer Reading Cover to Cover." National Council of Teachers of English. https://ncte.org/blog/2020/06/rethinking-summer-reading-cover-cover/.

Brandt, Deborah. 2001. *Literacy in American Lives*. Cambridge, UK: Cambridge University Press.

Brandt, Deborah. 2015. *The Rise of Writing: Redefining Mass Literacy*. Cambridge, UK: Cambridge University Press.

Breakstone, Joel, Sarah McGrew, Mark Smith, Teresa Ortega, and Sam Wineburg. 2018. "Why We Need a New Approach to Digital Literacy." *Phi Delta Kappan* 99 (6):

27–32. https://kappanonline.org/breakstone-need-new-approach-teaching-digital-literacy/.

Breakstone, Joel, Mark Smith, Sam Wineburg, Amie Rapaport, Jill Carle, Marshall Garland, and Anna Saavedra. 2021. "Students' Civic Online Reasoning: A National Portrait." *Educational Researcher* 50 (8): 505–515. https://doi.org/10.3102/0013189X211017495.

Brereton, John C., ed. 1995. *The Origins of Composition Studies in the American College, 1875–1925: A Documentary History*. Pittsburgh, PA: University of Pittsburgh Press.

Brereton, John C. 2012. "A Closer Look at the Harvard Entrance Examinations in the 1870s." In *Writing Assessment in the Twenty-First Century: Essays in Honor of Edward M. White*, edited by Norbert Elliot and Les Perelman, 31–43. Cresskill, NJ: Hampton.

Brewer, Meaghan. 2020. *Conceptions of Literacy: Graduate Instructors and the Teaching of First-Year Composition*. Logan: Utah State University Press.

Brodsky, Jessica E., Patricia J. Brooks, Donna Scimeca, Ralitsa Todorova, Peter Galati, Michael Batson, Robert Grosso, Michael Matthews, Victor Miller, and Michael Caulfield. 2021. "Improving College Students' Fact-Checking Strategies through Lateral Reading Instruction in a General Education Civics Course." *Cognitive Research: Principles and Implications* 6 (23). https://doi.org/10.1186/s41235-021-00291-4.

Bruffee, Kenneth A. 1982. *A Short Course in Writing*, 2nd ed. Cambridge, MA: Winthrop.

Bruggink, Marian, Nicole Swart, Annelies van der Lee, and Eliane Segers. 2022. *Putting PIRLS to Use in Classrooms across the Globe: IEA Research for Educators*. Cham, Switzerland: Springer. https://doi-org.huaryu.kl.oakland.edu/10.1007/978-3-030-95266-2_4.

Bunch, Will. 2022. *After the Ivory Tower Falls: How College Broke the American Dream and Blew Up Our Politics—and How to Fix It*. New York: William Morrow/HarperCollins.

Butler, Walter D., Aloha Sargent, and Kelsey Smith. 2021. *Introduction to College Research*. Creative Commons Attribution 4.0 International License. https://oer.pressbooks.pub/collegeresearch/chapter/the-sift-method/.

Calhoon-Dillahunt, Carolyn, Darin L. Jensen, Sarah Z. Johnson, Howard Tinberg, and Christie Toth. 2017. "TYCA Guidelines for Preparing Teachers of English in the Two-Year College." *College English* 79 (6): 550–560.

Campbell, Joanne. 1992. "Controlling Voices: The Legacy of English A at Radcliffe College 1883–1917." *College Composition and Communication* 43 (4): 472–485.

Canagarajah, Suresh. 2012. *Translingual Practice: Global Englishes and Cosmopolitan Relations*. New York: Routledge, Taylor, and Francis.

Carillo, Ellen C. 2015. *Securing a Place for Reading in Composition: The Importance of Teaching for Transfer*. Logan: Utah State University Press.

Carillo, Ellen C. 2017a. "A Place for Reading in the Framework for Success in Postsecondary Writing: Recontextualizing the Habits of Mind." In *The Framework for Success in Postsecondary Writing: Scholarship and Applications*, edited by Sherry Rankins-Robertson, Nicholas Behm, and Duane Roen, 38–53. Anderson, SC: Parlor Press.

Carillo, Ellen C. 2017b. *A Writer's Guide to Mindful Reading*. Fort Collins, CO: WAC Clearinghouse.

Carillo, Ellen C. 2018. *Teaching Readers in Post-Truth America*. Logan: Utah State University Press.

Carillo, Ellen C. 2022. *The MLA Guide to Digital Literacy*, 2nd ed. New York: Modern Language Association.

Carillo, Ellen C. Forthcoming. "The Case for Teaching Skim Reading in First-Year Writing Courses." In *What Is College Writing 2.0*, edited by Howard Tinberg, Patrick Sullivan, and Sheridan Blau.

Carillo, Ellen C., and Alice S. Horning, guest eds. 2021a. "Reading and Writing in the Era of Fake News-Introduction." *Pedagogy* 21 (2): 197–203.

Carillo, Ellen C., and Alice S. Horning, eds. 2021b. *Teaching Critical Reading and Writing in the Era of Fake News*. New York: Peter Lang.

Carillo, Ellen C., and Alice S. Horning. 2022. "Effectively and Efficiently Reading the Credibility of Online Sources." In *Writing Spaces: Readings on Writing*, volume 4, edited by Dana Lynn Driscoll, Megan Heise, Mary K. Stewart, and Matthew Vetter, 35–50. Anderson, SC: Parlor Press.

Carr, Nicholas. 2020. *The Shallows: What the Internet Is Doing to Our Brains*. New York: W. W. Norton.

Cavazos, Alyssa, G. 2019. "Encouraging Languages Other than English in First-Year Writing Courses: Experiences from Linguistically Diverse Writers." *Composition Studies* 47 (1): 38–56.

Cervetti, Gina N., P. David Pearson, Annemarie S. Palincsar, Peter Afflerbach, Panayiota Kendeou, Gina Biancarosa, Jennifer Higgs, Miranda S. Fitzgerald, and Amy I. Berman. 2020. "How the Reading for Understanding Initiative's Research Complicates the Simple View of Reading Invoked in the Science of Reading." *Reading Research Quarterly* 55 (S1): S161–S172. https://doi.org/10.1002/rrq.343.

Chen, Xianglei. 2016. *Remedial Coursetaking at U.S. Public 2- and 4-Year Institutions: Scope, Experiences, and Outcomes* (NCES 2016–405). US Department of Education. Washington, DC: National Center for Education Statistics. http://nces.ed.gov/pubs2016/2016405.pdf.

Cheney-Lippold, John. 2017. *We Are Data: Algorithms and the Making of Our Digital Selves*. New York: New York University Press. https://nyupress.org/9781479857593/we-are-data/.

Clifford, Geraldine Joncich. 1987. *A Sisyphean Task: Historical Perspectives on the Relationship between Writing and Reading Instruction*. Technical Report 7. ED 297 318. Washington, DC, and Berkeley: Center for the Study of Writing, Office of Educational Research and Improvement (ED), and Center for the Study of Writing, School of Education, University of California, Berkeley.

Coburn, Cynthia E., P. David Pearson, and Sarah Woulfin. 2010. "Reading Policy in the Era of Accountability." In *Handbook of Reading Research*, volume 4, edited by Michael L. Kamil, P. David Pearson, Elizabeth Birr Moje, Peter Afflerbach, and Peter B. Mosenthal, 561–593. ProQuest Ebook Central. New York: Taylor and Francis Group.

Cohen, Arthur M., Florence B. Brawer, and Carrie B. Kisker. 2014. *The American Community College*, 6th ed. San Francisco: Jossey-Bass/John Wiley.

Cohn, Jenae. 2021. *Skim, Dive, Surface: Teaching Digital Reading*. Morgantown: West Virginia University Press.

College Board. 2015. *Test Specifications for the Redesigned SAT*. New York: College Board. https://satsuite.collegeboard.org/media/pdf/test-specifications-redesigned-sat-1.pdf.

College Board. 2023. *Total Group SAT Suite of Assessments Annual Report*. New York: College Entrance Examination Board. https://reports.collegeboard.org/media/pdf/2023-total-group-sat-suite-of-assessments-annual-report%20ADA.pdf.

College Entrance Exam Board. 1965. *Freedom and Discipline in English: Report of the Commission on English*. New York: College Entrance Examination Board.

Community College Research Center. 2021. *Investing in Student Success at Community Colleges: Lessons from Research on Guided Pathways*. New York: Community College Research Center, Teachers College Columbia University. https://ccrc.tc.columbia.edu/media/k2/attachments/policy-brief-guided-pathways.pdf.

Community College Research Center. 2022. *Community College Research Center FAQs*. New York: Community College Research Center, Teachers College Columbia University. https://ccrc.tc.columbia.edu/community-college-faqs.html.

Complete College America. 2021. *No Room for Doubt: Moving Corequisite Support from Idea to Imperative*. https://completecollege.org/wp-content/uploads/2021/04/CCA_NoRoomForDoubt_CorequisiteSupport.pdf.

Complete College America. 2022. *Building on Completion Gains: Amplifying Progress and Closing Persistent Gaps*. https:/completecollege.org/resource/BuildingOnCompletionGains.

Conference on College Composition and Communication. 2021. *CCCC Position Statement on the Role of Reading in College Writing Classrooms*. https://cccc.ncte.org/cccc/the-role-of-reading.

Connolly, Steve. 2019. "W(h)ither Media in English?" In *The Future of English Teaching Worldwide: Celebrating 50 Years from the Dartmouth Conference*, edited by Andrew Goodwyn, Cal Durrant, Wayne Sawyer, Lisa Scherff, and Don Zancanella, 175–190. New York: Routledge/National Association for the Teaching of English (NATE).

Copeland, Charles Townsend, and Henry Milner Rideout. 1901. *Freshman English and Theme-Correcting in Harvard College*. New York: Silver Burdett. https://books.google.com/books?id=kxMCAAAAYAAJ&printsec=frontcover&source=gbs_ge_summary_r&cad=0#v=onepage&q=reading&f=false.

Core Curriculum. N.d. Boston University Core Curriculum. https://www.bu.edu/academics/cas/programs/core-curriculum/.

Council of Writing Program Administrators, National Council of Teachers of English, and the National Writing Project. 2011. *Framework for Success in Postsecondary Writing*. http://www.wpacouncil.org/aws/CWPA/pt/sd/news_article/242845/_PARENT/layout_details/false.

Counihan, Beth. 2021. "Article 1: An Open Educational Resource for Teaching Revision: Flesch-Kincaid Readability Statistics." *HETS Online Journal* 11 (2): 6+. *Gale Academic OneFile*. https://link.gale.com/apps/doc/A669329701/AONE?u=anon~8f07d3a&sid=googleScholar&xid=c727a951.

Crisp, Robert B. 2021. *Using Film to Unlock Textual Literacy: A Teacher's Guide*. Urbana, IL: National Council of Teachers of English.

Cui, Wenqi. 2019. "Rhetorical Listening Pedagogy: Promoting Communication across Cultural and Societal Groups with Video Narrative." *Computers and Composition* 54. https://doi.org/10.1016/j.compcom.2019.102517.

Dahl, Roald. 2006. "Poison." In *Collected Stories*, edited by Jeremy Treglown 259–269. New York: Alfred S. Knopf. Original work published in *Collier's Magazine*, 1950.

D'Angelo, Barbara J., Sandra Jamieson, Barry Maid, and Janice R. Walker, eds. 2016. *Information Literacy: Research and Collaboration across Disciplines*. Fort Collins, CO: WAC Clearinghouse. https://doi.org/10.37514/PER-B.2016.0834.

Dartmouth Institute. 2016. "College Writing: From the 1966 Dartmouth Seminar to Tomorrow." https://dartmouthwritinginstitute.wordpress.com/institute/.

Davis, Leslie, and Richard Fry. 2019. *College Faculty Have Become More Racially and Ethnically Diverse, but Remain Far Less So Than Students*. Washington, DC: Pew Research Center. https://www.pewresearch.org/fact-tank/2019/07/31/us-college-faculty-student-diversity/.

de Brey, Cristobal, Thomas D. Snyder, Anlan Zhang, and Sally A. Dillow 2021. *Digest of Education Statistics 2019* (NCES 2021–009). Washington, DC: National Center for Education Statistics, Institute of Education Sciences, US Department of Education.

Dehaene, Stanislas. 2009. *Reading in the Brain: The Science and Evolution of a Human Invention*. New York: Viking/Penguin.

Del Principe, Annie, and Rachel Ihara. 2019. "Reading Is Not One Thing." Blog post. https://style.mla.org/variability-of-reading-practices/.

Del Rio, Giulia McDonnell Nieto. 2021. "University of California Drops Admissions Tests." *New York Times*, May 16, Section 1, 26.

Deniz, Fatma, Anwar O. Nunez-Elizalde, Alexander G. Huth, and Jack L. Gallant. 2019. "The Representation of Semantic Information across Human Cerebral Cortex during Listening versus Reading Is Invariant to Stimulus Modality." *Journal of Neuroscience* 39 (39): 7722–7736. https://doi.org/10.1523/JNEUROSCI.0675-19.2019.

Digest of Education Statistics. 2023. "Total Undergraduate Fall Enrollment . . ." Washington, DC: US Department of Education, National Center for Education Statistics. https://nces.ed.gov/programs/digest/d13/tables/dt13_303.70.asp.

Discard Studies. 2024. "About Discard Studies." https://discardstudies.com/about/.

Dixon, John. 1967. *Growth through English*. Caversham, Reading, UK: National Association for the Teaching of English.

Donahue, Christiane. 2015. "College Writing: From the 1966 Dartmouth Seminar to Tomorrow." Blog post. Impact of the 1966 Seminar. https://dartmouthwritinginstitute.wordpress.com/1966-seminar/impact/.

Doolittle, Peter. N.d. *Constructivism and Education—EDEP 6224: 25-Word Summaries*. Twenty-five-Word Summary Guide. https://peterdoolittle.org/courses/constructivism-and-education/syllabus.pdf.

Dreyfus, Hubert L., and Stuart E. Dreyfus. 1986. *Mind over Machine: The Power of Human Intuition and Expertise in the Era of the Computer*. New York: Free Press.

Driscoll, Dana Lynn, Megan Heise, Mary K. Stewart, and Matthew Vetter. 2022. *Writing Spaces: Readings on Writing*, volume 4. Anderson, SC: Parlor Press.

Durst, Russel K. 2009. "Writing at the Postsecondary Level." In *The Norton Book of Composition Studies*, edited by Susan Miller, 1655–1689. New York: W. W. Norton.
Eastman, Arthur M., Caesar R. Blake, Hubert M. English, Alan B. Howes, Robert T. Lenaghan, Leo F. McNamara, and James Rosier, eds. 1965. *The Norton Reader: An Anthology of Expository Prose*. New York: W. W. Norton.
Elbow, Peter, and Pat Belanoff. 1989. *Sharing and Responding*. New York: Random House.
Elliot, Norbert. 2005. *On a Scale: A Social History of Writing Assessment in America*. New York: Peter Lang.
Elliot, Norbert. 2008. "A Midrash for Louise Rosenblatt." *Rhetoric Review* 27 (3): 281–304. https://doi.org/10.1080/07350190802126235.
Fader, Daniel N., and Elton B. McNeil. 1966. *Hooked on Books: Program and Proof*. New York: G. P. Putnam's Sons.
Fader, Daniel N., and Morton H. Shaevitz. 1966. *Hooked on Books*. New York: Berkley Medallion Books.
Farris, Christine. 2020. "Reclaiming English's Disciplinary Responsibility in the Transition from High School to College." In *Improving Outcomes: Disciplinary Writing, Local Assessment, and the Aim of Fairness*, edited by Diane Kelly-Riley and Norbert Elliot, 127–138. New York: Modern Language Association.
Fish, Stanley. 1980. *Is There a Text in This Class? The Authority of Interpretive Communities*. Cambridge, MA: Harvard University Press.
Flippo, Rona F., and Thomas W. Bean, eds. 2018. *Handbook of College Reading and Study Strategy Research*, 3rd ed. New York: Routledge/Taylor and Francis.
Foorman, Barbara, Michael Coyne, Carolyn A. Denton, Joseph Dimino, Lynda Hayes, Laura Justice, Warnick Lewis, and Richard Wagner. 2016. *Foundational Skills to Support Reading for Understanding in Kindergarten through Third Grade* (NCEE 2016–4008). Washington, DC: National Center for Education Evaluation and Regional Assistance (NCEE), Institute of Education Sciences, US Department of Education. https://ies.ed.gov/ncee/WWC/Docs/PracticeGuide/wwc_foundationalreading_040717.pdf.
Freire, Paulo. 1983. "The Importance of the Act of Reading." *Journal of Education* 165 (1): 5–11. https://doi.org/10.1177/002205748316500103.
Freire, Paulo. 1993. *The Pedagogy of the Oppressed: New Revised 20th Anniversary Edition*. New York: Continuum.
Fulkerson, Richard. 2005. "Composition at the Turn of the Twenty-First Century." *College Composition and Communication* 56 (4): 654–687.
Gable, Rachel. 2021. *The Hidden Curriculum: First Generation Students at Legacy Universities*. Princeton, NJ: Princeton University Press.
Gallagher, Kelly. 2009. *Readicide: How Schools Are Killing Reading and What You Can Do about It*. Portland, ME: Stenhouse.
Gannett, Cinthia, and John C. Brereton. 2020. "Framing and Facing Histories of Rhetoric and Composition." In *Talking Back: Senior Scholars and Their Colleagues Deliberate on the Past, Present, and Future of Writing Studies*, edited by Norbert Elliot and Alice S. Horning, 139–152. Logan: Utah State University Press.

Genung, John F. 1886. *The Practical Elements of Rhetoric*. Boston: Ginn. https://catalog.hathitrust.org/Record/100414729.

Genung, John F. 1902. *The Practical Elements of Rhetoric with Illustrative Examples*. Boston: Ginn.

Gere, Anne Ruggles. 1997. *Intimate Practices: Literacy and Cultural Work in U.S. Women's Clubs 1880–1920*. Urbana: University of Illinois Press.

Gere, Anne Ruggles, Anne Curzan, J. W. Hammond, Sarah Hughes, Ruth Li, Andrew Moos, Kendon Smith, Kathryn Van Zanen, Kelly L. Wheeler, and Crystal J. Zanders. 2021. "Communal Justicing: Writing Assessment, Disciplinary Infrastructure, and the Case for Critical Language Awareness." *College Composition and Communication* 72 (3): 384–412.

Gilpin, Gregory, Ezra Karger, and Peter Nencka. 2021. *The Returns to Public Library Investment*. Chicago: Federal Reserve Bank. WP 2021-06. https://doi.org/10.21033/wp-2021-06.

Ginestet, Emilie, Jalyssa Shadbolt, Rebecca Tucker, Marie-Line Bosse, and S. Hélène Deacon. 2021. "Orthographic Learning and Transfer of Complex Words: Insights from Eye Tracking during Reading and Learning Tasks." *Journal of Research in Reading* 44: 51–69. https://doi.org/10.1111/1467-9817.12341.

Giordano, Joanne Baird. 2020. "Second-Chance Pedagogy: Integrating College-Level Skills and Strategies into a Developmental Writing Course." In *Sixteen Teachers Teaching: Two-Year College Perspectives*, edited by Patrick Sullivan, 221–242. Logan: Utah State University Press.

Giordano, Joanne Baird, and Holly Hassel. 2019. "Intersections of Privilege and Access: Writing Programs, Disciplinary Knowledge, and the Shape of a Field." *WPA: Writing Program Administration* 43 (1): 33–53. https://wpacouncil.org/aws/CWPA/asset_manager/get_file/471719?ver=7.

Giordano, Joanne Baird, and Holly Hassel. 2021. "Developing Critical Readers in the Age of Literacy Acceleration." *Pedagogy* 21 (2): 241–258.

Glass, Gene V., and David C. Berliner. 2020. "Review of *Slaying Goliath: The Passionate Resistance to Privatization and the Fight to Save America's Public Schools*." *Education Review* 27. http://dx.doi.org/10.14507/er.v27.2879.

Glau, Gregory R. 2007. "'Stretch' at 10: A Progress Report on Arizona State University's 'Stretch' Program." *Journal of Basic Writing* 26 (2): 30–48. http://www.jstor.org/stable/43444083.

Goen, Sugie, and Helen Gillotte-Tropp. 2003. "Integrating Reading and Writing: A Response to the Basic Writing 'Crisis.'" *Journal of Basic Writing* 22 (2): 90–113. http://www.jstor.org/stable/43443776.

Goldthwaite, Melissa A., Joseph Bizzup, Anne E. Fernald, John C. Brereton, Brian Goedde, and Charles Hood. 2020a. *A Guide to the Norton Reader*, 15th ed. New York: W. W. Norton.

Goldthwaite, Melissa A., Joseph Bizzup, Anne E. Fernald, and John C. Brereton. 2020b. *The Norton Reader*, 15th ed. New York: W. W. Norton.

Graff, Harvey J. 2022. *Searching for Literacy: The Social and Intellectual Origins of Literacy Studies*. Cham, Switzerland: Palgrave Macmillan/Springer. https://doi-org.proxy.lib.umich.edu/10.1007/978-3-030-96981-3.

Graham, Steve. 2020. "The Sciences of Reading and Writing Must Become More Fully Integrated." *Reading Research Quarterly* 55 (S1): S35–S44. https://doi.org/10.1002/rrq.332.

Graham, Steve, Xinghua Liu, Angelique Aitken, Clarence Ng, Brendan Bartlett, Karen R. Harris, and Jennifer Holzapel. 2018a. "Effectiveness of Literacy Programs Balancing Reading and Writing Instruction: A Meta-Analysis." *Reading Research Quarterly* 53 (3): 279–304.

Graham, Steve, Xinghua Liu, Brendan Bartlett, Clarence Ng, Karen R. Harris, Angelique Aitken, Ashley Barkel, Colin Kavanaugh, and Joy Talukdar. 2018b. "Reading for Writing: A Meta-Analysis of the Impact of Reading and Reading Instruction on Writing." *Review of Educational Research* 88 (2): 243–284.

Grayson, Mara. 2022. "Writing Toward Racial Literacy." In *Writing Spaces: Readings on Writing*, volume 4, edited by Dana Lynn Driscoll, Megan Heise, Mary K. Stewart, and Matthew Vetter, 166-183. Anderson, SC: Parlor Press.

Greenlaw, Edwin, and Clarence Stratton. 1922. "Learning to Read: An Introduction." In *Literature and Life, Book 2*, edited by Dudley Miles, Clarence Stratton, Robert C. Pooley and Edwin Greenlaw, 1–5. Chicago: Scott, Foresman. https://books.google.com/books?id=bAUBAAAAYAAJ&lpg=PR3&ots=PO1_fWvuov&dq=%22literature%20and%20life%22%20anthology%20series&pg=PA1#v=onepage&q=%22literature%20and%20life%22%20anthology%20series&f=false.

Griffiths, Brett. 2020. "Compassionate Writing Instruction." In *Sixteen Teachers Teaching: Two-Year College Perspectives*, edited by Patrick Sullivan, 71–84. Logan: Utah State University Press.

Hairston, Maxine. 1982. "The Winds of Change: Thomas Kuhn and the Revolution in the Teaching of Writing." *College Composition and Communication* 33 (1): 76–88.

Hall, G. Stanley. 1886. *How to Teach Reading and What to Read in School*. Boston: D. C. Heath.

Hardwick, Jennifer. 2021. "Open and Closed: Open Education Projects, Indigenous Studies, and Teaching Undergraduate Students about the Ethics of Information Access." In *Integrating Digital Literacy in the Disciplines*, edited by Lauren Hays and Jenna Kammer, 83–94. ProQuest Ebook Central. Sterling, VA: Stylus.

Harkin, Patricia. 1999. *Acts of Reading*. Upper Saddle River, NJ: Prentice-Hall.

Harkin, Patricia. 2005. "The Reception of Reader-Response Theory." *College Composition and Communication* 56 (3): 410–425.

Harris, Joseph. 1991. "After Dartmouth: Growth and Conflict in English." *College English* 53 (6): 631–646. http://www.jstor.com/stable/377888.

Harris, Joseph. 1997. *A Teaching Subject: Composition since 1966*. Upper Saddle River, NJ: Prentice-Hall.

Hart, James Morgan. 1884. "The College Course in English Literature, How It May Be Improved." *Transactions of the Modern Language Association of America* 1: 84–95. https://doi.org/10.2307/456000.

Hartocollis, Anemona. 2021. "2020's Turmoil Alters Diversity of Class of '25." *New York Times*, April 18, 1.

Harvard University. 1896. *Twenty Years of School and College English*. Cambridge, MA: The University. https://babel.hathitrust.org/cgi/pt?id=loc.ark:/13960/t9d51cw09;view=1up;seq=7.

Hassel, Holly. 2020. "Social Justice and the Two-Year College: Cultivating Critical Information Literacy Skills in First-Year Writing." In *Sixteen Teachers Teaching: Two-Year College Perspectives*, edited by Patrick Sullivan, 133–150. Logan: Utah State University Press.

Hassel, Holly, and Joanne Baird Giordano. 2013. "Occupy Writing Studies: Rethinking College Composition for the Needs of the Teaching Majority." *College Composition and Communication* 65 (1): 117–139. http://www.jstor.org/stable/43490809.

Have, Iben, and Birgitte Stougaard Pedersen. 2020. "Reading Audiobooks." In *Beyond Media Borders: Intermedial Relations among Multimodal Media*, edited by Lars Elleström, 197–215. Cham, Switzerland: Palgrave Macmillan.

Hayles, Katherine. 2007. "Hyper and Deep Attention: The Generational Divide in Cognitive Modes." *Profession* 13 (1): 187–199.

Hazelrigg, Nick. 2019. "What the Freshmen Are Reading." *Inside Higher Ed*, June 11. https://www.insidehighered.com/news/2019/06/11/common-freshman-reading-2019.

Head, Alison J. 2012. "Learning the Ropes: How Freshmen Conduct Research Once They Enter College." *Project Information Literacy Research Report*. https://projectinfolit.org/publications/first-year-experience-study/.

Head, Alison J. 2021. "Reading in the Age of Distrust." Provocation Series. https://projectinfolit.org/pubs/provocation-series/essays/reading-in-the-age-of-distrust.html.

Head, Alison J., Barbara Fister, and Margy MacMillan. 2020. *Information Literacy in the Age of Algorithms: Student Experiences with News and Information, and the Need for Change*. Project Information Literacy Research Institute. https://projectinfolit.org/publications/algorithm-study/.

Head, Alison J., John Wihbey, P. Takis Metaxas, Margy MacMillan, and Dan Cohen. 2018. "How Students Engage with News: Five Takeaways for Educators, Journalists, and Librarians." *Project Information Literacy Institute*. http://www.projectinfolit.org/uploads/2/7/5/4/27541717/newsreport.pdf.

"History of NWP." National Writing Project: Improving Writing and Learning in the Nation's Schools. 2022. https://archive.nwp.org/cs/public/print/doc/about/history.csp.

Hobbs, Catherine, and James Berlin. 2001. "A Century of Writing Instruction in School and College English." In *A Short History of Writing Instruction: From Ancient Greece to Modern America*, 3rd ed., edited by James J. Murphy, 247–289. Mahwah, NJ: Lawrence Erlbaum Associates.

Holland, Norman. 1973. *Poems in Persons: An Introduction to the Psychoanalysis of Literature*. New York: W. W. Norton.

Holland, Norman. 1975. *Five Readers Reading*. New Haven, CT: Yale University Press.

Hook, Julius N. 1979. *A Long Way Together: A Personal View of NCTE's First Sixty-Seven Years*. Urbana, IL: National Council of Teachers of English.

Horning, Alice S. 1978. "The Connection of Writing to Reading: A Gloss on the Gospel of Mina Shaughnessy." *College English* 40 (3): 264–268. https://doi.org/10.2307/375785.

Horning, Alice S. 1987. *Teaching Writing as a Second Language*. Carbondale, IL: Southern Illinois University Press.

Horning, Alice S. 2012. *Reading, Writing, and Digitizing: Understanding Literacy in the Electronic Age*. Newcastle upon Tyne, UK: Cambridge Scholars.

Horning, Alice S. 2017. "Enhancing the *Framework for Success*: Adding Experiences in Critical Reading." In *The Framework for Success in Postsecondary Writing: Scholarship and Applications*, edited by Sherry Rankins-Robertson, Nicholas Behm, and Duane Roen, 54–68. Anderson, SC: Parlor Press.

Horning, Alice S. 2018. *Literacy Then and Now: A Study of Modern and Contemporary Literacy Practices*. New York: Peter Lang.

Horning, Alice S. 2021a. *Literacy Heroines: Women and the Written Word*. New York: Peter Lang.

Horning, Alice S. 2021b. "Now More Than Ever: Developing *Crafty Readers* in Writing Classes and across the Curriculum." In *Reading and Writing Instruction in the Twenty-First Century: Recovering and Transforming the Pedagogy of Robert Scholes*, edited by Ellen C. Carillo, 38–53. Logan: Utah State University Press.

Hosic, James. 1911. *Reorganization of English in Secondary Schools*. Bulletin 1917, no. 2. Report of the Joint National Commission. Washington, DC: Department of the Interior, Bureau of Education. http://www.ncte.org/library/NCTEFiles/Centennial/Reorganization.pdf.

Hosic, James. 1912. "The Influence of the Uniform Entrance Requirements in English: A Brief Chapter of Educational History, Together with a Summary of the Facts So Far Obtained by a Committee of the National Education Association and a List of References." *English Journal* 1 (2): 95–121. https://doi.org/10.2307/801190.

Howard, Rebecca Moore, Tricia Serviss, and Tanya K. Rodrigue. 2010. "Writing from Sources, Writing from Sentences." *Writing and Pedagogy* 2 (2): 177–192. https://doi-org.huaryu.kl.oakland.edu/10.1558/wap.v2i2.177.

Huey, Edmund B. 1908. *The Psychology and Pedagogy of Reading*. New York: Macmillan.

Hurlbut, Byron S. 1896. "College Requirements in English." In *Twenty Years of School and College English*, edited by Harvard University, 46–53. Cambridge, MA: The University.

Hutton, Elizabeth B. 2018. "Textual Transactions: Recontextualizing Louise Rosenblatt's Transactional Theory for the College Writing Classroom." PhD dissertation, University of Michigan, Ann Arbor.

Hymes, Dell. 1964. "Introduction: Toward Ethnographies of Communication." *American Anthropologist* 66 (6): 1–34. https://doi.org/10.1525/aa.1964.66.suppl_3.02a00010.

Hymes, Dell. 1972 [1971]. "On Communicative Competence." In *Sociolinguistics: Selected Readings*, edited by J. B. Pride and Janet Holmes, 269–293. Hammondsworth, UK: Penguin Education.

Hypothes.is. 2022. "To Enable a Conversation over the World's Knowledge." Hypothesis Mission. https://web.hypothes.is/about/.

"Intended Meaning of NAEP." 2022. National Assessment of Educational Progress, National Center for Education Statistics. https://nces.ed.gov/nationsreportcard/guides/. Updated October 13, 2022.

International Literacy Association. 2022. "About Us." https://www.literacyworldwide.org/.

International Organization for Migration. 2022. *World Migration Report*. https://worldmigrationreport.iom.int/wmr-2022-interactive/.

International Reading Association. 2002. "History and Development, Projects and Programs, Organizational Structure." https://education.stateuniversity.com/pages/2126/International-Reading-Association.html.

Iser, Wolfgang. 1974. *The Implied Reader: Patterns of Communication in Prose Fiction from Bunyan to Beckett*. Baltimore, MD: Johns Hopkins University Press.

Iser, Wolfgang. 1978. *The Act of Reading: A Theory of Aesthetic Response*. London: Routledge and Kegan Paul.

Jabr, Ferris. 2013. "Why the Brain Prefers Paper." *Scientific American* 309 (5): 48–53. http://www.jstor.org/stable/26018148.

Jamieson, Sandra. 2013. "Reading and Engaging Sources: What Students' Use of Sources Reveals about Advanced Reading Skills." *Across the Disciplines* 10 (4). https://wac.colostate.edu/atd/special/reading/.

Jamieson, Sandra. 2017. "The Evolution of the Citation Project: Developing a Pilot Study from Local to Translocal." In *Points of Departure: Rethinking Student Source Use and Writing Studies Research Methods*, edited by Tricia Serviss and Sandra Jamieson, 33–61. Logan: Utah State University Press.

Jamieson, Sandra, and Rebecca Moore Howard. 2013. "Sentence-Mining: Uncovering the Amount of Reading and Reading Comprehension in College Writers' Researched Writing." In *The New Digital Scholar: Exploring and Enriching the Research and Writing Practices of Nextgen Students*, edited by Randall McClure and James P. Purdy, 111–133. Leesburg, VA: American Society for Information Science and Technology.

Jensen, Darin L. Forthcoming. "Basic Writing Is Dead: Long Live Basic Writing." In *Basic Writing in the Twenty-First Century*, edited by Laura Gray-Rosendale and Barbara Gleason. New York: Peter Lang.

Keller, Daniel. 2014. *Chasing Literacy: Reading and Writing in an Age of Acceleration*. Logan: Utah State University Press.

Kolers, Paul A. 1967. "Reading Is Only Incidentally Visual." In *Psycholinguistics and the Teaching of Reading*, edited by Kenneth S. Goodman and James T. Fleming, 8–16. Newark, DE: International Reading Association.

Kopko, Elizabeth, Hollie Daniels, and Dan Cullinan. 2023. *The Long-Term Effectiveness of Multiple Measures Assessment: Evidence from a Randomized Controlled Trial*. New York: Center for the Analysis of Postsecondary Readiness/Community College Research Center, Teachers College Columbia University. https://postsecondaryreadiness.org/long-term-effectiveness-multiple-measures-assessment/.

Kucer, Stephen B. 2014. *Dimensions of Literacy: A Conceptual Base for Teaching Reading and Writing in School Settings*, 4th ed. New York: Routledge.

Kuhn, Thomas S. 1996. *The Structure of Scientific Revolutions*, 3rd ed. Chicago: University of Chicago Press.

Kuncel, Nathan, and Paul Sackett. 2018. "The Truth about the SAT and ACT." *Wall Street Journal*, March 8. https://www.wsj.com/articles/the-truth-about-the-sat-and-act-1520521861.

Lacy, Tim. 2006. "Making a Democratic Culture: The Great Books Idea, Mortimer J. Adler, and Twentieth-Century America." Order 3229793. Chicago: Loyola University. https://www-proquest.com.huaryu.kl.oakland.edu/docview/305319330?pq-origsite=primo.

Lau, Sunny Man Chu, and Saskia Van Viegen. 2020. *Plurilingual Pedagogies: Critical and Creative Endeavors for Equitable Language in Education*. Cham, Switzerland: Springer. https://doi-org.proxy.lib.umich.edu/10.1007/978-3-030-36983-5.

Lemov, Doug, Colleen Driggs, and Erica Woolway. 2016. *Reading Reconsidered: A Practical Guide to Rigorous Literacy Instruction*. San Francisco: Jossey-Bass.

Levinson, David. 2005. *Community Colleges: A Reference Handbook*. Santa Barbara, CA: ABC-CLIO.

Li, Jinrong. 2020. "LILAC and Citation Project Workshop." *Georgia International Conference on Information Literacy* 78. https://digitalcommons.georgiasouthern.edu/gaintlit/2020/2020/78.

Lindemann, Erika. 1993. "Freshman Composition: No Place for Literature." *College English* 55 (3): 311–316. http://www.jstor.com/stable/378743.

Lindemann, Erika. 1995. "Three Views of English 101." *College English* 57 (3): 287–302. https://www.jstor.org/stable/378679.

Lloyd-Jones, Richard, and Andrea Lunsford, eds. 1989. *The English Coalition Conference: Democracy through Language*. ERIC ED 303815. Urbana, IL: National Council of Teachers of English.

Lockhart, Tara, Brenda Glascott, Chris Warnick, Juli Parrish, and Justin Lewis, eds. 2021. *Literacy and Pedagogy in an Age of Misinformation and Disinformation*. Philadelphia: New City Community Press/Parlor Press.

McClymer, John. 2005. *The AHA Guide to Teaching and Learning with New Media*. https://www.historians.org/teaching-and-learning/teaching-resources-for-historians/approaches-to-teaching/the-aha-guide-to-teaching-and-learning-with-new-media.

McGrew, Sarah, Teresa Ortega, Joel Breakstone, and Sam Wineburg. 2017. "The Challenge That's Bigger than Fake News: Civic Reasoning in a Social Media Environment." *American Educator* 41 (3): 4–9, 39.

Melzer, Dan. 2009. "Writing Assignments across the Curriculum: A National Study of College Writing." *College Composition and Communication* 61 (2): W240–W261.

MI School Data: Michigan's Official Education Data Source. 2022. Postsecondary Landing Page. https://www.mischooldata.org/postsecondary-landing-page/.

Mina, Lilian W., Jeanne Law Bohannon, and Jinrong Li. 2018. "Google, Baidu, the Library, and ACRL Framework: Assessing Information-Seeking Behaviors of First-

Year Multilingual Writers through Research-Aloud Protocols." In *Teaching Information Literacy and Writing Studies*, vol. 1: *First-Year Composition Courses*, edited by Grace Veach, 251–267. West Lafayette, IN: Purdue University Press.

MLA History. 2022. Modern Language Association. https://www.mla.org/About-Us/About-the-MLA/MLA-Archives/Time-Lines/MLA-History.

Moje, Elizabeth B., Peter P. Afflerbach, Patricia Enciso, and Nonie K. Lesaux. 2020. *Handbook of Reading Research, Volume V*. New York: Routledge. https://doi-org.10.4324/9781315676302.

Muller, Herbert J. 1967. *The Uses of English: Guidelines for the Teaching of English from the Anglo-American Conference at Dartmouth College*. New York: Holt, Rinehart, and Winston.

Muniz, Hannah. 2020. "What Is a Nontraditional Student?" https://www.bestcolleges.com/blog/what-is-a-nontraditional-student/.

Nash, Brady. 2021. "Constructing Meaning Online: Teaching Critical Reading in a Post-Truth Era." *Reading Teacher* 74 (6): 713–722. https://doi-org.huaryu.kl.oakland.edu/10.1002/trtr.1980.

National Academies of Sciences, Engineering, and Medicine. 2017. *Evaluation of the Achievement Levels for Mathematics and Reading on the National Assessment of Educational Progress*. Washington, DC: National Academies Press. https://doi.org/10.17226/23409.

National Assessment of Educational Progress. 2019. *Explore Results for the 2019 NAEP Reading Assessment*. Washington, DC: United States Department of Education. https://www.nationsreportcard.gov/reading?grade=12.

National Center for Education Statistics. 2022. "Undergraduate Retention and Graduation Rates." *Condition of Education*. Washington DC: United States Department of Education, Institute of Education Sciences. https://nces.ed.gov/programs/coe/pdf/2022/ctr_508.pdf.

National Education Association. 1894. *Report of the Committee of Ten on Secondary School Studies with the Reports of the Conferences Arranged by Committee*. New York: American Book Company. https://books.google.com/books?id=PfcBAAAAYAAJ&pg=PA3&lpg=PA3#v=onepage&q&f=false.

National Governors Association Center for Best Practices, Council of Chief State School Officers. 2010. *Common Core State Standards*. Washington, DC: National Governors Association Center for Best Practices, Council of Chief State School Officers. http://www.corestandards.org/ELA-Literacy/RI/11-12.

National Student Clearinghouse Research Center. 2020. *Completing College: National and State Reports*. Herndon, VA: National Student Clearinghouse Research Center. https://nscresearchcenter.org/completing-college/.

National Writing Project. 2022. "About NWP." National Writing Project: Improving Writing and Learning in the Nation's Schools. https://archive.nwp.org/cs/public/print/doc/about.csp.

NCTE. 2022. *Position Statement on Media Education in English Language Arts*. https://ncte.org/statement/media_education/.

NCTE Archive. 2009. NCTE/Professional Conference Files, 1955–1995. Urbana, IL: University of Illinois. https://archon.library.illinois.edu/archives/index.php?p=collections/controlcard&id=2473&q=NCTE+and+the+Dartmouth+Seminar.

Nichols, Laura. 2020. *The Journey before Us: First-Generation Pathways from Middle School to College*. New Brunswick, NJ: Rutgers University Press.

Noble, Safiya Umoja. 2018. *Algorithms of Oppression: How Search Engines Reinforce Racism*. New York: New York University Press. https://nyupress.org/9781479837243/algorithms-of-oppression/.

Norton, Bonny, and Kelleen Toohey, eds. 2010. *Critical Pedagogies and Language Learning*. New York: Cambridge University Press.

OECD. 2019. "How Does PISA Assess Reading." In *PISA 2018 Results (Volume I): What Students Know and Can Do*. Paris: OECD Publishing. https://doi.org/10.1787/8eebc6cc-en.

OECD. 2021a. *The Assessment Frameworks for Cycle 2 of the Programme for the International Assessment of Adult Competencies*. OECD Skills Studies. Paris: OECD Publishing. https://doi.org/10.1787/4bc2342d-en.

OECD. 2021b. *Twenty-First-Century Readers: Developing Literacy Skills in a Digital World*. Paris: OECD Publishing. https://doi.org/10.1787/a83d84cb-en.

Oliver, Amanda. 2022. *Overdue: Reckoning with the Public Library*. Chicago: Chicago Review Press.

Oliveri, Maria Elena, Robert J. Mislevy, and Norbert Elliot. 2020. "After Admissions: What Comes Next in Higher Education?" In *Higher Education Admission Practices: An International Perspective*, edited by Maria Elena Oliveri and Cathy Wendler, 347–375. New York: Cambridge University Press.

O'Mara, Joanne, and Catherine Beavis. 2019. "Reading for Pleasure in English Class." In *The Future of English Teaching Worldwide: Celebrating 50 Years from the Dartmouth Conference*, edited by Andrew Goodwyn, Cal Durrant, Wayne Sawyer, Lisa Scherff, and Don Zancanella, 215–226. New York: Routledge/National Association of Teachers of English.

Otte, George, and Rebecca Williams Mlynarczyk. 2010. *Reference Guide to Basic Writing*. West Lafayette, IN: Parlor Press and WAC Clearinghouse.

Pandya, Jessica Z., Raul A. Mora, Jennifer H. Alford, Noah A. Golden, and Roberto S. de Roock, eds. 2021. *Handbook of Critical Literacies*. Milton, UK: Taylor and Francis Group.

Parfitt, Matthew. 2016. *Writing in Response*, 2nd ed. Boston: Bedford/St. Martin's.

Peele, Thomas. 2010. "Working Together: Student-Faculty Interaction and the Boise State Stretch Program." *Journal of Basic Writing* 29 (2): 50–73. https://www.jstor.org/stable/43443899.

Perin, Dolores, and Jodi Patrick Holschuh. 2019. "Teaching Academically Underprepared Postsecondary Students." *Review of Research in Education* 43 (1): 363–393. https://doi.org/10.3102/0091732X18821114.

Perusall. 2022a. "About Us." https://perusall.com/about.

Perusall. 2022b. "Research on Perusall." https://www.perusall.com/research.

Plan of Organization for the College Entrance Examination Board of the Middle States and Maryland and a Statement of Subjects in Which Examinations Are Proposed by College Entrance Examination Board of the Middle States and Maryland. 1900. https://archive.org/details/cu31924031758109/page/n5/mode/2up.

Poe, Mya, Asao B. Inoue, and Norbert Elliot, eds. 2018. *Writing Assessment, Social Justice, and the Advancement of Opportunity*. Fort Collins, CO: WAC Clearinghouse. https://doi.org/10.37514/PER-B.2018.0155.

Poe, Mya, Jessica Nastal, and Norbert Elliot. 2019. "An Admitted Student Is a Qualified Student: A Roadmap for Writing Placement in the Two-Year College." *Journal of Writing Assessment* 12 (1). http://journalofwritingassessment.org/article.php?article=140.

PowerNotes. 2021a. "PowerNotes and Social Annotation: A Look at Hypothes.is and Perusall." https://www.blog.powernotes.com/powernotes-and-social-annotation-hypothosis-and-perusall.

PowerNotes. 2021b. "The Science behind PowerNotes." https://www.blog.powernotes.com/why-powernotes.

Programme for International Student Assessment. 2018. PISA 2018 Results. https://www.oecd.org/pisa/publications/pisa-2018-results.html How does PISA assess reading?—OECD iLibrary.

Project Information Literacy. 2021. https://projectinfolit.org/.

Ran, Florence Xiaotao, Susan Bickerstaff, and Nikki Edgecombe. 2022. *Improving College Success for Students in Corequisite Reading*. New York: Columbia College Research Center. https://ccrc.tc.columbia.edu/publications/improving-college-success-corequisite-reading.html.

Ratcliffe, Krista. 2005. *Rhetorical Listening: Identification, Gender, Whiteness*. Carbondale: Southern Illinois University Press.

Raucci, John. 2021. "A Replication Agenda for Composition Studies." *College Composition and Communication* 72 (3): 440–461.

Ravitch, Diane. 2020. *Slaying Goliath: The Passionate Resistance to Privatization and the Fight to Save America's Public Schools*. New York: Alfred A. Knopf.

Reece, Bryan. 2022. *Social Justice and Community College Education*. New York: Routledge.

Richardson, Brian. 1997. "The Other Reader's Response: On Multiple, Divided, and Oppositional Audiences." *Criticism: A Quarterly for Literature and the Arts* 39 (1): 31–53.

Roose, Kevin. 2021. *Futureproof: 9 Rules for Humans in the Age of Automation*. New York: Random House.

Rose, Mike. 1989. *Lives on the Boundary: The Struggles and Achievements of America's Educationally Underprepared*. New York: Penguin Books.

Rose, Mike. 2012. *Back to School: Why Everyone Deserves a Second Chance at Education*. New York: New Press.

Rosenberg, Lauren. 2015. *The Desire for Literacy: Writing in the Lives of Adult Learners*. Urbana, IL: Conference on College Composition and Communication/National Council of Teachers of English.

Rosenblatt, Louise M. 1938. *Literature as Exploration*. New York: D. Appleton-Century.

Rosenblatt, Louise M. 1978. *The Reader, the Text, the Poem*. Carbondale: Southern Illinois University Press.

Rosenblatt, Louise M. 1993. "The Transactional Theory: Against Dualisms." *College English* 55 (4): 377–386.

Rosenblatt, Louise M. 2018 [1994]. "The Transactional Theory of Reading and Writing." In *Theoretical Models and Processes of Literacy*, 7th ed., edited by Donna E. Alvermann, Norman J. Unrau, Misty Sailors, and Robert B. Ruddell, 451–477. Boca Raton, FL: Routledge.

Rothwell, Jonathan. 2020. *Assessing the Economic Gains of Eradicating Illiteracy Nationally and Regionally in the United States*. https://www.barbarabush.org/wp-content/uploads/2020/09/BBFoundation_GainsFromEradicatingIlliteracy_9_8.pdf.

RTI International. 2019a. *First-Generation College Students: Demographic Characteristics and Postsecondary Enrollment*. Washington, DC: National Association of Student Personnel Administrators. https://firstgen.naspa.org/files/dmfile/FactSheet-01.pdf.

RTI International. 2019b. *First Year Experience, Persistence, and Attainment of First-Generation College Students*. Washington, DC: National Association of Student Personnel Administrators. https://firstgen.naspa.org/files/dmfile/FactSheet-02.pdf.

Rubery, Matthew. 2016. *The Untold Story of the Talking Book*. Cambridge, MA: Harvard University Press.

Russell, David R. 1991. *Writing in the Academic Disciplines, 1870–1990: A Curricular History*. Carbondale: Southern Illinois University Press.

Rutschow, Elizabeth Zachry, Maria Scott Cormier, Dominique Dukes, and Diana E. Cruz Zamora. 2019. *The Changing Landscape of Developmental Education Practices: Findings from a National Survey and Interviews with Postsecondary Institutions*. New York: Center for the Analysis of Postsecondary Readiness. https://postsecondaryreadiness.org/changing-landscape-developmental-education-practices/.

Sabine, Gordon A. 1993. *Memoir of a Book: The Norton Reader, an Anthology of Expository Prose*. Ann Arbor: University of Michigan Library.

St. John's Reading List: A Great Books Curriculum. 2022. St. John's College. https://www.sjc.edu/academic-programs/undergraduate/great-books-reading-list.

Saxon, D. Patrick, Nara M. Martirosyan, Rebecca A. Wentworth, and Hunter R. Boylan. 2015. "Developmental Education Research Agenda: Survey of Field Professionals, Part I." *Journal of Developmental Education* 38 (2) (Winter): 32–34. https://www.proquest.com/scholarly-journals/developmental-education-research-agenda-survey/docview/1689345421/se-2.

Saxon, D. Patrick, and Edward A. Morante. 2021. "Effective Student Assessment and Placement: Challenges and Recommendations." *Journal of Developmental Education* 44 (3) (Spring): 12–17. https://www.proquest.com/scholarly-journals/effective-student-assessment-placement-challenges/docview/2548697295/se-2.

Schleicher, Andreas. 2019. *PISA 2018: Insights and Interpretations*. Paris: Organisation for Economic Cooperation and Development. https://www.oecd.org/pisa/publications/pisa-2018-results.htm.

Scott, Fred Newton. 1913. "The Undefended Gate." *English Journal* 3 (1): 1–14. https://www.jstor.org/stable/801013.

Scott, Jonathan. 2022. "Transaction Theory Rebooted: What Neuroscience's Research on Reading Means for Composition." *College Composition and Communication* 73 (3): 526–561.

Seeley, Sarah, Kelly Xu, and Matthew Chen. 2022. "Read the Room! Navigating Social Contexts." In *Writing Spaces: Readings on Writing*, volume 4, edited by Dana Lynn Driscoll, Megan Heise, Mary K. Stewart, and Matthew Vetter, 281–300. Anderson, SC: Parlor Press.

Seidenberg, Mark. 2017. *Language at the Speed of Sight: How We Read, Why So Many Can't, and What Can Be Done about It*. New York: Basic Books.

Shapiro, Shawna. 2022. *Cultivating Critical Language Awareness in the Writing Classroom*. New York: Routledge.

Shaughnessy, Mina P. 1977. *Errors and Expectations: A Guide for the Teacher of Basic Writing*. New York: Oxford University Press.

Shepherd, Dawn, Samantha Sturman, and Heidi Estrem. 2020. "Corequisite Writing Courses: Equity and Access." *Composition Studies* 48 (2): 9–17.

Shober, Arnold. 2016. *In Common No More: The Politics of the Common Core State Standards*. Santa Barbara, CA: ABC-CLIO.

Sills, Lauren. 2020. "Community: Student Perspective." In *Sixteen Teachers Teaching: Two-Year College Perspectives*, edited by Patrick Sullivan, 151–152. Logan: Utah State University Press.

Silverstein, Michael. 1979. "Language Structure and Linguistic Ideology." In *The Elements: A Parasession on Linguistic Units and Levels*, edited by Paul Clyne, William F. Hanks, and Carol L. Hofbauer, 193–247. Chicago: Chicago Linguistic Society.

Sireci, Stephen G., and Jennifer Randall. 2022. "Evolving Notions of Fairness in Testing in the United States." In *The History of Educational Measurement: Key Advancements in Theory, Policy, and Practice*, edited by Brian E. Clauser and Michael B. Bunch, 111–135. New York: Routledge/Taylor and Francis.

Slevin, James F. 2001. *Introducing English: Essays in the Intellectual Work of Composition*. Pittsburgh, PA: University of Pittsburgh Press.

Smagorinsky, Peter, Mary Guay, Tisha Lewis Ellison, and Arlette Ingram Willis. 2020. "A Sociocultural Perspective on Readers, Reading, Reading Instruction and Assessment, Reading Policy, and Reading Research." In *Handbook of Reading Research, Volume V*, edited by Elizabeth Birr Moje, Peter P. Afflerbach, Patricia Enciso, and Nonie K. Lesaux, 57–75. New York: Routledge.

Smilges, J. Logan. 2021. "Neuroqueer Literacies; or, Against Able-Reading." *College Composition and Communication* 73 (3): 103–125.

Smitherman, Geneva. 1977. *Talkin and Testifyin: The Language of Black America*. Boston: Houghton Mifflin.

Smitherman, Geneva. 2000. *Talkin That Talk: Language, Culture, and Education in African America*. London: Routledge.

Smitherman, Geneva. 2022. *My Soul Look Back in Wonder: Memories from a Life of Study, Struggle, and Doin Battle in the Language Wars*. London: Routledge.

Snyder, Thomas D., ed. 1993. *120 Years of American Education: A Statistical Portrait*. Washington, DC: National Center for Education Statistics.

Stanford History Education Group. 2016. *Evaluating Information: The Cornerstone of Civic Online Reasoning*. https://sheg.stanford.edu/upload/V3LessonPlans/Executive%20Summary%2011.21.16.pdf.

Stanford History Education Group and Gibson Consulting. 2019. *Students' Civic Online Reasoning: A National Portrait*. https://stacks.stanford.edu/file/gf151tb4868/Civic%20Online%20Reasoning%20National%20Portrait.pdf.

Stengel, Richard. 2019. *Information Wars: How We Lost the Global Battle against Disinformation and What We Can DO About It*. New York: Atlantic Monthly Press.

Stewart, Donald. 1992. "Harvard's Influence on English Studies: Perceptions from Three Universities in the Early Twentieth Century." *College Composition and Communication* 43 (4): 455–471.

Sullivan, Patrick. 2014. *A New Writing Classroom: Listening, Motivation, and Habits of Mind*. Logan: Utah State University Press.

Sullivan, Patrick. 2017. *Economic Inequality, Neoliberalism, and the American Community College*. New York: Palgrave Macmillan.

Sullivan, Patrick. 2021. *Democracy, Social Justice, and the American Community College: A Student-Centered Perspective*. Cham, Switzerland: Springer Books.

Sullivan, Patrick, Howard Tinberg, and Sheridan Blau. 2017. *Deep Reading: Teaching Reading in the Writing Classroom*. Urbana, IL: National Council of Teachers of English.

Sullivan, Patrick, Howard Tinberg, and Sheridan Blau. 2022. *Deep Reading, Deep Learning: Deep Reading, Volume 2*. New York: Peter Lang.

Tallal, Paula. 2016. "Neuroplasticity-Based Cognitive and Linguistic Skills Training Improves Reading and Writing Skills in College Students." Paper presented at College Writing from the 1966 Dartmouth Seminar to Tomorrow: Exploring the State of Writing Research in Higher Education. Hanover, NH, August 11.

Tampio, Nicholas. 2018. *National Education Standards and the Threat to Democracy*. Baltimore, MD: Johns Hopkins University Press.

Tampio, Nicholas. 2019. *Learning versus the Common Core*. Minneapolis: University of Minnesota Press.

Tate, Gary. 1993. "A Place for Literature in Freshman Composition." *College English* 55 (3): 317–321. https://www.jstor.org/stable/378744.

Taylor, Helen. 2019. *Why Women Read Fiction*. New York: Oxford University Press.

Teixeira, Ruy, William H. Frey, and Rob Griffin. 2015. "States of Change: The Demographic Evolution of the American Electorate, 1974–2060." Washington, DC: Center for American Progress, American Enterprise Institute, and Brookings Institution. https://www.americanprogress.org/article/states-of-change/.

Tierney, Robert J., and P. David Pearson. 2021. *A History of Literacy Education: Waves of Research and Practice*. New York: Teachers College Press.

Troyka, Lynn Quitman. 1987. "Defining Basic Writing in Context." In *A Sourcebook for Basic Writing Teachers*, edited by Theresa Enos, 2–15. New York: Random House.

Tulley, Christine E. 2018. *How Writing Faculty Write*. Logan: Utah State University Press.

Tyson, Lois. 1999. *Critical Theory Today: A User-Friendly Guide*. New York: Garland.

Uehling, Karen. Forthcoming. "The Council on Basic Writing: A Legacy of Sustained and Sustaining Conversation." In *Basic Writing in the Twenty-First Century*, edited by Laura Gray-Rosendale and Barbara Gleason. New York: Peter Lang.

Uncommon Schools. 2022. "About Us." Uncommonschools.org. https://uncommon schools.org/about-us/.

United States Bureau of Labor Statistics. 2021. *American Time Use Survey: Reading for Personal Interest, 2009–2019*. https://www.bls.gov/tus/database.htm.

United States Department of Education, Institute for Education Sciences. 2021. *Condition of Education: Undergraduate Retention and Graduation Rates*. https://nces.ed.gov/programs/coe/indicator/ctr?tid=74.

VanKooten, Crystal. 2020. *Transfer across Media: Using Digital Video in the Teaching of Writing*. Logan: Computers and Composition Digital Press/Utah State University Press. https://ccdigitalpress.org/book/transfer-across-media/index.html.

Vasquez, Vivian Maria. 2017. "Critical Literacy." *Oxford Research Encyclopedia of Education*. https://oxfordre.com/education/view/10.1093/acrefore/9780190264093.001.0001/acrefore-9780190264093-e-20.

Vee, Annette. 2020. *Introduction: What Was the Dartmouth Seminar?* WAC Clearinghouse Resource. https://wac.colostate.edu/resources/research/dartmouth/introduction-what-was-the-dartmouth-seminar/.

Waite, Stacey. 2017. *Teaching Queer: Radical Possibilities for Writing and Knowing*. Pittsburgh, PA: University of Pittsburgh Press. https://search-ebscohost-com.proxy.lib.umich.edu/login.aspx?direct=true&db=e000xna&AN=1542395&site=ehost-live&scope=site.

Walker, Allison S. 2019. "Perusall: Harnessing AI Robo-Tools and Writing Analytics to Improve Student Learning and Increase Instructor Efficiency." *Journal of Writing Analytics* 3: 227–263. https://doi.org/10.37514/JWA-J.2019.3.1.11.

Wardhaugh, Ronald, and Janet M. Fuller. 2015. *An Introduction to Sociolinguistics*, 7th ed. Chichester, UK: John Wiley and Sons.

Weingarten, Randi. 2021. "Reading Opens the World." *New York Times*, December 26, 10A.

Willingham, Daniel. 2017. *The Reading Mind: A Cognitive Approach to Understanding How the Mind Reads*. San Francisco: Jossey-Bass.

Wilner, Arlene Fish. 2020. *Rethinking Reading in College: An Across-the-Curriculum Approach*. Urbana, IL: National Council of Teachers of English.

Wineburg, Sam, Joel Breakstone, Sarah McGrew, Mark Smith, and Teresa Ortega. 2022. "Lateral Reading on the Open Internet." https://ssrn.com/abstract=3936112 or http://dx.doi.org/10.2139/ssrn.3936112.

Wineburg, Sam, Joel Breakstone, Nadav Ziv, and Mark Smith. 2020. *Educating for Misunderstanding: How Approaches to Teaching Digital Literacy Make Students Susceptible to Scammers, Rogues, Bad Actors, and Hate Mongers*. Working Paper A-21322. Stanford, CA: Stanford History Education Group. https://purl.stanford.edu/mf412bt5333.

Wineburg, Sam, and Sarah McGrew. 2017. *Lateral Reading: Reading Less and Learning More When Evaluating Digital Information*. Stanford History Education Group Working Paper 2017-A1. https://papers.ssrn.com/sol3/papers.cfm?abstract_id=3048994.

Wolf, Maryanne. 2018. *Reader Come Home: The Reading Brain in a Digital World*. New York: HarperCollins.

Wolf, Maryanne. 2021. "Foreword." In *How We Read Now: Strategic Choices for Print, Screen, and Audio* by Naomi Baron, ix–xi. New York: Oxford University Press.

World Population Review. 2021. *Common Core States 2021*. Walnut, CA: World Population Review. https://worldpopulationreview.com/state-rankings/common-core-states.

WPA. 2014. *WPA Outcomes Statement for First-Year Composition (3.0)*. http://wpacouncil.org/aws/CWPA/pt/sd/news_article/243055/_PARENT/layout_details/false.

Zickuhr, Kathryn, and Lee Rainie. 2014. *Younger Americans and Public Libraries: How Those under 30 Engage with Libraries and Think about Libraries' Role in Their Lives and Communities*. Pew Research Center, Internet and Technology. https://www.pewresearch.org/internet/2014/09/10/younger-americans-and-public-libraries/.

# Index

Page numbers followed by *f* indicate a figure; page numbers followed by *t* indicate a table.

AACC. *See* American Association of Community Colleges (AACC)
*Academic Discourse and Critical Consciousness* (Bizzell), 127–128
academic environment, 30, 42, 55
Accelerated Learning Program (ALP), 38, 46, 48–54, 133, 163
ACRL. *See* Association of College and Research Libraries (ACRL)
ACT (standardized test), 8–11, 14, 53, 63
*Act of Reading, The* (Iser), 120
*Acts of Reading* (Harkin), 120, 166–167
Adams, Peter, 38, 50–52, 54, 133, 159, 163
Adler, Mortimer J., 142–143
Administrative Procedures Act, 197–198
AFT. *See* American Federation of Teachers (AFT)
AHA. *See* American Historical Association (AHA)
ALA. *See* American Library Association (ALA)
Alexander, Patricia A., 157
algorithms, 169, 189, 203–204
Allen, Harold, 102
ALP. *See* Accelerated Learning Program (ALP)
Alvermann, Donna E., 100

American Association of Chemistry Teachers, 207
American Association of Community Colleges (AACC), 67
American Federation of Teachers (AFT), 205
American Historical Association (AHA), 208
American Library Association (ALA), 103–104
Anglo-American Seminar on the Teaching of English. *See* Dartmouth Conference
Anson, Chris, 33
Applebee, Arthur N., 31, 94–96, 99, 140–141
article evaluation, 22–23
Association of College and Research Libraries (ACRL), 17, 19–20, 103–105; Association of College and Research Libraries Framework, 17, 19–20
audiobooks, 58, 71–73, 75, 77, 130, 178, 186, 190–191
Aull, Laura L., 184

*Back to School* (Rose), 63
Bailey, Thomas R., 45
Baker-Bell, April, 35–36, 70
Barclay, Donald A., 190

Baron, Naomi, 170, 177–179, 181
Bartholomae, David, 134, 159–160, 162
BAWP. *See* Bay Area Writing Project (BAWP)
Bay Area Writing Project (BAWP), 138–139
Bazerman, Chuck, 114, 118, 157
Beam, Alex, 142–143
Bean, Thomas W., 144
Becker, Anne, 193
behaviorism, 158
Benjamin, Ruha, 34
Berlin, James, 157
Berliner, David C., 31
Bizzell, Patricia, 127–128
Black Language, 35–36
Blau, Sheridan, 118
Bleich, David, 120
Bloom, Lynn Z., 154, 159–160, 164
Boston University, 142
Boylan, Hunter R., 46
Brandt, Deborah, 63, 77, 114, 130
Brawer, Florence B., 134
Breakstone, Joel, 199–200
Brereton, John C., 87, 111, 155–156
Brewer, Meaghan, 181
Briggs, Lyman, 88
Bruffee, Kenneth, 157, 160
Bunch, Will, 20

Campbell, Joanne, 91
Canagarajah, Suresh, 37
Carillo, Ellen C., 33, 53, 68, 118–119, 140, 145, 148, 161, 167–170, 174, 178, 181–184
Carr, Nicholas, 57
Caulfield, Mike, 201
Cavazos, Alyssa G., 39
CCCC. *See* Conference on College Composition and Communication (CCCC)
CCRC. *See* Community College Research Center (CCRC)
CCSS. *See* Common Core State Standards (CCSS)
CEEB. *See* College Entrance Exam Board (CEEB)
*Chasing Literacy* (Keller), 62
Chautauqua program, 142
Chen, Xianglei, 6, 43, 133
Cheney-Lippold, John, 189
Chomsky, Noam, 158
Citation Project, 15–16, 42, 64, 181
CLA. *See* critical language awareness (CLA)
Clifford, Geraldine Joncich, 140
"cognitive patience," 79
cognitive rhetoric, 157

Cohen, Arthur M., 107, 133–134
Cohn, Jenae, 62
College Entrance Exam Board (CEEB), 94, 96–98
Columbia University, 142
common book programs, 70–71
Common Core State Standards (CCSS), 29–33, 43, 55, 92–93, 98, 140, 158
community college. *See* two-year colleges and open access institutions (TYCOAs)
Community College Research Center (CCRC), 44–45
Conference on College Composition and Communication (CCCC), 7–8, 32–34, 67–68, 79, 92, 96, 101–102, 116–118, 145–147, 146t, 181, 184, 206
Conference on English, 94–95
Connolly, Steve, 113–114
Copeland, Charles Townsend, 90
Council of Writing Program Administrators (CWPA), 139
Counihan, Beth, 203
COVID-19 pandemic, 30–31, 146, 150, 181, 183
CRAAP test (currency, relevance, authority, accuracy, and purpose), 25, 200–201
Crisp, Robert B., 195
critical language awareness (CLA), 175–176
critical literacy: Common Core State Standards and, 30; critical language awareness and, 175; defining, 4f, 58–63, 63f; equity and, 33; in Freire, 124–131; importance of, 7; lack of, 80; model of, 83, 84f, 152f, 190–196, 191f; as term, 59–60; texts and, 193–194. *See also* literacy
Cui, Wenqi, 192
culture: first-generation students and, 66; reading instruction and, 36–42; testing and, 14
Cushman, Ellen, 114
CWPA. *See* Council of Writing Program Administrators (CWPA)

Dartmouth Conference, 60, 71, 85–86, 107, 109–116, 157, 191–192
degree completion rates, 7
Dehaene, Stanislas, 186
Del Principe, Annie, 209
digital materials, 77–78, 161–162, 169–171, 202. *See also* online reading
discard studies, 60–61
disciplinary reading, 155
disinformation, 24, 57–58, 80, 175–176, 183, 190

Disrupters, 31
Dixon, John, 112
Donahue, Christiane, 114–116
Doolittle, Peter, 209
Driscoll, Dana Lynn, 170–171
Durst, Russel K., 128

Eastman, Arthur, 164
Ede, Lisa, 157
Elbow, Peter, 157, 166
Elliot, Norbert, 6, 42–43, 105, 121, 131, 190
English A (Harvard University), 27, 44, 60, 71, 77–78, 85–93, 156
Enos, Theresa, 134
*Errors and Expectations* (Shaughnessy), 6
evidence-based approaches, 197–198
"Experience Curriculum," 106–107
expressivism, 157

Fader, Daniel N., 140–141, 143–144
Farris, Christine, 92–93
Fish, Stanley, 120
Fleming, Jimmy, 173
Flesch-Kincaid Readability Statistics program, 203
Flippo, Rona F., 144
Flower, Linda, 157
Foundations for Evidence-Based Policymaking, 198
Fox, Emily, 157
Freire, Paulo, 124–131, 175
Fulkerson, Richard, 119

Galbraith, David, 114
Gallagher, Kelly, 207
Gannett, Cinthia, 111
gender, 69–70, 79–80, 124–125, 175, 196, 203
Genung, John F., 154–156, 179
Gerber, John, 102
Gere, Anne Ruggles, 85, 175
GI Bill, 105
Gillotte-Tropp, Helen, 54
Giordano, Joanne Baird, 34, 38, 46, 65–66, 138
Glass, Gene V., 31
Glau, Gregory R., 53, 138
Gleason, Barbara, 54
Goen, Sugie, 54
Goodman, Kenneth, 7, 158
Goodman, Yetta, 7, 158
graduation rates, 7
Graff, Harvey J., 20, 129–131
Graham, Steve, 48–50, 207
Gray, James, 139

Grayson, Mara, 171
Great Books, 116, 141–144, 150
Greenlaw, Edwin, 106
Griffiths, Brett, 39
Guided Pathways, 45–46

Hairston, Maxine, 153
Hall, G. Stanley, 99–100
*Handbook of College Reading and Study Strategy Research* (Flippo and Bean), 144–145
*Handbook of Reading Research*, 32
Hardwick, Jennifer, 196
Harkin, Patricia, 119–120, 166–167, 170
Harris, Joseph, 113
Hart, James Morgan, 93
Harvard University. *See* English A (Harvard University)
Hassel, Holly, 38–39, 46, 65–66, 138
Have, Iben, 73
Hayes, John, 157
HBCUs. *See* historically Black colleges and universities (HBCUs)
Head, Alison, 19, 21, 74
Hill, Adams Sherman, 86–88
historically Black colleges and universities (HBCUs), 67, 105
Hobbs, Catherine, 157
Holland, Norman, 120
Holschuh, Jodi Patrick, 198
homepage analysis, 23
Hook, Julius N., 102, 106
*Hooked on Books*, 116, 140–141, 144
Hosic, James, 97, 99
Howard, Rebecca Moore, 15
*How to Read a Book* (Adler), 143
*How We Read Now* (Baron), 177
*Hub, The* (Adams), 159
Huey, Edmund Burke, 99, 156
Hurlbut, Byron S., 88
Hutchins, Robert, 142
Hutton, Elizabeth H., 122
Hymes, Dell, 40–41
Hypothes.is, 173, 188

Ihara, Rachel, 209
ILA. *See* International Literacy Association (ILA)
incidental reading, 73–74
inequities, 29–30, 33–36, 45, 54–55, 125, 128
information acceleration, 77
information literacy, 19–22, 21f, 39, 104–105, 146–147, 185, 190, 196. *See also* Project Information Literacy (PIL)

Inoue, Asao, 7
International Literacy Association (ILA), 103, 157, 206–207
internet, effect on reading, 57–58. *See also* online reading
Iser, Wolfgang, 120, 166–167

Jabr, Ferris, 77–78
Jaggars, Shanna Smith, 45
Jamieson, Sandra, 15–16
Jenkins, Davis, 45
journals (academic), 147*t*, 147–148
justice: algorithmic, 204; social, 71, 125, 128, 157, 175, 192. *See also* linguistic justice

Keller, Daniel, 29, 62, 77
Kisker, Carrie B., 134
Kolers, Paul A., 188
Kucer, Stephen B., 69–70
Kuhn, Thomas S., 151, 153–154, 165, 179
Kuncel, Nathan, 14

Lacy, Tim, 141–142
Lahr, John, 167
language arts model, 190–197
Lau, Sunny Man Chu, 70
Lemov, Doug, 98
Levinson, David, 46
librarians, information literacy and, 19–22, 21*f*
libraries, 103–104
LILAC Project (Learning Information Literacy across the Curriculum), 17–19
Lindemann, Erika, 109, 116–118, 150
linguistic justice, 34–36, 55, 70–71, 75
lit/comp split, 116–119
literacy: defined, 13, 206; information, 19–22, 21*f*; meaning making and, 69; media, 80, 176; wars and, 105–107. *See also* critical literacy
*Literacy in American Lives* (Brandt), 130
*Lives in the Boundary* (Rose), 6
Lloyd-Jones, Richard, 114
Lunsford, Andrea, 64, 114, 157

Macrorie, Ken, 157
Martirosyan, Nara M., 46
Maxey Boys Training School, 140–141
McClymer, John, 208
McGrew, Sarah, 24, 200
"meaning making," 69
media literacy. *See* literacy
Melzer, Dan, 90
Microsoft Word, 203

mindful reading, 79, 167–168, 178
misinformation, 24, 57–58, 80, 175–176, 183, 190
Mislevy, Robert J., 6, 43
MLA. *See* Modern Language Association (MLA)
*MLA Guide to Digital Literacy* (Carillo), 167, 169–170
Mlynarczyk, Rebecca Williams, 134
mobile reading, 73
Modern Language Association (MLA), 92–94, 182–183
Muller, Herbert J., 112–113
Muniz, Hannah, 38
Murray, Donald, 157

NAEP. *See* National Assessment of Educational Progress (NAEP)
Nastal, Jessica, 42
National Assessment of Educational Progress (NAEP), 11–12, 15, 31, 61
National Council of Teachers of English (NCTE), 86, 92, 95–96, 98–102, 106, 111, 139, 194
National Education Association (NEA), 94
National Writing Project (NWP), 138–140, 150
NCTE. *See* National Council of Teachers of English (NCTE)
NEA. *See* National Education Association (NEA)
New Criticism, 113
newspapers, 74, 100–101
Nichols, Laura, 66
Noble, Safiya Umoja, 189
*Norton Reader*, 162–165
NWP. *See* National Writing Project (NWP)

Oliveri, Maria Elena, 6, 43
online reading, 22–26, 177–178, 203. *See also* digital materials
Otte, George, 134

pandemic, 30–31, 146, 150, 181, 183
paper-based reading, 77–78
Parfitt, Matthew, 165–166, 170, 174
Pearson, P. David, 124
*Pedagogy of the Oppressed* (Freire), 126
Pedersen, Birgitte Stougaard, 73
Peele, Thomas, 53–54
Perin, Dolores, 198
Perl, Sondra, 157
Perusall, 173–174, 201–202
Petrosky, Anthony, 134, 159–160, 162
PIL. *See* Project Information Literacy (PIL)

PISA. *See* Programme for International Student Assessment (PISA)
platforms, reading, 75–78, 76t
PN. *See* PowerNotes (PN)
Poe, Mya, 42
Pollan, Michael, 178
PowerNotes (PN), 172–173, 178, 188
*Practical Rhetoric* (Genung), 166
Programme for International Student Assessment (PISA), 12–13, 15, 114, 132
Project Information Literacy (PIL), 19, 74, 204
Prose, Francine, 80
psycholinguistics of reading, 7–8, 59, 99, 166, 181–182

"quote mining," 42

race: historically Black colleges and universities, 67, 105; intersectionality and, 124; linguistic justice and, 34–36, 70, 75; reform efforts and, 45; remedial courses and, 7, 36; in student demographics, 67
racism, 6, 35–36, 75, 189–190, 203
Radcliffe College, 91
Randall, Jennifer, 145
Ratcliffe, Krista, 192
Raucci, John, 198
Ravitch, Diane, 31
reader-response theory, 26, 110, 116, 119–124, 150, 166–167
*Readicide: How Schools Are Killing Reading and What You Can Do about It* (Gallagher), 207
reading: absence of, 144–148, 146t, 147t; changing conceptions of, 58; common book programs and, 70–71; Common Core State Standards and, 29–33; community colleges and, 107–108; critical, 175–177; current landscape of, 57–81; deep, 61–62, 155; disciplinary, 155; in Freire, 126–127; gender and, 70; guided, 163; habits of students, 71–75; incidental, 73–74; inequities in instruction, 29–30, 33–36; integrated, 48–50, 53; internet's effect on, 57–58; language and, 70; lateral, 169–170; linguistic justice and, 34–36; mindful, 79, 167–168, 178; mobile, 73; online, 22–26, 177–178, 203; paper-based, 77–78, 202; platforms, 75–78, 76t; psycholinguistics of, 7–8, 59, 99, 166, 181–182; readers in, 63–69; reasons for, 78–80; reform efforts and, 44–46; resources and, 33–36; technological approaches to, 165–172; technological help with, 172–174; technology resources and, 34; as term, 59–60; textbooks, 159–163;

165–168, 170–171; time spent, 75–77, 76t; varied approaches to, 28–56; what counts as, 72; writing classes and, 42–46. *See also* critical literacy; literacy
reading landscape, 60–61
reading processes, in PISA, 13
remedial courses, 6–7, 36, 88, 99, 132, 136
research skills, of students, 16–19, 18f. *See also* information literacy
Resisters, 31
*Rethinking Reading in College* (Wilner), 210
Richardson, Brian, 121
Rideout, Henry Milner, 90
*Rise of Writing, The* (Brandt), 63
Roose, Kevin, 191
Rose, Mike, 6, 63
Rosenberg, Lauren, 79
Rosenblatt, Louise M., 116, 119–123, 150
Ross, Valerie, 184
Russell, David R., 86, 143

Sabine, Gordon A., 164
Sackett, Paul, 14
sampling, standardized testing and, 14
SAT (standardized test), 10–11, 14, 53, 63, 86
Saxon, D. Patrick, 46
Scholes, Robert, 145
Scott, Fred Newton, 91, 98–101
Scott, Jonathan, 194
*Searching for Literacy* (Graff), 129
Seidenberg, Mark, 61–62, 181
Shanahan, Timothy, 138
Shaughnessy, Mina P., 6, 110, 131
SHEG. *See* Stanford History Education Group (SHEG)
*Short Course in Writing, A* (Bruffee), 160
Showalter, Elaine, 167
SIFT (stop, investigate, find, and trace), 201
Sills, Lauren, 39
Silverstein, Michael, 37
Sinfree, Makoni, 114
Sireci, Stephen G., 145
*Skim, Dive, Surface: Teaching Digital Reading* (Cohn), 62
Skinner, B. F., 158
Slevin, James F., 118, 175–176
Smilges, J. Logan, 69
Smith, Frank, 158
Smitherman, Geneva, 175
social constructionism, 157
social justice, 71, 125, 128, 157, 175, 192
social media, 21, 23, 57, 181, 190
socioeconomic status, 14–15, 33, 69, 201

Sommers, Nancy, 157
sources, in student research, 16
Spinuzzi, Clay, 114
standards. *See* Common Core State Standards (CCSS)
Stanford History Education Group (SHEG), 22–25, 144, 199–201
Stengel, Richard, 176
Stewart, Cora Wilson, 105
Stewart, Donald, 91
St. John's College, 142
stretch approach, 53–54
*Structure of Scientific Revolutions, The* (Kuhn), 153
student(s): demographics, 63–71; first-generation, 37–39, 63, 66–67; reading habits of, 71–75; socioeconomic status of, 14–15, 33, 69, 201
Sullivan, Patrick, 43, 54, 133, 138, 181, 192, 210

"taking bearings," 24–25
talking books, 72. *See also* audiobooks
Tallal, Paula, 115
Tampio, Nicholas, 31
Tate, Gary, 109, 116–117, 150
Taylor, Helen, 79–80
teachers: classroom experience of, 208–211; demographics and backgrounds of, 67–69; faculty development for, 181; preparing, to help with reading, 148
technological approaches, to reading, 165–172
technological help, with reading, 172–174
technology access, 29–30, 34
test blindness, 63
testing: College Entrance Exam Board, 94, 96–98; culture and, 14; dropping of, as admissions requirement, 64–65; fairness in, 145; issues regarding, 14–15; large-scale, 8–14; at nineteenth-century Harvard, 87; sampling and, 14; socioeconomic status and, 14–15
textbooks, 153–156, 158–171, 174–175, 179
Tierney, Robert J., 124
time spent reading, 75–77, 76*t*
Tinberg, Howard, 181, 183
Toohey, Kelleen, 70
Trevelyan, G. M. W., 93
Troyka, Lynn Quitman, 134–135, 138
*Trust Me: Are You Being Manipulated?* (film), 80

Tulley, Christine E., 148
two-year colleges and open access institutions (TYCOAs), 135–136; complexity in, 46–54; culture and, 38; *Norton Reader* and, 164; proportion of students starting at, 64; reading and, 107–108; reform efforts and, 44–45; roles of, 47
Tyson, Lois, 121

Uehling, Karen, 54
University of Chicago, 142

Van Doren, Charles, 143
VanKooten, Crystal, 69
Van Viegen, Saskia, 70
Vasquez, Vivian Maria, 124
Vee, Annette, 109–110
video evidence, 22–23

WAC. *See* writing across the curriculum (WAC)
Waite, Stacey, 70, 160
Walker, Allison S., 202
Walker, Janice R., 17
wars, literacy and, 105–107
*Ways of Reading*, 159–162
webpage comparison, 22–23
Wentworth, Rebecca A., 46
Willingham, Daniel, 73–74, 181
Wilner, Arlene Fish, 210
Wineburg, Sam, 24, 200
Wolf, Maryanne, 61–62, 77–79, 177–178, 181, 196–197, 202
Word (software), 203
World War I, 105
World War II, 105–106
*Writer's Guide to Mindful Reading, A* (Carillo), 167–169
writing across the curriculum (WAC), 86
writing classes: in graduate programs, 67–69; integrated, 48–50, 53; reading and, 42–46
*Writing in Response* (Parfitt), 165–166
*Writing Spaces*, 170–171
writing studies: developmental courses and, 43; as discipline, 109–150; Freire and, 127–128; graduate programs in, 67–68; history of, 85, 87; reading in, 4, 7, 48; textbooks, 153–156, 158–165; today, 144–148, 146*t*, 147*t*

www.ingramcontent.com/pod-product-compliance
Lightning Source LLC
Chambersburg PA
CBHW060555080526
44585CB00013B/576